Webster's Dictionary of Synonyms and Antonyms

This book is not published by the original publishers of WEBSTER'S DICTIONARY, or by their successors.

Galahad Books • New York City

DEFINITIONS

SYNONYMS — Words that have the same meaning
Example: big, large

ANTONYMS — Words that have opposite meanings
Example: large, small
Note: Antonyms appear in parentheses ( ) following the synonyms.

HOMONYMS — Words that sound alike, but are spelled differently and have different meanings
Example: one, won
Note: Homonyms begin on page 238.

ISBN: 0-88365-470-9
Library of Congress Catalog Card Number: 80-84330

A

abandon—*v.* abdicate, leave, jilt, desert, vacate, cease, resign, drop, waive, discontinue, yield, surrender, forsake, retire, quit, relinquish, let go, repudiate, part with. *(cherish, keep, retain, adopt, pursue, uphold, occupy, support, favor, depend, maintain, vindicate, assert, advocate, claim, seek, embrace.)*

abandoned—*adj.* cast aside, bad, forsaken, deserted, wicked, vacated, vicious, rejected, sinful, depraved, unprincipled, corrupt, left, discarded, dropped, demoralized, forlorn. *(good, honest, righteous, steady, pure, virtuous, cherished, correct, upright, loved, respectable.)*

abase—*v.* disgrace, debase, mock, scorn, belittle, mortify, reduce, degrade, dishonour, despise, shame, lower, expose, humble, confuse, humiliate. *(elevate, uplift, exalt, honour, cherish, respect, praise, dignify, glorify, lift, laud, extol.)*

abate—*v.* alleviate, terminate, wane, reduce, diminish, ebb, decrease, restrain, lessen, allay, lower, decline, subside, slacken, slow down, ease. *(increase, prolong, extend, intensify, enlarge, magnify, amplify, enhance, aggravate, grow, accelerate, speed.)*

abbreviate—*v.* curtail, shorten, clip, reduce, lessen, condense, prune, abridge, cut short, cut down, trim, diminish, compress. *(lengthen, increase, expand, distend, dilate, prolong, swell, amplify, enlarge, augment, add to, supplement.)*

abdicate—*v.* cede, renounce, yield, resign, abandon, give up, relinquish, quit, forego, surrender, waive. *(claim, retain, hold, assume, maintain, challenge, defy, seize, possess.)*

abet—*v.* help, encourage, assist, aid, condone, uphold, stimulate, sustain, support, promote, incite, subsidize, sanction. *(hinder, impede, thwart, obstruct, discourage, frustrate, deter, oppose, resist, counteract, dampen, baffle.)*

abeyance—*n.* inactivity, recess, suspension, expectation, rest, reservation, pause, adjournment, latency. *(continuation, operation, exercise, enjoyment, force, possession, revival, enforcement, renewal, action.)*

abhor—*v.* loathe, detest, avoid, abominate, shun,

scorn, distain, hate, dislike, recoil from. *(cherish, adore, prize, love, desire, enjoy, treasure, admire, value, approve, covet.)*

abide—*v.* stay, dwell, sojourn, rest, remain, lodge, anchor, exist, live, settle, tarry, confront, sit, bide, endure, await. *(move, proceed, go, leave, migrate, despise, journey, avoid, deport, mistake.)*

ability—*n.* aptitude, capability, power, energy, skill, talent, knack, cleverness, strength, qualification, flair, know-how, vigor. *(inability, weakness, helplessness, incompetence, ineffectiveness, unreadiness, inadequacy.)*

abject—*adj.* base, mean, degrade, low, vile, worthless, contemptible, dishonourable, sordid, miserable, hangdog, outcast, hopeless, wretched, fawning, servile. *(noble, haughty, proud, dignified, honorable, magnificent, lofty, bold, arrogant, worthy, aristocratic, vain, respected, exalted, hopeful, staunch, manly.)*

abjure—*v.* disclaim, deny, assert, demand, repudiate, reject, discard, disown, abrogate, revoke, unsay, renege, disavow, forswear. *(attest, profess, demand, affirm, maintain, hug, certify, justify, praise, cherish, vindicate, approve, command, laud.)*

able—*adj.* skillful, adroit, competent, strong, accomplished, gifted, clever, capable, expert, proficient, adept, powerful, apt, talented, highly qualified. *(incapable, weak, incompetent, inept, unqualified, inefficient, mediocre, indifferent, useless, stupid, delicate, fair.)*

ablution—*n.* purification, bathing, cleansing, washing, lavation, ceremonial washing. *(soil, soiling, tainting, pollution, contaminating, taint, defiling.)*

abnegation—*n.* abstinence, refusal, relinquishment, denial, rejection, surrender, abandonment, temperance, giving up. *(abandon, self-indulgence, indulgence, concession, intemperance, affirmation.)*

abnormal—*adj.* eccentric, weird, exceptional, irregular, unnatural, peculiar, atypical, bizarre, strange, devious, monstrous, queer, odd, unconventional. *(natural, customary, common, routine, normal, ordinary, familiar, usual, conventional, typical.)*

abode—*n.* residence, home, nest, pad, lodgings,

berth, habitat, domicile, house, address, quarters. *(halt, tent, pilgrimage, ramble, perch, bivouac, peregrenation.)*

abolish—*v.* eliminate, efface, annihilate, destroy, cancel, repeal, annul, erase, revoke, repudiate, nullify, end, suppress, obliterate, quash, extinguish, overturn. *(introduce, enforce, restore, support, sustain, establish, continue, create, renew, enact, repair, promote, reinstate, legalize.)*

abominable—*adj.* vile, detestable, despicable, contemptible, hateful, horrid, revolting, repugnant, wretched, offensive, nauseous, infamous, foul, atrocious. *(choice, select, delightful, attractive, pure, charming, typical, routine, conventional, admirable, familiar, enjoyable.)*

aboriginal—*adj.* original, native, earliest, indigenous, ancient, primary, first, prime, primitive. *(foreign, immigrant, alien, late, imported, exotic, recent, modern.)*

abortion—*n.* disaster, failure, miscarriage, unsuccessful attempt, fiasco, blunder, termination, ending, mishap, misproduction. *(achievement, delivery, success, childbirth, perfection, development, realization, feat, parturition, completion.)*

abound—*v.* swarm, increase, flow, multiply, teem, overflow, be numerous, swell, luxuriate, flourish, be rich in, revel, be well supplied, stream, superabound. *(lack, have too few, fail, want, waste, decay, be scant, dry, die, lessen, vanish, wane, fail, need, be destitute of.)*

about—*adj.* around, nearly, regarding, relative to, concerning, approximately, connected with, over, surrounding, generally, almost, round, touching, respecting. *(unlike, afar, precisely, exactly, remote, distant, separated.)*

above—*adv.* over, aloft, overhead, beyond, higher, on top of, exceeding. *(within, beneath, below, under.)*

abridge—*v.* condense, compress, curtail, abbreviate, lessen, reduce, diminish, digest, epitomize, recap, summarize, telescope, shorten. *(amplify, expand, extend, spread out, enlarge, lengthen, detail.)*

abrogate—*v.* cancel, abolish, annul, nullify, quash, repeal, revoke, recind, set aside, invalidate, override, reverse. *(enforce, maintain, ratify, create, institute,* *establish, found, uphold, sanction, revive, continue, confirm.)*

abrupt—*adj.* rude, curt, harsh, sudden, craggy, zigzag, jagged, sharp, brusque, uneven, violent, broken, blunt. *(civil, easy, blending, gliding, gracious, polite, polished, smooth.)*

absent—*v.* depart, not appear, play truant, withdraw. *(attend, appear at, stay, remain.)*

absent—*adj.* missing, listless, gone away, truant, pre-occupied, oblivious, inattentive, elsewhere, dreamy, out, heedless. *(present, aware.)*

absolute—*adj.* unrestricted, pure, perfect, dogmatic, full, supreme, irrespective, complete, unqualified, despotic, certain, arbitrary, unconditional, entire. *(mild, conditional, gentle, dubious, meek, relative, imperfect, incomplete, dependent, accountable, docile, qualified.)*

absolve—*v.* pardon, acquit, clear, excuse, exonerate, forgive, release, deliver, condone, liberate. *(accuse, bind, blame, censure, condemn, hold to, convict, compel.)*

absorb—*v.* sponge up, suck up, swallow, devour, monopolize, drink in, drown, engulf, consume, engross, exhaust, merge. *(impart, cast off, emit, belch, dissipate, distil, eject, disperse, distract, disgorge, eliminate, weary.)*

abstain—*v.* avoid, eschew, withhold, forgo, scruple, decline, forbear, refrain, discontinue, refuse, desist, avoid, demur. *(yield to, wanton, overdue, reveal, indulge, exceed.)*

abstemious—*adj.* teetotal, sober, temperate, non-indulgent, self-denying, sparing, abstinent, frugal, moderate. *(greedy, intemperate, self-indulgent, sensual, excessive, gluttonous, uncontrolled.)*

abstract—*v.* discriminate, subtle, abridge, purloin, outline, separate, appropriate, detach, take away, eliminate, steal, withdraw. *(mend, add, unite, concrete, return, specific, restore, impose, conjoin, adduce, surrender.)*

absurd—*adj.* ludicrous, silly, stupid, comical, ridiculous, funny, unreasonable, asinine, monstrous, senseless, foolish, listless. *(smart, judicious, wise, sensical, prudent, sensible, reflective, sound, rational, consistent, logical, sagacious, reasonable.)*

accessory—*n.* retainer, associate, colleague, complement, aide, additional, assistant, crutch, auxiliary, accomplice, henchman, helper. *(opponent, spy, adversary, rival, enemy, foe, antagonist, irrelevant, immanent, superfluous, cumbersome.)*

accident—*n.* hazard, collision, chance, wreck, fortuity, crash, calamity, misadventure, incident, mishap, adventure, misfortune. *(intent, design, purpose, plan, decree, appointment, law, ordainment, provision.)*

accommodate—*v.* oblige, provide, aid, suit, help, supply, fit, adapt, serve, harmonize, reconcile, lodge. *(disturb, impede, deprive, censure, aggravate, inconvenience, hinder, hissing, block.)*

accommodating—*adj.* courteous, gracious, neighborly, polite, kind, yielding, obliging, unselfish, considerate. *(churlish, exacting, rude, disobliging, selfish, imperious, dictatorial, hostile.)*

accomplice—*n.* cohort, coworker, assistant, aide, supporter, ally, colleague, henchman, partner, accessory, associate, helper. *(objector, rival, foe, denouncer, opponent, betrayer, enemy, antagonist.)*

accomplish—*v.* conclude, do, discharge, effect, perform, carryout, fulfil, perfect, realize, attain, execute, achieve, associate, manage, finish. *(give up, leave undone, fall short, defeat, baffle, fail, destroy, spoil.)*

accord—*v.* give, admit, cede, allow, tally, render, agree, answer, consist, consent, grant, bequeath. *(deny, disagree, clash, collide, differ, refuse, misfit, withhold, discord.)*

accordingly—*adv.* whence, whereupon, thence, suitably, conformably, hence, agreeably, conversely. *(conversely.)*

accost—*v.* solicit, confront, stop, waylay, greet, salute. *(avoid, shun, overlook, slight.)*

abundant—*adj.* enough, copious, replete, overflowing, profuse, large, liberal, lavish, rich, plentiful, teeming, luxuriant. *(meager, poor, scant, skimpy, uncommon, rare, drained, deficient, scarce, short, sparing, dry, exhausted.)*

abuse—*v.* harm, hurt, injure, misuse, desecrate, disparage, damage, ill-use, revile, malign, pervert, maltreat, upbraid, prostitute, defame, asperse, vilify.

(eulogize, shield, care for, extol, laud, cherish, flatter, tend, regard, consider, respect, protect, sustain.)

abuse—*n.* unfair use, ill treatment, imposition, invective, improper use, ribaldry, reproach, insolence, ill usage, disgrace, blame, censure. *(praise, laudation, commendation, approval, sanction, deference, respect, kindness, good treatment.)*

academic—*adj.* learned, lettered, classical, bookish, scholarly, collegiate, pedantic. *(non-scholarly, untaught, unschooled, illiterate, ordinary, plain.)*

accelerate—*v.* quicken, rush, spur, urge, hasten, further, speed, hurry, promote, expedite, forward, precipitate. *(slow, hinder, resist, embarrass, impede, clog, delay, retard, obstruct, drag.)*

accent—*n.* stress, force, cadence, modulation, beat, pulsation, emphasis, rhythm. *(flow, smoothness, babble, monotony, inaccentuation, equableness.)*

accept—*v.* receive, concur, hail, allow, recognize, take, avow, admit, accede to, believe, agree. *(yield, spurn, disown, disacknowledge, deny, decline, refuse, ignore.)*

acceptable—*adj.* fitting, suitable, worthy, good, gratifying, agreeable, grateful, welcome, pleasant. *(repugnant, unfitting, annoying, poor, below par, disagreeable, unpleasant, unsuitable, ungrateful.)*

account—*n.* narrative, reckoning, value, charge, bill, recital, motive, description. *(riddle, silence, puzzle, unknown quantity, mystery, project.)*

account—*v.* think, judge, view as, rate, calculate, estimate, deem, value, hold, explain, reckon. *(leave unexplained, leave unsolved, mystify, perplex.)*

accountable—*adj.* answerable, censurable, responsible, beholden, liable, delegated, guilty, subordinate, blameworthy. *(innocent, despotic, autocratic, guiltless, absolute, supreme, unreliable.)*

accredit—*v.* delegate, commission, license, entrust, authorize, endorse, believe, sanction. *(distrust, discard, recall, supersede, disbelieve, suspect, dismiss.)*

accumulate—*v.* gather, pile up, amass, hoard, collect, add to, garner, augment, assemble, accrue. *(waste, scatter,* *disperse, distribute, dissipate, get rid of, throw out.)*

accumulation—*n.* store, amassing, agglomeration, gathering, heap, hoard, pile, mass, bulk, lot. *(division, separation, scattering, unit, individual, segregation, dispersal.)*

accurate—*adj.* minute, careful, nice, unerring, true, scrupulous, just, correct, close, strict, exact, faithful, truthful. *(false, wrong, deceptive, careless, faulty, loose, inexact, defective, sloppy.)*

accuse—*v.* indict, summon, impeach, against, incriminate, tax, blame, censure, taunt. *(plea, pardon, blame, vindicate, acquit, condone, exonerate, deny, rebut.)*

accustom—*v.* form, ingrain, train, discipline, harden, incure, reconcile, familiarize. *(disaccustom, estrange, alienate, dishabituate, wean.)*

achieve—*v.* accomplish, dispatch, attain, fulfill, realize, win, procure, finish. *(be deprived of, lose, fail, miss.)*

achievement—*n.* realization, fulfillment, exploit, performance, accomplishment. *(frustration, defeat, failure, loss, waste.)*

acknowledge—*v.* recognize, admit, confess, accept, profess, concede, yield, own, grant. *(disclaim, slight, reject, repudiate, ignore, deny, abandon.)*

acme—*n.* height, peak, apex, summit, zenith, pinnacle, crown. *(bottom, depth, base, nadir, low point, foundation.)*

acquaint—*v.* familiarize, inform, reveal, advertise, enlighten, divulage, notify, tell, apprise. *(hide, misinform, withhold, reserve, deceive, conceal, delude.)*

acquaintance—*n.* relationship, experience, dealings, association, knowledge, intimacy. *(stranger, ignore, inexperience, ignorance.)*

acquiesce—*v.* allow, yield, concur, assent, comply, submit, bow to, grant. *(contest, demur, protest, veto, resist.)*

acquire—*v.* get, obtain, attain, gain, secure, achieve. *(lose, relinquish, give up, forgo, be deprived of.)*

acquit—*v.* clear, excuse, release, discharge, exonerate, vindicate, deliver, pardon.

(convict, declare, charge, constrain, compel, bind, condemn, damn, indict, accuse.)

acquittance—*n.* discharge, voucher, release, receipt. *(obligation, bond, charge, claim.)*

across—*prep.* & *adv.* against, transversely, athwart, crosswise, thwart. *(lengthwise, parallel, along, concurrently.)*

act—*n.* statute, movement, play, degree, bill, performance, operation, measure, pose, deed, *(inactivity, quiet, repose, inertia, rest, stop, procrastinate, suspension, immobility, sluggishness.)*

activate—*v.* turn on, drive, stimulate, impel, energize, nudge. *(stop, halt, paralyze, weaken, turn off, check.)*

active—*adj.* energetic, vigorous, brisk, supple, nimble, busy, vibrant, agile, prompt, dexterous, ambitious, forceful, bubbling. *(quiet, dormant, sluggish, heavy, inactive, inert.)*

actual—*adj.* concrete, positive, authentic, tangible, sure, certain, unquestionable, prevailing. *(fictional, hypothetical, probable, possible, potential, fabulous, unreal, made-up.)*

acumen—*n.* insight, keenness, sharpness, cleverness, wisdom, intelligence. *(dullness, ignorance, apathy, slowness, stupor, bad judgment.)*

acute—*adj.* clever, ingenious, severe, sharp, shrewd, violent, astute, sagacious, smart, fierce. *(stupid, obtuse, dense, mild, dull, stolid, blunt, heavy.)*

adamant—*adj.* determined, unbending, stubborn, firm, set, insistent, immovable. *(lax, yielding, flexible, indifferent, easy-going, undemanding.)*

adapt—*v.* adjust, temper, qualify, fit, attune, harmonize, comply, assimilate. *(confuse, jumble, misapply, misfit, disturb, displace.)*

add—*v.* enlarge, extend, increase, affix, append, adduce, sum up, count up, amplify. *(deduct, subtract, remove, withdraw, reduce, exclude.)*

addicted—*adj.* attached, prone, devoted, given, accustomed, disposed, dedicated. *(unaddicted, averse, free, contrary, opposed, indisposed, reluctant.)*

addition—*n.* totaling, appendage, enlargement, increase, adjunct, summation, enumeration, extension. *(sub-*

traction, loss, deterioration, deduction, decrease, shrinkage.)

address—*n.* speech, discourse, tact, oration, ability. *(awkwardness, rudeness, folly, stupidity.)*

address—*v.* approach, implore, solicit, greet, salute, appeal, invoke, hail, memorialize. *(pass, shun, elude, avoid, ignore.)*

adept—*n.* soothsayer, wizard, expert, master, peer, artist, performer, magician. *(faker, blunderer, novice, hypocrite, pretender, awkward, clumsy.)*

adequate—*adj.* suitable, fit, equal, capable, ample, able, enough, satisfactory, competent. *(unsuited, imperfect, inadequate, incompetent, unfit, inferior, worthless.)*

adherence—*n.* loyalty, attachment, endearment, fidelity, allegiance, devotion, constancy, adhesion. *(slickness, disunion, infidelity, unfaithfulness, desertion, disloyalty, breaking.)*

adherent—*n.* accessory, ally, follower, devotee, fan, disciple, backer, pupil, admirer. *(detractor, betrayer, opponent, renegade, opposer, adversary.)*

adhesive—*adj.* glutinous, gummy, waxy, sticky, adherent. *(attachment, free, apart, unattachable, oily, open, loose.)*

adieu—*n.* farewell, departure, parting, leave, good-bye, leave-taking, setting out. *(salutation, greeting, recognition, welcome.)*

adipose—*adj.* fat, greasy, obese, oily, corpulent, sebaceous, oleoginous. *(thin, bony, leathery, mummified.)*

adjacent—*adj.* next to, beside, neighboring, close, bordering, attached, adjoining, near. *(beyond, afar, remote, distant, detached, apart.)*

adjoin—*v.* border upon, near to, annex, adjacent to, connect, unite, add, touch, affix, join on, approximate, abut. *(dismember, part, remote, disunite, detach, disconnect, removed, distant, recede.)*

adjourn—*v.* suspend, recess, close, postpone, defer, delay, procrastinate, put off, dismiss. *(convene, stimulate, conclude, hasten, gather, convoke, expedite, consummate, protract, impel.)*

adjunct—*n.* accessory, auxiliary, addition, complement, attachment, aid, acquisition, dependency. *(lessening, removal. hindrance, essence, clog, separation, impediment, drawback, detriment.)*

adjust—*v.* arrange, regulate, harmonize, localize, organize, acclimate, callocate, set in order, compose, classify, prepare. *(scatter, disorder, dislocate, jumble, dismember, derange, disturb, involve, confuse.)*

ad-lib—*n.* wisecrack, extemporaneous, improvisation, speak off the cuff, speak impromptu. *(follow the script, speak from notes.)*

administer—*v.* supply, direct, accord, dole, furnish, govern, award, discharge, afford, execute, superintend, distribute, dispense. *(foil, resign, withhold, frustrate, refuse, resume, deny, nullify, betray, forego.)*

admirable—*adj.* worthy, excellent, captivating, pleasing, praiseworthy, astonishing, enticing, good. *(repelling, ridiculous, displeasing, unworthy, hateful, mediocre, repulsive.)*

admissible—*adj.* worthy, permissible, probable, proper, fair, just, likely, reasonable, qualified. *(intolerable, wrong, irrelevant, absurd, preposterous, unfair, excluded, inadmissible.)*

admit—*v.* invest, pass, accept, own, avow, welcome, acknowledge, receive, grant, tell. *(deny, shut, debar, repel, reject, dismiss, eject, repudiate, disavow, confute.)*

admonish—*v.* counsel, advise, rebuke, remind, censure, scold, criticize, forewarn, reprove, warn. *(laud, urge, extol, instigate, applaud, chide, abet, praise.)*

adolescent—*n.* teenager, lad, lass, youth, schoolboy, schoolgirl, young man or woman. *(adult, grown-up, child, mature.)*

adopt—*v.* acknowledge, select, affiliate, elect, endorse, espouse, avow, choose, accept, conform to, assume. *(annul, reject, discard, disinherit, repudiate, abrogate, decline, disclaim, disown.)*

adoration—*n.* worship, exaltation, glorification, veneration, honor, magnification, devotion. *(denunciation, blasphemy, reviling, execration, belittling.)*

adore—*v.* exalt, revere, praise, admire, idolize, glorify, hallow, reverence. *(loathe, dislike, revile, exercrate, abhor, blaspheme, abominate.)*

adorn—*v.* beautify, gild, garnish, embellish, bejewel, illustrate, ornament. *(mock, despise, curse, condemn, strip, bare, simplify, mar, spoil.)*

adulation—*n.* compliment, praise, fawning, flattering, courtship, cringing, fulsome, incense. *(loathing, dislike, hatred, defamation, obloquy, satire, sarcasm, detraction, abuse, censure.)*

advance—*v.* prosper, rise, go, proceed, promote, elevate, lend, increase, exalt, allege. *(stop, withhold, depress, hesitate, halt, withdraw, degrade, retreat, oppose, yield.)*

advantage—*n.* boon, success, interest, blessing, comfort, gain, help, superiority, utility, profit, victory, avail. *(hindrance, curse, loss, frustration, obstacle, disadvantage, dilemma, disservice, burden, barrier.)*

adventurous—*adj.* challenging, brave, risky, gallant, bold, fearless, rash, audacious, valiant. *(cautious, nervous, hesitant, dull, routine, boring, hesitating, cowardly, unenterprising.)*

adversary—*n.* opponent, rival, enemy, competitor, foe, antagonist. *(colleague, aider, friend, teammate, accessory, ally, accomplice, help, cooperation.)*

adverse—*adj.* contrary, negative, hostile, harmful, antagonistic, unfriendly, detremental, injurious. *(favorable, helpful, supporting, agreeable, auspicious, beneficial.)*

adversity—*n.* trial, calamity, woe, misfortune, misery, disaster, bad luck, affliction, ruin, unsuccess. *(blessings, prosperity, help, aid, happiness, approval.)*

advertise—*v.* call attention to, publicize, show, circulate, inform, advise, notify, proclaim, tout, display. *(hide, warn, deliberate, conceal, ignore, proclaim, hush, misinform, hoodwink.)*

advise—*v.* counsel, direct, acquaint, warn, deliberate, prompt, inform, admonish, show, apprise. *(fool, deter, curb, mislead, dissuade, inhibit, remonstrate, delude, misinform.)*

advocate—*n.* counsellor, propagator, champion, defender. *(opponent, impugner, accuser, enemy, antagonist.)*

aerial—*adj.* dreamy, ethereal, fanciful, airy, airborne, air, by air, wind-created, atmospheric. *(land, on the ground, by land, real, practical, pragmatic.)*

affable—*adj.* kindly, genial, courteous, condescending, polite, easy, civil, pleasant, mild, gracious. *(haughty, exclusive, sour, arrogant, surly, distant, unapproachable, contemptuous.)*

affect—*v.* soften, favor, assume, thrill, agitate, influence, like, overcome, interest, subdue, modify. *(repudiate, dislike, scorn, repel, shed, shun, feign.)*

affectation—*n.* airs, artifice, mannerism, pretext, frills, simulation, hypocrisy, pretense, sham. *(sincerity, naturalness, simplicity, artlessness, genuineness, unaffectedness.)*

affection—*n.* friendship, state love, desire, fondness, solicitude, mood, warmth, attachment, tenderness. *(hate, repugnance, indifference, insensibility, antipathy, loathing, coldness.)*

affinity—*n.* relation, harmony, attraction, alliance, connection, sympathy, compatibility, likeness, homology, interdependence. *(aversion, antipathy, disconnection, repugnance, repulsion, discordance, dissimilarity.)*

affirm—*v.* swear, tell, ratify, validate, declare, endorse, warrant, approve, state, aver, maintain. *(refute, deny, rescind, dispute, demur, impugn, oppose, veto, nullify, disallow.)*

affix—*v.* attach, fasten, fix, add on, set to, seal, glue, paste, stick. *(detach, unfasten, take off, unglue.)*

affliction—*n.* calamity, distress, trial, pain, curse, misery, woe, torment, misfortune. *(relief, blessing, pleasure, joy, solace, comfort, consolation, boon.)*

affluent—*adj.* rich, wealthy, prosperous, moneyed, well-off, well-fixed. *(poor, indigent, impoverished, impecunious, destitute.)*

afford—*v.* supply, offer, produce, yield, furnish, impart, grant, give, extend, bestow. *(grudge, retain, stint, withhold, deny, withdraw.)*

affront—*v.* insult, outrage, wrong, vex, provoke, abuse, annoy, displease, shame. *(compliment, placate, soothe, mollify, please.)*

afloat—*adj.* loose, distracted, dazed, adrift, wrong. *(snug, tight, close, fast, collected, ashore, concentrated.)*

afoot—*adj.* instituted, started, established, afloat, launched, working, agoing. *(contemplated, designed, pro-*

jected, incomplete, uncommenced, proposed.)

afraid—*adj.* panicky, alarmed, terrified, faint-hearted, apprehensive, uneasy, aghast, cautious, fearful. *(unafraid, bold, hopeful, fearless, inapprehensive, unsolicitous, secure, reckless, eager, audacious, confident.)*

afresh—*adv.* over again, anew, repeatedly, again, intermittently, frequently. *(unintermittently, connectedly, uniformly, continuously, uninterruptedly.)*

after—*prep.* afterwards, following, latter, behind, subsequent. *(introducing, preceeding, afore, before.)*

again—*adv.* another, frequently, over, afresh, once more, anew. *(uninterruptedly, uniformly, continuously, once, unintermittently.)*

against—*prep.* abreast of, close to, over, despite, counter, opposing, fronting, resisting. *(aiding, promoting, with, accompanying, suiting, for.)*

age—*n.* generation, date, forever, millennium, era, century, senility, duration, period, epoch. *(infancy, moment, instant, childhood, adolescence, second.)*

agent—*n.* executor, performer, force, mechanic, deputy, doer, operator, cause, envoy, delegate. *(opponent, neutralizer, counteragent, counteraction, counteractor.)*

aggravate—*v.* annoy, provoke, vex, intensify, nettle, affront, irritate, exasperate, enhance, embitter, inflame, worsen. *(soften, soothe, mitigate, diminish, assuage, neutralize, lessen, alleviate.)*

agile—*adj.* limber, active, brisk, quick, dexterous, lithe, fleet, nimble, supple, swift, rapid, lively, graceful. *(sluggish, inert, awkward, bulky, clumsy, lethargic, ponderous, slow.)*

agitate—*v.* trouble, ruffle, shake, excite, oscillate, fluster, convulse. *(soothe, compose, quiet, pacify, smooth, still.)*

agog—*adj.* thrilled, astir, awestruck, enthralled, excited. *(bored, uninterested, indifferent.)*

agony—*n.* torture, distress, affliction, anxiety, pain, anguish, torment, woe, suffering. *(pleasure, enjoyment, ease, consolation, ecstacy, comfort, joy, relief, gratification.)*

agree—*v.* match, tally, harmonize, concur, chime, suit, consent, consort, coincide, dovetail, square. *(dispute, op-*

pose, protest, demur, refute, contradict, revolt, disagree.)

agreeable—*adj.* concurring, pleasant, enticing, suitable, acceptable, amenable, ready, willing, accommodating, loving. *(unfitting, harsh, unpleasant, ungrateful, offensive, unacceptable, disobliging, repugnant, revolting, odious.)*

agreement—*n.* compact, unison, mutuality, welcome, harmony, contract, bond, undertaking, concord, bargain, compliance. *(disagreement; difference, discrepancy, discord.)*

aid—*v.* assist, support, minister to, favor, help, sustain, serve, protect, encourage, befriend, foster, promote, instigate, encourage. *(harm, oppose, resist, hurt, obstruct, thwart, discourage, baffle, deter, impede, hinder.)*

ailment—*n.* malady, sickness, disease, infection; complaint, affliction, weakness. *(health, fitness, sanity, robusiness, vigor, convalescence.)*

aim—*n.* goal, design, aspiration, purpose, endeavor, wish, tendency, scope. *(oversight, neglect, carelessness.)*

airy—*adj.* light, sprightly, frolicsome, jaunty, animated, joyous, fairylike. *(heavy, gloomy, dark, doleful, stony, ponderous, cheerless.)*

akin—*adj.* homogeneous, allied, related, analogous, similar, sympathetic, agnate, cognate. *(unrelated, dissimilar, unconnected, alien, unsympathetic, hostile, antagonistic.)*

alacrity—*n.* agility, briskness, animation, compliance, speed, promptitude, eagerness, zeal, alertness. *(repugnance, apathy, dislike, slowness, lethargy, dullness, laziness.)*

alarm—*n.* terror, fright, distress, fear, misgiving, dread, panic, apprehension, agitation. *(quiet, security, calmness, coolness, tranquillity, peace, repose.)*

alarming—*adj.* imminent, formidable, perilous, terrible, frightful, ominous, fearful. *(assuring, hopeful, attractive, soothing, inviting, alluring.)*

alert—*adj.* diligent, brisk, lively, vigilant, watchful, sprightly, hustling, prompt, nimble, wary. *(lazy, oblivious, heavy, stupid, lethargic, languid, dilatory, slow, absent, lackadaisical.)*

alien—*adj.* foreign, strange, remote, undomesicated, hostile, estranged, irrelevant. *(germane, akin, alike, congenial, pertinent, proper, naturalized, native.)*

alike—*adj.* identical, uniform, similar, equal, same, kindred, parallel, homogeneous, resembling. *(apart, unlike, distinct, different, heterogeneous.)*

alive—*adj.* together, animate, breathing, equal, vivacious, alert, brisk, agile, resembling, safe. *(departed, lifeless, inanimate, cold, dull, dead, apathetic, morose, drowsy.)*

allay—*v.* ease, soften, soothe, pacify, diminish, appease, quiet, calm, tranquilize. *(agitate, aggravate, provoke, stimulate, stir, arouse, intensify, magnify.)*

allege—*v.* profess, affirm, assert, contend, accuse, cite, plead, maintain, state, aver. *(neutralize, repel, retract, deny, refute, disclaim, contradict, quash.)*

allegiance—*n.* homage, devotion, loyalty, fealty, faithfulness, deference, fidelity, duty. *(treason, rebellion, treachery, sedition, alienation, deceit, ressistance, disloyalty.)*

alleviate—*v.* soften, lessen, mitigate, diminish, subdue, mollify, remove. *(enhance, embitter, intensify, increase, multiply, augment.)*

alliance—*n.* treaty, union, junction, coalition, partnership, friendship, confederation, association, syndicate. *(secession, enmity, discord, disunion, rebellion, separation, divorce, revolution.)*

allot—*v.* destine, award, tabulate, grant, mete out, catalogue, classify, distribute, parcel, yield. *(resume, repudiate, grasp, resist, withstand, guard, shuffle, refuse, protest, retain.)*

allow—*v.* acknowledge, confess, apportion, recognize, authorize, warrant, approve, avow, grant, tolerate, concede, admit. *(withdraw, forbid, prohibit, withstand, reject, deny, resume, protest, disallow.)*

alloy—*n.* deterioration, lower impairment, debasement, adulteration, admixture, abatement, degradation. *(enhancement, integrity, purity, genuineness.)*

allude—*v.* mention, glance, hint, point, refer, insinuate, cite, quote, imply, remark. *(keep secret, state, declare,* *be closemouthed about, specify.)*

ally—*n.* supporter, helper, confederate, league, affiliate, accomplice, colleague. *(rival, competitor, foe, opponent, antagonist, adversary, enemy.)*

aloft—*adv.* overhead, heavenward, high up, in the clouds, above. *(down, below, beneath, lower, earthward, low.)*

aloud—*adv.* plainly, clearly, audibly, sonorously, clamorously, loudly. *(silently, suppressedly, softly, inaudibly.)*

alter—*v.* transform, substitute, vary, convert, modify, diversify, recast, regulate, twist. *(keep, retain, stay, arrest, refrain, continue, stereotype, solidify, preserve.)*

altercation—*n.* disagreement, controversy, wrangle, spat, fracas, dissension, dispute. *(union, accord, agreement, unity, peace, harmony, consonance.)*

alternative—*n.* option, choice, preference, pick, election. *(necessity, fix, quandry, urgency, obligation, coercion.)*

altogether—*adv.* thoroughly, collectively, totally, quite, fully, perfectly, completely, on the whole. *(incompletely, partially, separately, partly, somewhat, individually.)*

altruistic—*adj.* humane, kind, charitable, philanthropic, generous. *(selfish, self-centered, malevolent, mean.)*

amass—*v.* assemble, heap, aggregate, muster, pile up, gather, collect, hoard. *(squander, dispense, scatter, portion, divide, waste, parcel, distribute.)*

amazement—*n.* admiration, wonder, awe, shock, astonishment, confusion, perplexity, surprise. *(indifference, coolness, calmness, anticipation, preparation, composure, steadiness.)*

ambiguous—*adj.* indefinite, puzzling, vague, equivocal, uncertain, perplexing, dubious, doubtful, misleading, cryptic. *(explicit, clear, obvious, necessary, frank, uncertain, perplexing, plain, lucid, unequivocal.)*

ambition—*n.* goal, aim, hope, longing, intent, yearning, dream, desire, enterprise. *(indolence, sloth, indifference, laziness, modesty, simplicity.)*

ameliorate—*v.* correct, raise, amend, reform, rectify, elevate, advance, promote.

(impair, injure, depress, debase, vitiate, mar, spoil.)

amend—*v.* better, rectify, mend, repair, meliorate, promote, cleanse, mitigate, correct. *(harm, corrupt, spoil, vitiate, blemish, tarnish, mar, impair, hurt.)*

amiable—*adj.* gentle, engaging, benevolent, cordial, pleasing, gracious, lovable, fascinating, charming, polite, genial. *(hostile, hateful, churlish, sullen, surly, offensive, abminable, repellent.)*

amiss—*adj.* untrue, bad, faulty, mistaken, defective, wrong, incorrect, false, inappropriate, erroneous. *(good, proper, suitable, right, complete, successful, opportune, expedient.)*

amnesty—*n.* absolution, pardon, truce, reprieve, condonation, dispensation, remission. *(penalty, retribution, requital, trial, retaliation, account, punishment.)*

ample—*adj.* abundant, liberal, copious, generous, enough, bountiful, adequate. *(sparse, narrow, scant, mean, insufficient, meager, scrimpy, bare, stint.)*

amplify—*v.* increase, augment, widen, dilate, expand, stretch, magnify, develop, swell, unfold, deepen. *(gather, epitomize, curtail, reduce, amputate, condense, collect, lessen, compress, abbreviate, shorten.)*

amuse—*v.* divert, occupy, charm, cheer, entertain, please, engross. *(bore, sadden, tire, wear, annoy, vex.)*

analogy—*n.* resemblance, metaphor, relation, affinity, parallelism, simile, comparison, likeness. *(difference, dissimilarity, incongruity, inaffinity, heterogeneousness, disharmony.)*

analysis—*n.* judgement, separation, partition, reduction, segregation, investigation, inquiry. *(synthesis, combination, union, aggregation, coalition, uniting.)*

anarchy—*n.* chaos, tumult, riot, misrule, rebellion, insubordination, disorder. *(control, law, order, organization, government, subjection.)*

anatomy—*n.* structure, framework, dissection, segregation, resolution, division. *(structure, union, organization, synthesis, body, form, collocation.)*

ancestry—*n.* family, parentage, genealogy, progenitors, pedigree, line, stock. *(posterity, descendants, issue, progeny.)*

ancient—*adj.* aged, old-time, antiquated, obsolete, archaic, primeval, olden, remote. *(modern, new, recent, fresh, young, newfangled, modish, juvenile.)*

anger—*n.* outrage, vexation, gall, bile, exasperation, petulance, fury, irritation, grudge, hostility, hatred, ire, choler. *(patience, peace, contentment, mildness, goodwill, peacefulness, gratitude.)*

anger—*v.* ruffle, vex, fret, provoke, embitter, annoy, irritate, wound. *(compose, calm, please, delight, soothe, conciliate, heal, gratify.)*

animosity—*n.* rancor, anger, hatred, feud, acrimony, enmity, malice, resentment, bitterness, virulence, strife, dislike. *(love, friendship, harmony, sympathy, congeniality, companionship, alliance, kindliness.)*

annex—*v.* attach, incorporate, acquire, subjoin, unite, add, expropriate, seize, appendage. *(detachment, detach, disconnect, remove, separate, disengage.)*

annihilate—*v.* nullify, destory, exterminate, eradicate, abolish, extirpate, liquidate, demolish, efface, erase, uproot, end. *(create, keep, cherish, build, make, develop, augment, cultivate, construct, foster, perpetuate, let live.)*

announce—*v.* speak, enunciate, circulate, herald, trumpet, broadcast, declare, publish, report, divulge, reveal. *(refrain, hush, suppress, withhold, silence, hide, stifle, smother, reserve, bury.)*

annoy—*v.* bore, badger, irritate, tease, plague, nag, exasperate, provoke, pester, incommode, harass, chafe, inconvenience, molest. *(appease, calm, foster, mollify, console, conciliate, cherish, solace, calm, please.)*

anomaly—*n.* rarity, abnormality, eccentricity, exception, aberration, oddity, peculiarity. *(the norm, the rule, conformity, specimen, illustration, regularity, exemplification.)*

anonymous—*adj.* nameless, unsigned, unacknowledged, unattested, authorless, unauthenticated, unnamed. *(acknowledged, signed, identified, known, attested, verified, named, authorized.)*

answer—*n.* plea, reply, defense, solution, vindication, apology, retort, counterpart, acknowledgment, confutation, response. *(question, inquiry, call, summons, interrogation, challenge, ask.)*

antecedent—*adj.* anterior, earlier, prior, previous, preliminary, former. *(later, posterior, consequent, succeeding, following.)*

anticipate—*v.* await, expect, prevent, count upon, hope for, prepare, forecast, forsee, apprehend, forestall. *(despair of, fear, remember, cure, doubt, dread, misapprehend, remedy, recollect.)*

anticipation—*n.* prospect, awaiting, foresight, prevention, preclusion, preconception, prelibation, provision, antepast. *(non-expectation, realization, unprepardness, surprise, consummation, enjoyment.)*

antipathy—*n.* dislike, hatred, aversion, enmity, rancor, bitterness, repugnance, ill-will, digust, abhorrence. *(affinity, respect, regard, sympathy, love, approval, esteem, reverence, affection.)*

antique—*adj.* ancient, quaint, relic, curio, objet d'art. trinket, antiquated, pristene, immemorial. *(new, modern, recent, modish, fashionable, current, up-to-date, stylish.)*

anxiety—*n.* unease, worry, trouble, solicitude, misgiving, anguish, concern, apprehension, fear. *(contentment, relief, apathy, ease, aplomb, nonchalance, tranquility, composure.)*

anxious—*adj.* uneasy, keen, watchful, solicitous, ardent, concerned, careful, intent, restless. *(careless, cool, inert, certain, confident, ease, unruffled, nonchalent.)*

apathy—*n.* insensibility, unconcern, passiveness, indifference, coolness, lack of interest. *(concern, interest, care, sensibility, eagerness, fervor, zeal, irritability.)*

ape—*v.* simulate, copy, mimic, echo, mock, follow, imitate, emulate. *(vary, change, modify, not to imitate, originate.)*

apiece—*adv.* analytically, each, respectively, severally, individually. *(together, en masse, synthetically, collectively, overall, as a group.)*

apology—*n.* explanation, plea, defense, confession, pretext, evasion, vindication, excuse, acknowledgment of error. *(wrong, censure, offense, impeachment, insult, charge, complaint, accusation, injury.)*

appal—*v.* daunt, dismay, shock, alarm, horrify, revolt, discourage, abash, sicken, frighten, cow, nauseate. *(rally, calm, reassure, please, at-*

tract, console, comfort, encourage.)

apparel—*n.* garments, robes, attire, vesture, habit, togs, costume, dress, clothing, gear. *(rags, nudity, divestiture, dishabille, tatters.)*

apparent—*adj.* understandable, evident, obvious, visible, likely, overt, presumable, ostensible, conspicuous, certain, distinct, open. *(hidden, real, veiled, disguised, obscure, uncertain, improbable, inapparent, dubious.)*

appeal—*v.* invoke, beseech, urge, request, apply, plea, petition, solicit, address, invite, apostrophize. *(deny, disclaim, recall, refuse, repudiate, protest, reject, disavow.)*

appearance—*n.* advent, arrival, appearing, aspect, manner, look, pretense, manifestation, emergence, coming. *(vanishing, passing, concealment, departure, unlikelihood, presumption.)*

append—*v.* add, attach, join, supplement, fasten, affix, hang. *(remove, omit, separate, disconnect, subtract, detach, take away.)*

appetite—*n.* passion, yearning, craving, tendency, gusto, thirst, proclivity, zest, impulse, want, propension. *(apathy, dislike, surfeit, loathing, repugnance, aversion, fill, revulsion, hatred.)*

applause—*n.* plaudits, eulogy, cheers, acclamation, ovation, fanfare, praise, commendation, homage, compliments, encoring, approval. *(disapproval, blame, condemnation, criticism, contempt, ridicule, hissing, obloquy, vituperation.)*

applicable—*adj.* germane, useful, apropos, pertinent, appropriate, apt, suitable. *(unfit, wrong, irrelevant, inconducive, useless, unsuitable.)*

appoint—*v.* establish, arrange, allot, apportion, nominate, select, employ, choose, fix, prescribe, elect, invest, institute, ordain. *(fire, cancel, dismiss, discharge, reverse, withdraw, suspend, disappoint, strip, dismantle, divest, recall.)*

apportion—*v.* allocate, ration, distribute, administer, dole out, dispense, share, deal, consign, prorate, adjust. *(resume, reappoint, collect, give all, divert, assemble, retain, receive, reserve, withhold, gather.)*

appreciate—*v.* cherish, recognize, regard, value, relish, admire, savor, acknowledge, respect, treasure. *(disparage, depreciate, misconceive, ignore, misjudge, deflate, underrate, belittle.)*

apprehend—*v.* seize, detect, arrest, dread, comprehend, fear, discern, anticipate, catch, capture, understand, perceive. *(lose, liberate, ignore, misconjecture, misapprehend, release, free, discharge, let go.)*

apprentice—*n.* pupil, novice, neophyte, beginner, student, indentured assistant. *(master, expert, professional.)*

approach—*v.* advance, gain upon, near. *(leave, retreat, diverge, exist, retire.)*

appropriate—*v.* take, confiscate, expropriate, allocate, allot, set apart, assign, earmark. *(donate, relinquish, cede.)*

approve—*v.* praise, sanction, respect, authorize, second, prize, cherish, value. *(repudiate, censure, dislike, criticize, reject, refute, disown.)*

approximate—*adj.* resemble, near, border, nearly equal, abut, closely resemble, suggest, verge on. *(precise, vary, exact, accurate, correct, recede, deviate, differ.)*

apt—*adj.* clever, suitable, proper, liable, relevant, pertinent, ready, seemly, apropos, appropriate. *(awkward, averse, slow, inapt, illtimed, dull, improper.)*

arbitrary—*adj.* despotic, harsh, willful, capricious, fanciful, tyrannical, selfish, irresponsible, domineering, whimsical. *(lenient, impersonal, modest, objective, limited, constitutional, lawful.)*

arbitrate—*v.* adjust, compose, mediate, adjudicate, settle, umpire, judge, referee, decide. *(claim, negotiate, dispute, litigate, misjudge, appeal.)*

ardent—*adj.* fervent, eager, warm, passionate, vehement, fierce, emotional, lusty, keen, feverish, zealous, burning, earnest. *(cold, nonchalant, apathetic, unloving, frigid, phlegmatic, passionless, detached, indifferent.)*

argue—*v.* dispute, battle, wrangle, reason, question, imply, demonstrate, bicker, quibble, denote. *(propound, agree, concur, assert, doubt, conceal, command, assent.)*

argument—*n.* controversy, quarrel, dispute, reasoning, debate, embroilment, altercation, clash. *(assumption,* *agreement, harmony, assertion, rebuttal, response, accord.)*

arid—*adj.* barren, sterile, dry, unproductive, lifeless, dreary, dull. *(damp, fertile, lush, pithy, luxuriant, moist, productive, lively, verdant.)*

aright—*adv.* well, truly, correctly, justly, properly, appropriately, suitably, without error. *(wrongly, awry, incorrectly, erroneously, properly, defectively.)*

aromatic—*adj.* sweet smelling, scented, fragrant, spicy, pungent, odoriferous. *(unscented, rank, putrid, acrid, bad smelling, malodorous.)*

arouse—*v.* stimulate, animate, spur, kindle, stir, incite, provoke, foster, quicken, whet, goad, excite. *(mollify, pacify, still, alleviate, calm, quell, allay, mitigate, dampen.)*

arraign—*v.* impute, cite, accuse, indict, impeach, denounce, prosecute. *(condone, pardon, discharge, acquit, vindicate, absolve, exonerate.)*

arrange—*v.* array, classify, marshall, rank, adjust, pose, systematize, sort, harmonize, prepare, order, parcel. *(scatter, disarray, strip, jumble, confuse, disperse, derange, divest, disturb.)*

array—*v.* deploy, don, garnish, place, dispose, arrange, attire, decorate. *(confuse, jumble, strip, mess up, disarray, denude.)*

arrest—*v.* capture, hold, halt, retain, apprehend, catch, detain, hinder, obstruct, suspend, incarcerate. *(free, release, let go, discharge, liberate, dismiss.)*

arrive—*v.* approach, near, enter, attain, land, come, reach, succeed, make good. *(start, leave, depart, retire, embark, withdraw.)*

arrogance—*n.* contemptuousness, hauteur, assurance, loftiness, vanity, conceit, egoism, self-importance, discourtesy, swagger, contempt. *(shyness, modesty, meekness, bashfulness, humility, simplicity, deference, courtesy, politeness, self-effacement.)*

artful—*adj.* maneuvering, subtle, shrewd, diplomatic, scheming, contriving, deceitful, underhand. *(innocent, open, natural, candid, unsophisticated, frank, naive, simple.)*

artificial—*adj.* false, invented, manmade, imitation, fake, simulated, concocted, unnatural, phony, synthetic. *(genuine, real, natural, spontaneous, artless, unaffected, sincere, candid, actual, frank.)*

ascertain—*v.* establish, verify, confirm, prove, learn, detect, settle, ferret out. *(surmise, suppose, conjecture, presume, guess.)*

ascribe—*v.* credit, refer, render, trace to, charge, arrogate, impute, assign. *(discount, refuse, dissociate, deny, disconnect.)*

askew—*adv., adj.* crooked, awry, lopsided, aslant, crookedly. *(line, aligned, plumb, straight as an arrow.)*

aspiration—*n.* ambition, hope, yearning, endeavor, daydream, purpose, desire, effort, craving. *(dullness, inertia, aversion, aimlessness, callousness, repudiation.)*

assembly—*n.* throng, council, conclave, meeting, conference, collection, pack, gathering, body, flock, congregation. *(disunion, dismissal, disruption, dissipation.)*

assent—*v.* accede, acquiesce, agree, approve, allow, comply, concur, yield, permit, acknowledge. *(differ, dissent, deny, repudiate, disclaim, reject, negate, refuse, veto.)*

assign—*v.* name, apportion, refer, allot to, convey, specify, stipulate, determine, prescribe. *(retain, disconnect, withhold, discharge, keep, open, divest, hold in abeyance.)*

assist—*v.* collaborate, reinforce, succor, support, cooperate, aid, boost, help, second, uphold, abet, serve. *(hamper, impede, obstruct, antagonize, clog, counteract, oppose.)*

assistant—*n.* aider, attendant, ally, partner, adjutant, aide, auxiliary, colleague, accomplice, helper. *(rival, foe, opposer, hinderer, antagonist.)*

association—*n.* companionship, alliance, membership, society, fellowship, partnership, corporation, league, intimacy, friendship, community. *(solitude, avoidance, severance, disunion, disconnection, separation, alienation, independence.)*

assortment—*n.* quantity, stock, collection, variety, miscellany, lot, motley, store, conglomeration, diversity, array. *(misplacement, sameness, monotony, mixing, heaping together, displacement.)*

assume—*v.* arrogate, postulate, uphold, certify,

wear, fancy, infer, presume, judge, surmise, gather. *(allow, render, concede, know, prove, leave, relinquish, put aside.)*

assure—*v.* promise, rally, encourage, aid, uphold, guarantee, clinch, secure, confirm, ensure, advise, certify. *(deter, warn, age, unsettle, intimidate, deny, refute, lie, disavow, fib, doubt.)*

astonish—*v.* amaze, surprise, startle, stun, shock, alarm, stupefy, daze, stagger, dumb, perplex, confuse, bewilder. *(rally, embolden, encourage, assure, anticipate, foresee, bore, count upon.)*

astray—*adj., adv.* loose, missing, erring, wrong, amiss, afield, off, into error. *(close, safe, at home, right, on course.)*

athletic—*adj.* muscular, powerful, brawny, burly, strong, strapping, manly, vigorous, herculean, sinewy, hardy. *(puny, feeble, effeminate, fragile, weak, frail, strengthless.)*

atrocious—*adj.* diabolical, wicked, shameful, infamous, ruthless, savage, monstrous, cruel, flagrant, nefarious, brutal. *(humane, kind, admirable, benevolent, gentle, chivalrous, merciful, noble.)*

attach—*v.* conciliate, tie, adhere, couple, add, secure, bind, unite, fasten, append, annex, join. *(loosen, detach, estrange, untie, release, disconnect, alienate.)*

attack—*v.* censure, invade, besiege, storm, threaten, assault, aggress, criticize. *(vindicate, retreat, defend, support, sustain, excuse, uphold, resist, befriend, cover.)*

attack—*n.* assault, onset, pelt, invasion, stone, aggression, onslaught, trespass. *(protection, aid, withdrawal, support, flight, defense, resistance.)*

attain—*v.* grasp, acquire, procure, win, master, fulfill, execute, reach, accomplish, reap, score. *(forfeit, lose, miss, let go, fail at, abandon, fall short of.)*

attempt—*v.* strive, venture, force, experiment, undertake, effort, violate, aim, hazard. *(abandon, dismiss, neglect, shun, disregard, drop, pretermit.)*

attend—*v.* observe, escort, oversee, listen, mark, watch, superintend, mind, notice, guard, serve, note. *(disregard, forsake, miss, leave, skip, ignore, desert, disassociate, abandon, wander.)*

attention—*n.* alertness, care, consideration, study, respect, civility, concentration, thought, note, observation, concern. *(remission, carelessness, absence, neglect, rudeness, abstraction, negligence, unconcern.)*

attest—*v.* certify, corroborate, display, support, vouch, aver, show evidence, seal, testify, prove, authenticate, imply, ratify, warrant, demonstrate, suggest. *(contradict, exclude, refute, deny, belie, disprove, gainsay, negate, falsify, exclude.)*

attire—*v.* garb, costume, dress, outfit. *(strip, bare, undress, disrobe, unclothe.)*

attract—*v.* dispose, allure, pull, fascinate, enchant, evoke, influence, captivate, invite, precipitate. *(estrange, repel, alienate, disgust, offend, deter.)*

attractive—*adj.* magnetic, winning, alluring, enticing, handsome, fetching, chic, elegant, tasteful, charming, lovely, fair, captivating. *(repugnant, deformed, loathsome, ugly, repulsive, repellent, unattractive, unpleasant, deterrent.)*

attribute—*v.* assign, arrogate, refer, connect, credit, blame, associate. *(disconnect, divorce, dissever, dissociate.)*

attribute—*n.* characteristic, sign, indication, reduction, erosion, weakening, quality. *(essence, substance, its correlative, viz, etc. misnomer, mask, semblance.)*

attrition—*n.* repentance, erosion, remorse, friction, sorrow, self-reproach, grinding. *(callousness, buildup, relentlessness, strengthening, impenitence.)*

audacious—*adj.* adventurous, reckless, rash, hardy, brave, valiant, impudent, insolent, fearless, dauntless. *(cautious, timid, unenterprising, shy, humble, polite, cowardly, unventuresome.)*

audacity—*n.* temerity, boldness, daring, recklessness, spunk, nerve, effrontery, arrogance. *(self-preservation, prudence, forethought, calculation, caution, timidity, meekness, gentility.)*

augment—*v.* enlarge, swell, inflate, increase, add, acquire, supply, deepen, amplify, widen, magnify. *(withdrawal, lose, reduce, diminish, subside, curtail, detract, waste, abridge, narrow, shrink, lessen.)*

augury—*n.* omen, prediction, conjecture, forerunner,

indication, herald, forecasting. *(science, experience, observation.)*

august—*adj.* dignified, lofty, solemn, eminent, venerable, majestic, exalted, pompous, regal. *(common, paltry, mean, undignified, ridiculous, despicable, unstately, lowly, petty.)*

auspicious—*adj.* lucky, successful, hopeful, timely, felicitous, right, golden, fortunate, opportune, encouraging. *(unfavorable, abortive, hopeless, ill-fated, unpromising, doomed, pathetic, unlucky.)*

austere—*adj.* rigid, strict, spartan, grave, severe, stiff, rigorous, harsh, chaste, stark. *(affable, tender, cheerful, sunny, mild, lavish, indulgent, relaxed.)*

authentic—*adj.* real, true, accurate, genuine, actual, bona fide, legitimate, reliable, dependable, factual, accredited, trustworthy. *(false, fake, disputed, unauthorized, sham, unreliable, deceptive, corrupt, fraudulent, counterfeit, fictitious, untrue, phony.)*

authoritative—*adj.* conclusive, sure, potent, imperious, sanctioned, ruling, lordly, dogmatic, firm, arrogant, autocratic, tyrannical, commanding, peremptory. *(vague, vacillating, deceptive, weak, inconclusive, servile, meek, bland, indefinite, conciliatory, affable, frivolous, invalid.)*

authority—*n.* authenticity, control, weight, supremacy, jurisdiction, sufferance, prestige, rule, esteem, force, command, direction, respect, administration, influence. *(indecision, weakness, groundlessness, servility, wrong, inconclusiveness, servitude, incompetency, inoperativeness.)*

autocratic—*adj.* arbitrary, absolute, tyrannical, depotic, czaristic, dictatorial, irresponsible. *(subordinate, limited, democratic, lenient, indulgent, constitutional, responsible.)*

auxilliary—*adj.* abetting, conducive, helping, secondary, backup, ancillary. *(superfluous, cumbersome, chief, primary, irrelevant, unassisting.)*

avail—*v.* hold, endure, service, aid, utilize, profit, answer, suffice, benefit, use. *(fail, betray, harm, ignore, hinder, disappoint.)*

available—*adj.* convertible, handy, on tap, obtainable, accessible, applicable, helpful, suitable. *(inappropriate, in-*

operative, inconducive, unobtainable, unserviceable.)

avarice—*n.* cupidity, stinginess, griping, venality, greed, covetousness, penury, miserliness, greediness, rapacity. *(bountifulness, extravagance, waste, generosity, liberality, munificence.)*

aver—*v.* oblige, protest, affirm, insist, profess, avow, maintain. *(contradict, repudiate, disclaim, doubt, dispute, deny, be uncertain.)*

avidity—*n.* eagerness, longing, varacity, hankering, greed, ravenousness, desire. *(apathy, nausea, repugnance, loathing, coldness, unwillingness, disdain, aversion.)*

avoid—*v.* abandon, forsake, eschew, shun, fly, elude, escape, dodge, shirk, evade. *(approach, address, court, invite, pursue, find, solicit, accost.)*

award—*v.* attribute, accord, divide, give, confer on, assign, decree, grant, determine. *(withdraw, retain, withhold, refuse, deny, misappropriate.)*

aware—*adj.* sensible, certified, knowledgeable, mindful, conversant, cognizant, informed, known. *(insensible, unaware, ignorant, unmindful, oblivious, unconscious.)*

awful—*adj.* appalling, ugly, dreadful, solemn, horrendous, deplorable, ghastly, hideous, portentous. *(unalarming, alluring, terrific, pretty, unnoticeable, likeable, delightful, unimposing.)*

awkward—*adj.* clownish, unhandy, unskillful, uncouth, boorish, stiff, gauche, ungainly. *(agile, neat, dexterous, deft, adroit, supple, nimble.)*

axiom—*n.* Truth, aphorism, postulate, maxim, principle, self-evidence. *(absurdness, paradox, absurdity, nonsense, contradiction.)*

B

babble—*n.* dribble, gabble, jabbering, twaddle, cackle, chatter, prattle, chitchat. *(sense, wisdom, learning, knowledge, understanding, erudition.)*

babel—*n.* clamor, din, clang, turmoil, confusion, bedlam, hubbub, discord, jargon. *(articulation, calm, intonation, monotony, elocution, enunciation, tranquility, distinctness, consecutiveness.)*

backing—*n.* help, assistance, sanction, endorsement, succor, aid, championing, cooperation. *(opposition,* *hindrance, resistance, subversion, repudiation.)*

bad—*adj.* defective, useless, imperfect, faulty, unfit, awful, inferior, below par, inadequate. *(excellent, fine, first rate, superior, exemplary, healthful, agreeable, pleasant.)*

baffle—*v.* disconcert, defeat, mystify, frustrate, elude, neutralize, amaze, counteract, perplex, dodge, foil, mar, restrain, balk, estop, counterfoil, upset, mock. *(aid, promote, transmit, point, assist, allow, encourage, advance, abet, enforce.)*

bait—*n.* decoy, allurement, hound, snare, inducement, badger, morsel, tease. *(intimidation, calm, deterrent, soothing, warning, prohibition, lull, dissuasion.)*

balance—*v.* estimate, weigh, pit, equalize, counteract, adjust, set, redress. *(tilt, subvert, overbalance, upset, cant, mispoise.)*

balderdash—*n.* flummery, fustian, drivel, froth, nonsense, bombast, twaddle, rhodomontade. *(wisdom, truth, sense, reason, fact, logic.)*

balk—*v.* thwart, nullify, defeat, impede, baffle, circumvent, hinder, prevent, bar, foil, estop, frustrate, stop, counteract. *(promote, aid, cooperate, encourage, instigate, progress, advance, abet.)*

balm—*n.* solve, emollient, sedative, narcotic, panacea, comfort, tranquilizer. *(stimulant, abrasive, irritant, nuisance.)*

balmy—*adj.* mild, pleasant, temperate, soft, gentle, refreshing, soothing. *(inclement, stormy, unpleasant, irritating, chafing, sensible, sound, normal.)*

banish—*v.* abandon, extrude, relegate, exile, repudiate, eject, eliminate, expel, expatriate, disclaim, eradicate. *(admit, cherish, protect, accept, foster, encourage, entertain, harbor, domiciliate, locate, retain.)*

banquet—*n.* festivity, carouse, dine, feast, treat, entertainment, cheer, repast. *(starvation, fast, snack, abstinence.)*

banter—*n.* mockery, irony, chaff, joshing, jesting, ridicule, badinage, ragging. *(discourse, kid, needle, argument, discussion, jolly, ride.)*

bar—*v.* obstruct, hinder, impede, thwart, restrain, exclude, forbid. *(allow, permit, let, accept, admit, welcome, receive, invite.)*

bargain—*n.* business, gain, agreement, speculation, pact, profit, treaty, transaction, hawking, haggling. *(misprofit, extravagance, swindle, loss.)*

barren—*adj.* depleted, useless, futile, ineffectual, dull, unfruitful, prosaic, uninformative, unrewarding, stale. *(productive, fertile, prolific, lush, rich, luxuriant, fruitful, interesting, instructive.)*

base—*adj.* vile, sordid, mean, pedestal, infamous, ignoble, source, cheap, corrupt, worthless, shameful, vulgar, dishonorable. *(exalted, noble, esteemed, correct, pure, precious, virtuous, shrill, honored, lofty, refined, valued.)*

bashful—*adj.* diffident, shy, timorous, modest, sheepish, retiring, reserved. *(impudent, forward, brazen, bold, impudent, arrogant, pert, unreserved, conceited.)*

basic—*adj.* fundamental, vital, essential, cardinal, key, necessary, care, prime, prerequisite. *(supporting, secondary, frill, trivial, accessory, superfluous, extra.)*

battle—*n.* skirmish, contest, engagement, fight, massacre, action, encounter, conflict, combat. *(harmony, truce, council, peace, reconcile, arbitrament, mediation.)*

bawl—*v.* roar, bellow, yell, clamor, vociferate, shout. *(babble, whisper, whimper, mumble, weep, wail.)*

beach—*n.* coast, seaboard, shore, seashore, rim, sands, water edge. *(deep, main, ocean, sea.)*

beaming—*adj.* radiant, bright, transparent, happy, gleaming, glowing, beautiful, translucid. *(opague, wan, gloomy, dingy, matt, sullen, morose.)*

bear—*v.* transport, maintain, brace, tolerate, sustain, lift, undergo, buttress, carry, admit, suffer, support, harbor, enact, endure, generate, produce. *(protest, eject, stroke, surrender, shed, resent, defend, relinquish, drop, reject, repel, decline.)*

beat—*v.* whack, conquer, pound, pommel, strike, batter, overcome, truncheon, surpass, vanquish, thrash, belabor. *(stroke, shield, defend, submit, relinquish, fall, surrender, protect, caress.)*

beauty—*n.* grace, exquisiteness, embellishment, radiance, picturesqueness, adornment, attractiveness, bloom, comeliness. *(ugliness, bareness, repulsiveness, foulness, hideousness, homeliness, unattractiveness.)*

because—*conj.* consequently, accordingly, owing, on account of. *(independently, inconsequently, unconnectedly, irrespectively.)*

beck—*n.* signal, instructions, control, mandate, authority, gesture, indication, command, summons, call, nod, influence, sign, subserviency. *(unsubservience, independence.)*

becoming—*adj.* neat, proper, seemly, enhancing, comely, graceful, befitting, pleasing, decorous, improving, beseeming, fit. *(unseemly, indecent, unattractive, uncomely, unbecoming, ungraceful, unsuitable, incongruous, derogatory.)*

befitting—*adj.* becoming, expedient, proper, relevant, desirable, appropriate, consistent, seemly, fitting, decent. *(unsuitable, improper, obligatory, unseemly, improper, inexpedient, compulsory, meaningless, incomptible, unbecoming.)*

before—*adv.* anteriorly, prior to, foremost, precedently, first. *(subsequently, later, afterwards, following, behind, after.)*

beg—*v.* request, supplicate, implore, plead, ask, petition, pray, crave, solicit. *(exact, require, demand, insist, give, bestow.)*

beggarly—*adj.* miserable, scant, niggardly, despicable, poor, wretched, miserly, stingy, scant. *(princely, liberal, magnificent, noble, sumptuous, prodigal, stately, gorgeous.)*

begin—*v.* prepare, originate, inaugurate, initiate, start, arise, create, commence. *(complete, conclude, stop, finish, achieve, consummate, terminate, expire.)*

beginning—*n.* start, rise, outbreak, opening, source, foundation, precedent, prelude, inception, commencement, preface, threshold, outset, initiation, preparation. *(finale, close, conclusion, completion, end, termination, consummation.)*

behavior—*n.* comportment, manner, deportment, actions, conduct, demeanor, proceeding, attitude. *(misbehavior, misconduct, misdemeanor.)*

belief—*n.* credence, faith, opinion, acceptance, trust, confidence, creed, persuasion, admission, concession, avowal, reliance, permission. *(distrust, misgiving, skepticism, unbelief, denial, incredulity, disavowal, rejection.)*

belligerent—*adj.* hostile, pugnacious, quarrelsome, combative, defiant, argumentative, warlike, embattled, cantankerous. *(easygoing, cool, compromising, pacific, conciliatory, amicable.)*

belonging—*adj.* connected, obligatory, congenial, cognate, accompanying, related. *(alien, uninvolved, independant, optional, unrelated, discretional, irrelevant, unconnected, impertinent, unimplied, uncongenial.)*

bemuse—*v.* muddle, obscure, stupefy, confound, confuse, disorient, unsettle, daze. *(enlighten, clarify, illuminate, simplify, straighten out.)*

bend—*v.* incline, swerve, curve, bias, buckle, mold, influence, accompany, twist, deviate, lean. *(extend, advance, straighten, proceed, stiffen, crush, resist, continue.)*

benediction—*n.* commendation, blessing, thanksgiving, gratitude, boon, dedication, prayer. *(censure, curse, calumniation, obloquy, execration, malediction, disapproval.)*

benefactor—*n.* contributor, upholder, welldoer, backer, subscriber, friend, donor, subsidizer, well-wisher. *(antagonist, foe, rival, backfriend, oppressor, disfavor, opponent.)*

beneficial—*adj.* salutory, wholesome, valuable, profitable, healthful, advantageous, good. *(noxious, detrimental, prejudicial, destructive, unprofitable, hurtful, baneful.)*

benefit—*n.* service, utility, good, profit, asset, advantage, blessing, reward, favor, avail, use. *(damage, injury, privation, detriment, handicap, calamity, bereavement, hinder.)*

benign—*adj.* kindly, warm, generous, amiable, benevolent, altruistic, affable. *(cold, hostile, violent, malign, nasty, mean, inclement.)*

bequeath—*v.* grant, devise, bestow, endow, give, impart, demise, leave, render, *(alienate, withhold.)*

bereavement—*n.* affliction, loss, destitution, adversity, tragedy, deprivation. *(donation, restoration, gift, substitution, consolation, blessing.)*

besotted—*adj.* steeped, drunk, gross, befuddled, intoxicated, prejudiced, dazed, stupefied. *(temperate, clear, steady, unbiased, enlight-*

ened, refined, self-possessed.)

bespeak—*v.* forestall, indicate, prearrange, suggest, betake, signify, provide. *(contradict, resign, negate, belie, countermand.)*

bestial—*adj.* animalistic, barbaric, wild, brutish, inhuman, disgusting. *(human, benevolent, compassionate, gentle, humane.)*

better—*adj.*superior, finer, preferable, choicer, worthier. *(poorer, worse, inferior, lesser, second-rate.)*

betimes—*adv.* early, prepared, readily, beforehand, soon, seasonably. *(slowly, sluggishly, belatedly, behindhand.)*

betray—*v.* delude, circumvent, abandon, deceive, dupe, defect, reveal, manifest, dishonor, ensnare. *(foster, dare, overlook, be faithful, support, protect, guard, cherish, adhere, preserve, cover.)*

beware—*v.* refrain, heed, take warning, care, fear, mind, consider, avoid. *(overlook, neglect, brave, dare, incur, ignore.)*

bewilder—*v.* confound, puzzle, muddle, astonish, nonplus, disconcert, daze, perplex, fluster, mystify, mislead. *(inform, instruct, advise, guide, edify, lead, educate.)*

bewitch—*v.* fascinate, charm, entrance, beguile, enchant, enrapture, captivate. *(disgust, disillusionize, exorcise, disenchant, repulse.)*

bias—*n.* prejudice, bent, proclivity, feeling, idea, preconception, inclination, bigotry. *(fairness, impartiality, objectivity, tolerance, dispassionateness.)*

bid—*v.* request, direct, tell, charge, offer, summon, command, propose, enjoin, greet. *(deter, restrain, forbid, prohibit, ban, dissallow.)*

bide—*v.* remain, stay, await, continue, tolerate, tarry, anticipate, suffer, stand, expect, abide. *(depart, move, resent, abominate, quit, move, repel, go, migrate, rebel, resist.)*

big—*adj.* wide, proud, fat, arrogant, mammoth, huge, pompous, enormous, massive, large, bulky. *(narrow, slight, easy, microscopic, lean, affable, petite, small, minute, little.)*

bilious—*adj.* irritable, peevish, angry, grumpy, cranky, grouchy, petulant, snappish, cantankerous. *(good, fine, attractive, amicable, gentle,* *mild, sympathetic, cordial, happy.)*

binding—*adj.* restraining, costive, mandatory, obligatory, styptic, compelling, astringent, restrictive. *(enlarging, flexible, loosening, elastic, opening, distending.)*

birth—*n.* nativity, origin, parentage, lineage, inception, source, race, nobility, beginning, rise, family, extraction. *(plebeianism, death, miscarriage, extinction, end.)*

bitter—*adj.* sharp, tart, severe, caustic, acrimonious, intense, afflictive, astringent, harsh, sarcastic, sad, stinging, pungent, cutting, acrid. *(pleasant, trivial, light, kindly, bland, mellow, genial, insipid, affable, mitigated, sweet.)*

blacken—*v.* befowl, defame, calumniate, asperse, discredit, malign, bespatter, slander, vilify, smear, dishonor, decry. *(eulogize, praise, vindicate, clear, exalt.)*

blackguard—*n.* rapscallion, villain, scamp, rogue, rascal, scoundrel. *(hero, gentleman.)*

blame—*v.* chide, reproach, dispraise, reprove, condemn, accuse, reprobate, reprehend, rebuke, censure, vituperate, disapprove, burden. *(exonerate, praise, approve, excuse, acquit, encourage, vindicate, exculpate.)*

bland—*adj.* gentle, courteous, gracious, monotonous, soft, complaisant, mild, tender, benign, prosaic, affable. *(abrupt, exciting, harsh, severe, rough.)*

blank—*adj.* vacant, clean, dull, empty, hollow, plain, futile, void. *(full, marked, busy, alert, sharp, valuable, significant, consequential.)*

blast—*v.* wither, shrivel, destroy, blight, ruin, wreck. *(swell, restore, expland, enlarge.)*

blast—*n.* explosion, burst, destruction, gale, tempest, tornado, squall, breeze, afflation, flurry, squall, frustration. *(neutralization, zephyr, gentle breeze, puff.)*

blatant—*adj.* gross, cheap, unpolished, harsh, noisy, crude, uncouth, tawdry, vulgar, tasteless. *(subtle, delicate, cultured, agreeable, unobtusive, acquiescent, genteel.)*

bleak—*adj.* bare, exposed, stormy, grim, open, dreary, nipping, blank, cold. *(verdant, halcyonic, balmy, warm, sheltered, lush, luxuriant, zephyrous, flourishing.)*

blemish—*n.* blot, speck, stain, obvious, blur, spot, tarnish, dishonor, gross, taint, disfigurement, disgrace, defect, daub, flow, discoloration. *(honor, purity, perfection, intactness, refinement, unsulliedness.)*

blend—*v.* harmonize, combine, merge, fuse, mingle, coalesce, amalgamate, unite, complement, assimilate. *(divide, separate, split, run, dissociate, confound, divide.)*

bless—*v.* gladden, endow, thank, consecrate, enrich, cheer, sanctify, felicitate, rejoice. *(ignore, sadden, condemn, deprive, curse, impoverish, harm, anathematize.)*

blind—eyeless, ignorant, visionless, unseeing, unaware, depraved, prejudiced, unperceptive, unconscious, undiscerning, irrational. *(penetrating, keen, clear-sighted, aware, concerned, conscious, rational, far-sighted, sensitive, discriminating.)*

blink—*v.* connive, ignore, wink, squint, overlook, peer. *(note, mark, visit, notice, be aware of.)*

bliss—*n.* joy, rapture, luxury, ectasy, blessedness, paradise. *(woe, suffering, agony, condemnation, misery, accursedness, grief, gloom.)*

blithe—*adj.* merry, happy, radiant, light, vivacious, gay, glee, blithesome, bonny, gladsome, cheerful, lively, elastic. *(dejected, sad, dull, morose, heavy, sullen.)*

blockhead—*n.* dunce, dullard, booby, numskull, clod, dolt, ignoramus, ninny, chump, simpleton, dunderhead, loggerhead. *(luminary, adept, sage, savant, scholar, philosopher, schoolman.)*

bloom—*v.* blossom, height, perfection, prime, flourish, prosper, succeed, blush, florescence. *(decay, dwindle, wane, languish, waste away.)*

blooming—*adj.* flowering, young, flourishing, vigorous, beautiful, fair, blossoming, exuberant. *(blighted, old, fading, unsightly, withering, waning, paralysed, deformed, declining, blasted.)*

blot—*v.* tarnish, sully, discolor, obliterate, blur, blotch, smear, stain, erase, daub, obscure, pollute, smutch, spoil, stigma. *(clear, perpetuate, cleanse, honor, elucidate, conserve, credit.)*

blow—*n.* breath, knock, bang, puff, stroke, crack, shock, wound, calamity, disappointment, blast, affliction, misfortune, tragedy. *(consolation, comfort, sparing, calm, assuagement, relief, caress.)*

bluff—*adj.* bold, frank, rude, swaggering, blunt, gruff, surly, open, brusk, discourteous, rough, bullying, hectoring, coarse, blustering. *(courteous, polite, inclined, undulating, suave, inabrupt, reserved, polished.)*

blunder—*n.* mistake, fault, inaccuracy, indescretion, slip, oversight, delusion, fumble, error, omission. *(exactness, prevention, correction, success, foresight, accuracy, achievement, truthfulness, faultlessness, atonement, hit.)*

blush—*n.* flush, carnation, confusion, bloom, glow, color, shame, self-reproach, guiltiness, aspect, complexion. *(unconsciousiness, purity, effrontery, paleness, innocence, ashen, boldness, guiltlessness.)*

boast—*v.* brag, swell, bluster, flaunt, truimph, vapor, glory, exhibit. *(be ashamed, disclaimer, cover up, deprecate, disavow.)*

body—*n.* mass, collection, organization, assemblage, association, whole, matter, substantiality, corporation, substance, denseness. *(soul, individual, intellect, spirit, mind.)*

boggle—*v.* blunder, halt, demur, blotch, spoil, vacillate, botch, hesitate, falter, dubitate. *(advance, face, beautify, clear, perfect, refine, encounter, advance, complete.)*

boisterous—*adj.* tumultuous, rowdy, obstreperous, shrill, clamorous, rambunctious, unruly, wild, loud. *(well-behaved, orderly, quiet, restrained, calm, tranquil, sedate, serene, disciplined.)*

bold—*adj.* fearless, brave, forward, dauntless, audacious, courageous, stout, daring, intrepid, brazen, lionhearted, adventurous. *(bashful, fearful, meek, timid, shy, weak, retiring.)*

bombast—*n.* braggadocio, bluster, pomposity, fustian, extravagance, tumidity, rhodomontade, gasconade, bravado. *(humility, truthfulness, refrain, modesty, veracity, reserve, shyness.)*

bond—*n.* association, compact, obligation, cement, link, tie, chain, security, fastening, manacle. *(honor, option, freedom, discretion, detachment.)*

bondsman—*n.* serf, captive, vassal, toiler, prisoner, slave. *(freeman, yeoman, master, lord, gentleman, aristocrat.)*

bonny—*adj.* pleasant, fair, cheerful, gay, pretty, shapely, merry, buxom, lively. *(dull,* *quiet, ill-favored, deformed, unseemly.)*

boost—*v.* lift, hoist, raise, elevate, pitch, shove, press, push, promote. *(reduce, decline, diminish, lessen, curtail, ease, deduct, belittle.)*

border—*n.* brink, rim, edge, circumference, limit, boundry, perimeter, hem, confine, enclosure, brim, band. *(tract, space, middle, center, land, inside, interior.)*

border on—*v.* be adjacent to, adjoin, be conterminous with, approach, come near. *(be remote from, be away from.)*

botch—*v.* jumble, mar, blunder, fumble, patch, disconcert, muff, cabble, spoil, mess, fail. *(trim, mend, perform, embroider, master, harmonize, beautify, handle, manipulate, perfect.)*

bother—*n.* worry, fuss, excitement, confusion, flurry, trouble. *(orderliness, quiet, comfort, calm, composure, peace, solace.)*

boundless—*adj.* infinite, illimitable, immense, unlimited, endless, unbounded, immeasurable. *(limited, circumscribed, restricted, small, confined, narrow, bounded.)*

bounty—*n.* benevolence, donation, charity, assistance, munificence, gratuity, liberality, gift, generosity, aid. *(closeness, stinginess, niggardliness, avarice, hardness, churlishness, greed.)*

brag—*v.* swagger, extol, bully, boast, crow, vaunt. *(whimper, deprecate, cringe, whine.)*

branch—*n.* bough, member, limb, channel, shoot, twig, ramification, relative, tributary, scion, bifurcation, offspring. *(house, trunk, stock, race, family, mass, stem, conglomerate.)*

brave—*adj.* courageous, valiant, heroic, dauntless, unafraid, plucky, fearless, stalwart. *(cowardly, fearful, craven, timid, timorous, frightened, faint hearted.)*

break—*v.* rupture, shatter, destroy, fragment, demolish, fracture, tame, burst, mangle, infringe, violate, subdue, smash, shiver, sever, split, tear. *(conjoin, observe, obey, repair, heal, conserve, rally, service, protect, piece.)*

breath—*n.* inspiration, respiration, exhalation, aspiration, expiration, inhalation. *(passing, death, perishing, cessation, departure, dying.)*

breeding—*n.* education, training, nurture, manners, air, decorum, discipline, gentility, culture. *(ill-training, ill-manners, ill-breeding, ignorance, ill-behavior.)*

brevity—*n.* compendiousness, abbreviation, terseness, curtness, shortness, conciseness, closeness, briefness, pointedness. *(diffuseness, tediousness, verbosity, length, elongation, prolixity, extension, garrulity.)*

bright—*adj.* luminous, happy, joyous, glowing, shining, cheerful, brilliant, intense, burnished, lucid, witty, radiant, sparkling, vivid. *(dull, joyless, imbecile, pallid, opaque, dead, sullen, cheerless, morose, muddy, slow, stupid.)*

brilliant—*adj.* shining, beaming, glorious, gleaming, flashing, radiant, luminous, resplendent, sparkling, lustrous. *(opaque, dull, tarnished, lusterless, lifeless.)*

bring—*v.* convey, bear, import, transport, fetch, carry, induce, produce, initiate, procure, cause. *(debar, prevent, subtract, quash, remove, exclude, dispel, abstract, export.)*

brisk—*adj.* vivacious, alert, quick, animated, vigorous, lively, active, prompt, spry, spirited, nimble, sprightly. *(dull, indolent, lethargic, slow, stagnant, heavy, lazy, inactive, unenergetic.)*

broad—*adj.* expansive, liberal, indelicate, voluminous, wide, coarse, extensive, spacious, generic, unreserved, ample. *(confined, prejudiced, narrow-minded, slender, restricted, pointed, delicate, veiled, shaded, precise, specific, enigmatical, illiberal, reserved, bigoted.)*

brotherhood—*n.* association, fellowship, society, affiliation, sodality, comradeship. *(no antonyms).*

brutal—*adj.* inhuman, violent, intemperate, fierce, savage, rude, bloodthirsty, stolid, cruel, primitive, unfeeling, vindictive, dense, ignorant, barbarous, brutish, sensual. *(civilized, self-controlled, sympathetic, generous, chivalrous, polished, intelligent, conscientious, merciful.)*

bubble—*n.* fancy, trash, effervescence, conceit, froth, percolate, trifle, toy, bead. *(treasure, good, advantage, be flat, reality, verity, acquisition, substance, prize, jewel.)*

budge—*v.* change, influence, persuade, sway, convince, shift. *(remain, stay, stick, halt, pause.)*

bugbear—*n.* goblin, ghoul, ogre, specter, bugaboo,

scarecrow, spook, spirit, hobgoblin.

building—*n.* architecture, fabric, structure, house, erection, frame, construction, domicile. *(dismantlement, delapidation, demolition, ruin, destruction.)*

bulk—*n.* entirety, mass, body, bigness, weight, dimension, largeness, bigness, enormity, whole, integrity, volume, magnitude, majority, size, greatness. *(diminution, atom, disintegration, tenuity, lesser part, smallest part, minority, portion, section.*

bungler—*n.* fumbler, novice, clown, blunderer, botcher, muffer, lubber. *(artist, professor, expert, master, proficient, adept, workman, adroit.)*

buoyant—*adj.* vivacious, light, spirited, floating, elated, sprightly, energetic, lively, joyous, elastic, hopeful. *(moody, heavy, cheerless, sullen, joyless, depressed, doleful, dejected, desponding.)*

burden—*n.* incubus, load, grief, stress, weight, affliction, hamper, difficulty, obstruction, oppression. *(expedition, lightness, ease, abjugation, free, facility, consolation, mitigation, airiness, alleviation, lighten, facility, disburdenment, assuagement, light-heartedness.)*

burn—*v.* brand, cauterize, flash, scorch, ignite, consume, cremate, glow, singe, kindle, rage, incinerate, smoulder, blaze. *(cool, wane, pale, chill, lower, extinguish, soothe, glimmer, stifle.)*

bury—*v.* conceal, suppress, cancel, compose, screen, hush, entomb, inter, obliterate, repress, veil. *(resuscitate, bruit, expose, reveal, exhume, aggravate, excavate, air.)*

business—*n.* profession, affair, office, concern, career, trade, duty, interest, occupation, calling, activity, vocation, employment, matter. *(inactivity, hobby, leisure, stagnation, avocation.)*

bustle—*n.* stir, commotion, excitement, scramble, business, flurry, haste, energy, dash, eagerness, hurry. *(indifference, calm, stagnation, procrastinate, idleness, inactivity, indolence, quiet, loaf, desertion, vacation, coolness.)*

busy—*adj.* diligent, engaged, industrious, laboring, occupied, toiling, assiduous. *(indolent, slothful, relaxed, idle, unoccupied, lazy.)*

but—*conj.* except, yet, moreover, save, beside, excluding, notwithstanding, still, though, barring. *(nevertheless, not withstanding, inclusive, with, including, however.)*

C

cage—*n.* coop, pen, receptacle, cell, enclosure, box. *(free, liberate, let out.)*

calamity—*n.* misfortune, trouble, mishap, fatality, disaster, catastrophe, affliction, tragedy, reverse. *(blessing, luck, boon, God-send.)*

calculate—*v.* weigh, reckon, apportion, consider, compute, estimate, investigate, count, rate, gauge, proportion. *(chance, stake, guess, hit, risk, speculate, conjecture, miscalculate.)*

calculation—*n.* consideration, regard, care, judgement, estimation, balance, caution, apportionment, vigilance, investigation, watchfulness, anticipation, reckoning, computation, forethought, thought. *(exception, inconsideration, carelessness, incaution, omission, exclusion, inconsiderateness, indiscretion, miscalculation, misconception, supposition, mistake.)*

calibre—*n.* diameter, capacity, force, endowment, character, strength, quality, power, scope.

called—*v.* denominated, termed, named, designated. *(misnamed, unnamed, misdesignated, undesignated.)*

calm—*v.* compose, still, appease, sedate, smooth, tranquilize, assuage, quiet, soothe, allay, relax. *(agitate, lash, stir, disconcert, tense, ruffle, heat, discompose, excite.)*

calumny—*n.* libel, opprobrium, slander, aspersion, defamation, back-biting, traducement, detraction, scandal. *(eulogy, panegyric, vindication, testimonial, clearance.)*

cancel—*v.* annul, obliterate, erase, delete, efface, nullify, discharge, abolish, repeal, blot out, expunge, countervail, quash, rescind, abrogate, revoke. *(ratify, contract, enforce, confirm, perpetuate, re-enact, enact.)*

candid—*adj.* frank, aboveboard, plain, ingenious, blunt, open, fair, unreserved, impartial, transparent, honest, artless, just. *(biased, jesuitical, unfair, mysterious, shuffling, reserved, disingenuous, close, insincere.)*

candidate—*n.* claimant, aspirant, petitioner, solicitor, canvasser, applicant, nominee, contender. *(abjurer, decliner, waiver, abandoner, resigner, noncompetitor.)*

cantankerous—*adj.* crotchety, cranky, irritable, cross, contrary, bad-tempered, quarrelsome, perverse. *(serene, affable, pleasant, equable, debonair, good-humored.)*

canvass—*v.* examine, request, question, challenge, discuss, sift, test, analyze, ventilate, investigate, contemplate, solicit. *(admit, pretermit, pass, allow, disregard, misexamine, ignore, misinvestigate.)*

capacity—*n.* volume, space, scope, calibre, talents, comprehensiveness, magnitude, accommodation, range, parts, competency, cleverness, tonnage, aptitude, size, ability, faculty. *(restriction, coarctation, contractedness, narrowness, incapacity.)*

capital—*n.* important, high, wealth, chief, cleverness, wherewithal, cardinal, principal. *(minor, defective, inferior, poor, unimportant, subordinate, awful.)*

capricious—*adj.* humorsome, uncertain, erratic, wayward, crotchety, whimsical, fanciful, fitful, inconstant, changeful, fickle, giddy. *(unchanging, constant, steadfast, firm, inflexible, unswerving, decided.)*

captivated—*adj.* smitten, enslaved, taken, enthralled, enchanted, captured, charmed. *(free, unscathed, insensitive, uninfluenced, unaffected, insensible, unfeeling.)*

capability—*n.* capacity, skill, competence, power, talent, flair, knack, qualification, attainment. *(inadequacy, impotency, inability, ineptitude, incompetence.)*

care—*n.* prudence, attention, thrift, consideration, pains, economy, heed, wariness, anxiety, foresight, effort, caution, preservation, custody, regard, solicitude, circumspection, prevention, trouble, concern. *(unguardedness, neglect, incaution, recklessness, inattention, improvidence, disregard, remissness, indifference, temerity, carelessness, abandon.)*

career—*n.* walk, progress, way of life, employment, course, race, history, passage, activity. *(unsuccess, miscarriage, avocation, misproceeding, misdeportment.)*

caress—*n.* stroking, embrace, endearment, wheedling, blandishment, fondling.

(annoyance, persecution, melancholy, vexation, provocation, irritation, teasing.)

careless—*adj.* negligent, rash, thoughtless, heedless, slack, unthinking, inconsiderate, slipshod. *(cautious, alert, careful, wary, mindful, diligent, concerned, neat, orderly.)*

caricature—*n.* parody, farce, mimicry, travesty, satire, extravagance, burlesque, exaggeration, hyperbole, monstrosity. *(justice, representation, portraiture, resemblance, truthfulness, fidility, likeness.)*

carnival—*n.* festivity, revel, masquerade, rout, celebration. *(mortification, retirement, fast, lent.)*

carpet—*n.* consideration, table, consultation, board, mat. *(disposal, rejection, oblivion, shelf, discharge.)*

carriage—*n.* bearing, vehicle, gait, transportation, coach, conveyance, deportment, bearing, behavior, walk, mien, conduct, manner, stance. *(misconduct, misconveyance, miscarriage, misconsignment.)*

case—*n.* contingency, plight, episode, condition, fact, instance, predicament, occurrence, circumstance, event, incident. *(supposition, hypothesis, presumption, theory, fancy, conjecture.)*

cast—*v.* throw, fling, frame, construct, pattern, mold, hurl, impel, project, pitch, send down. *(dissipate, approve, retain, ignore, dismember, misprovide, erect, raise, dislocate, break, recover, elevate, accept, carry, miscalculate.)*

cast—*n.* plight, fact, event, condition, subject, instance, occurrence, predicament, contingency, catapult. *(supposition, theory, hypothesis, fancy, conjecture, speculation.)*

caste—*n.* rank, blood, order, station, class, lineage, race, respect, dignity. *(taboo, reproach, degradation, disrepute, abasement, depravation.)*

casual—*adj.* occasional, contingent, fortuitous, accidental, chance, incidental, unforeseen. *(ordinary, fixed, systematic, calculated, regular, certain, periodic.)*

catastrophe—*n.* disaster, blow, misadventure, visitation, calamity, devastation, revolution, reverse, misfortune, tragedy. *(triumph, success, benefit, blessing, godsend, felicitation, ovation, achievement, victory.)*

catch—*v.* capture, corner, snag, grab, seize, arrest, apprehend, snare, trap. *(free, liberate, let go, fumble, lose, release, give up, drop.)*

cause—*n.* agent, inducement, suit, reason, action, source, motive, producer, stimulus, object, origin, creator, account, purpose, principle, motivation. *(result, end, production, issue, preventive, effect, accomplishment, conclusion.)*

cease—*v.* desist, pause, quit, stop, leave off, adjourn, intermit, abstain, refrain, end, discontinue. *(commence, persist.)*

celebrated—*adj.* notable, renowned, distinguished, exalted, popular, famed, eminent, noted, famous, glorious. *(disgraced, obscure, mean, insignificant, unrenowned, unknown, nondescript.)*

celebrity—*n.* eminence, honor, renown, fame, notoriety, personality, notability, distinction, star, glory. *(cipher, obscurity, ingloriousness, indolence, meaness, ignominy, disgrace, nobody, contempt.)*

celestial—*adj.* ethereal, elysian, heavenly, atmospheric, blissful, godlike, supernatural, radiant, angelic, immortal, divine. *(hellish, earthly, mundane, infernal, mortal, terrene, sublunary, human, wordly.)*

censure—*n.* reprimand, blame, dispraise, stricture, rebuke, reproach, criticism, disapproval, admonition. *(eulogy, encouragement, praise, approbation, support, commendation.)*

ceremonial—*adj.* functional, imposing, scenic, ritualistic, pompous, sumptuous, official, ministerial. *(unostentatious, private, casual, undramatic, unimposing, ordinary.)*

certain—*adj.* regular, infallible, sure, actual, convinced, real, confident, unfailing, unmistakable, indubitable, incontrovertible, undoubtful, true, fixed, established, secure, reliable. *(undecided, casual, dubious, irregular, unsettled, uncertain, occasional, doubtful, exceptional, vacillating, unsure, fallible.)*

certify—*v.* prove, aver, vouch, demonstrate, protest, assure, inform, ratify, evidence, testify, acknowledge, avow, declare, avouch, underwrite. *(misinform, repudiate, disprove, misadvise, disavow.)*

challenge—*v.* dare, question, brave, demand, defy, investigate, canvass, summon. *(allow, believe, pass, grant, acquiesce, concede, yield.)*

chance—*n.* hazard, luck, fate, fortuity, befallment, accident, haphazard, casualty, destiny, fortune. *(design, consequence, rule, intent, certainty, law, causation, sequence, purpose, premeditation, casualty.)*

changeless—*adj.* settled, firm, consistent, constant, immovable, reliable, regular, uniform, immutable, steady, stationary, undeviating, resolute, fixed, abiding. *(mutable, irregular, plastic, unsettled, wavering, fluctuating, vacillating, capricious, unsteady, irresolute, variable.)*

character—*n.* mark, symbol, sign, record, letter, figure, nature, type, genius, class, quality, tone, part, disposition, temperament, repute, cast, kind, order, individuality, species, stamp, makeup. *(vagueness, non-description, dishonesty, anonymousness, disrepute, dishonor.)*

characteristic—*n.* singularity, distinction, specialty, peculiarity, idiosyncrasy, individuality, personality. *(miscellany, nondescription, mannerism, generality, abstractedness.)*

charge—*v.* command, instruct, bid, direct, call, order, accuse, incriminate, assign, indict, blame. *(vindicate, pardon, withdraw, retreat, imply, absolve, exonerate, acquit.)*

charitable—*adj.* benevolent, kind, inextreme, forgiving, liberal, compassionate, generous, placable, philanthropic, considerate, inexacting, benign. *(extreme, harsh, revengeful, exacting, stingy, retaliative, uncharitable, selfish, censorious, uncompassionate, unforgiving, illiberal, unkind, parsimonious.)*

charm—*v.* enchant, subdue, transport, delight, captivate, attract, entrance, bewitch, fascinate, soothe, entice, lay, mesmerize, gratify. *(irritate, rouse, annoy, disgust, terrify, excite, offend, disenchant, disturb, disillusionize, repel, alarm.)*

charm—*n.* attraction, incantation, allurement, spell, magnetism, spell, enchantment. *(repulsion, disgust, fear, disenchantment, displeasure.)*

chaste—*adj.* uncontaminated, nice, pure, virtuous, modest, celibate, incorrupt, unaffected, undefiled, simple, spotless, wholesome. *(meretricious, flashy, impure, lewd,* *corrupt, gaudy, overdecorated.)*

cheap—*adj.* low-priced, mean, inexpensive, vile, economical, common, uncostly, worthless. *(worthy, honorable, valuable, high, costly, expensive, rare, noble.)*

cheat—*v.* fleece, inveigle, gull, silence, beguile, hoodwink, dissemble, deceive, overreach, victimize, prevaricate, trick, cozen, defraud, juggle, dupe, deprive, shuffle, swindle.

cheat—*n.* charlatan, fraud, imposter, artifice, fake.

check—*v.* halt, constrain, brake, curb, harness, arrest, prevent, stay, restrain, suppress, retard, impede, thwart. *(initiate, unleash, encourage, aid, support, begin, accelerate, spur, foster, help, abet.)*

cheer—*n.* conviviality, hope, comfort, hospitality, plenty, happiness, optimism. *(unsociableness, dejection, gloom, niggardliness, pessimism, sullenness, churlishness, dearth, inhospitableness, starvation.)*

cheerful—*adj.* joyous, lively, happy, sprightly, joyful, merry, jovial, gay, buoyant, blithe, in good spirits, bonny, glad, enlivening, pleasant, bright. *(despiriting, lifeless, unhappy, depressing, dull, dejected, melancholy, gloomy, morose, sullen, joyless, depressed.)*

chief—*n.* boss, administrator, supervisor, master, chairman, overseer, chieftain, overlord, monarch, potentate, director. *(underling, subject, subordinate, secondary, subsidiary, follower.)*

childish—*adj.* silly, paltry, foolish, infantine, adolescent, weak, trivial, trifling, imbecile, puerile. *(chivalrous, judicious, strong, polite, mature, resolute, wise, manly, sagacious, profound.)*

chivalrous—*adj.* generous, heroic, gallant, valiant, courtly, high-minded, spirited, handsome, courageous, adventurous, knightly, polite. *(dirty, ungenerous, unhandsome, sneaking, ungentlemanly, recreant, scrubby, dastardly, pettifogging, borish, cruel.)*

choice—*n.* preference, selection, option, election, discretion, alternative, adoption. *(indifference, refusal, compulsion, rejection, refuse, coercion, necessity, unimportance.)*

chuckle—*v.* cackle, laugh, grin, crow, chortle. *(grumble,* *wail, whine, cry, whimper, moan.)*

churlish—*adj.* brusque, crusty, petulant, irritable, bilious, sour, rude, grouchy, sullen. *(amiable, kind, pleasant, gallant, noble, cultivated, humble, polite.)*

cipher—*n.* dot, button (fig.), rush, straw, nonentity, naught, pin, nothing, trifle, mole-hill, nil. *(colossus, notability, triton, star, somebody, infinity, something, bigwig, celebrity.)*

circumstance—*n.* feature, point, event, incident, position, topic, episode, detail, specialty, condition, particular, occurrence, situation, fact. *(case, deed, transaction, performance.)*

civil—*adj.* political, polite, respectful, well-mannered, civilized, affable, obliging, accommodating, courteous, well-bred, complaisant, cordial. *(unaccommodating, boorish, churlish, impolite, uncivil, clownish, disrespectful, disobliging.)*

claim—*v.* ask, insist, privilege, maintain, profess, demand, require, title, right, pretense, request, avow. *(abandon, surrender, waive, deny, abjure, disavow, concede, repudiate, disclaim, forego.)*

claim—*n.* vindication, demand, right, assertion, pretension, title, arrogation, request, privilege. *(surrender, abjuration, waiving, disclaimer, denial.)*

claimant—*n.* appellant, assertor, vindicator, petitioner, litigrant. *(conceder, abjurer, relinquisher, quiter, resigner, waiver, renouncer.)*

classification—*n.* nature, sect, designation, genus, order, section, division, species, character, description, assortment, category, kind, group, cast, stamp. *(isolation, division, hetergeneity, specialty, individuality, compartment, exclusion, alienation, singularity, distinction.)*

clause—*n.* paragraph, article, section, chapter, passage, portion, term, stipulation, proviso, condition, provision. *(instrument, document, muniment, charter.)*

clear—*v.* exonerate, disentangle, clarify, emancipate, extricate, whitewash, disencumber, set free, disembarrass, liberate, absolve, retrieve, acquit, justify, exculpate, eliminate, release, rid. *(pollute, embarrass, clog, implicate, contaminate, condemn, encumber, involve, befowl.)*

clear—*adj.* intelligible, pure, lucid, transparent, obvious, open, plain, free, unobstructed, patent, unequivocal, conspicuous, manifest, apparent, evident, unclowded, serene, acquitted, absolved, disentangled, disengaged, disencumbered. *(condemned, dubious, muddy, thick, opague, fowl, entangled, convicted, encumbered, blurred, indistinct, turbid, unintelligible, limpid.)*

clemency—*n.* mercy, compassion, leniency, forbearance, tolerance, charity, understanding, sympathy, benevolence. *(vindictiveness, cruelty, illwill, vengefulness, intolerance, brutality.)*

clever—*adj.* talented, gifted, expert, well-contrived, adroit, nimble, able, skillful, ingenious, quick-witted, dexterous, quick, ready. *(botched, weak, clumsy, dull, slow, awkward, incompetent, bungling, stupid, ill-contrived, uninventive, doltish, inept.)*

cling—*v.* adhere, hug, hang, fasten, embrace, linger, hold, twine, cleave, stick. *(surrender, drop, relax, swerve, abandon, forsake, apostatize, forego, secede, recede.)*

cloak—*v.* extenuate, conceal, screen, mask, disguise, cover, mitigate, camouflage, veil, palliate, hide. *(propound, exhibit, promulge, expose, reveal, protray, unmask, aggravate, demonstrate.)*

close—*adj.* condensed, compressed, dense, niggardly, secret, narrow, fast, limited, adjacent, restricted, shut, reserved, firm, compact, packed, solid. *(liberal, ample, frank, wide, spacious, rarefied, vaporous, public, roomy, open, advertised, open- handed, patent, airy, subtle, dispersed, unconfined.)*

cloudy—*adj.* misty, smoky, gray, overcast, hazy, vaporous, soupy, dreary, gloomy. *(clear, fair, bright, sunny, cloudless, azure, transparent.)*

clownish—*adj.* foolish, cloddish, bucolic, clumsy, comical, rude, rustic, untutored, boorish, awkward. *(intelligent, civil, polite, educated, urbane, high-bred, sedate, courtly, affable, graceful, polished, refined.)*

clumsy—*adj.* uncouth, bungling, unhandy, botching, ill-shaped, awkward, inept, unwieldy, inexpert, maladroit, unskillful. *(dexterous, artistic, adroit, neat, expert, workmanlike, handy, nimble, skillful.)*

coarse—*adj.* indelicate, rough, immodest, unrefined, crude, vulgar, common, unpolished, ordinary, gross, rude. *(choice, refined, elegant, delicate, gentle, fine, polished.)*

cognizance—*n.* recognition, notice, observation, knowledge, perception, experience. *(oversight, neglect, connivance, inadventure, ignorance, unawareness, inexperience.)*

coherent—*adj.* complete, compact, consecutive, united, close, sensible, logical, consistent, adhering. *(illogical, loose, inconsecutive, discursive, rambling, confused, aberrant, disunited, silly, inconsistent.)*

coincide—*v.* square, tally, agree, accord, harmonize, dovetail, correspond, equal, meet. *(diverge, conflict, differ, disagree, clash.)*

coincidence—*n.* consent, casualty, contemporaneousness, chance, agreement, fortuity, simultaneous, concurrence, harmony, correspondence, commensurateness. *(purpose, difference, incommensurateness, design, variation, premeditation, adaption, discordance, disharmony, asynchronism, anachronism.)*

colleague—*n.* adjutant, partner, helper, associate, assessor, companion, ally, collaborator, confederate, coadjutor, assistant. *(competitor, co-rival, counteragent, adversary, co- opponent, co-antagonist.)*

collect—*v.* gather, sum, muster, accumulate, collate, marshal, garner, convoke, glean, convene, amass, congregate, infer, learn, assemble. *(arrange, sort, dispose, classify, deal, scatter, dispense, distribute, divide.)*

collection—*n.* store, assemblage, collation, gathering, compilation, assembly. *(disposal, division, classification, arrangement, distribution, assortment, dispersion, dispensation.)*

color—*n.* complexion, speciousness, falsification, perversion, hue, pretense, pigment, varnish, tint, distortion, garbling, tinge. *(transparency, achromatism, pallor, nakedness, paleness, openness, truthfulness, genuineness.)*

combination—*n.* association, coalition, co-operation, cabal, blending, union, synthesis, alliance, league, confederacy, concert, consortment. *(analysis, resistance, inter-repellence, separation, division, opposition, disunion, disruption, dispersion, dissolution.)*

comely—*adj.* becoming, tasteful, proper, pleasant,

charming, appealing, unaffected, decorous, nice, simple. *(homely, unsightly, ugly, faded, unattractive, improper, repulsive, affected, plain, unbecoming.)*

comfortable—*adj.* convenient, snug, consoled, satisfied, agreeable, congenial, commodious, cozy, pleasant. *(disagreeable, uncomfortable, forlorn, unhappy, dissatisfied, unsuitable, cheerless, wretched, troubled, miserable.)*

command—*v.* govern, conduct, guide, supervise, administer, rule, boss, direct, superintend. *(supplicate, follow, plead, beg, deter, discourage, repel, obey.)*

commerce—*n.* merchandize, barter, dealing, trade, intercourse, communication, exchange, business, industry, traffic. *(interdict, stagnation, dullness, inactivity, embargo, standstill, exclusion.)*

commodious—*adj.* ill- contrived, discommodious, inconvenient, cramped, incommensurate, incommodious, narrow. *(suitable, easy, comfortable, convenient, ample, spacious, luxurious.)*

common—*adj.* everyday, universal, ordinary, mean, habitual, low, prevalent, familiar, coarse, frequent, vulgar. *(exceptional, rare, egregious, unusual, excellent, peculiar, scarce, uncommon, partial, refined, sporadic, infrequent.)*

community—*n.* association, unity, aggregation, homogeneity, polity, society, brotherhood, co-ordination, fellowship, similarity, nationality, commonwealth, fraternity, class, order, sympathy. *(contrariance, segregation, heterogeneity, hostility, estrangement, secession, polarity, animosity, independence, disconnection, dissociation, dissimilarity, rivalry.)*

company—*n.* union, aggregation, firm, sodality, concourse, assembly, order, congregation, association, audience, society, fraternity, corporation, guild, assemblage, community, gang, troop, posse, crew, establishment. *(antagonism, competition, counter-association, rivalry, isolation, opposition, counter-agency, disqualification.)*

compass—*v.* complete, circumvent, encompass, effectuate, embrace, consummate, surround, enclose, achieve, circumscribe. *(misconceive, liberate, expand, miscontrive, mismanage, despond, discard, fail, exclude, amplify,* *display, dismiss, bungle, unfold.)*

compatible—*adj.* consentaneous, consonant, consistent, congenial, harmonious, sympathetic, co-existent, agreeable, accordant, congruous. *(inter-repugnant, impossible, contradictory, divergent, incompatible, destructive, hostile, insupposable, adverse, incongruous, antagonistic, discordant, inconsistent.)*

compel—*v.* coerce, force, blind, make, oblige, constrain, domineer, drive, necessitate. *(cozen, persuade, liberate, induce, thwart, release, convince, egg, tempt, coax, seduce, acquit, allure.)*

compensation—*n.* restoration, pay, damages, remuneration, restitution, indemnification, amercement, equivalent, settlement, wages, allowance, satisfaction, atonement, expiation. *(fraudulence, deprivation, damage, loss, injury, donation, non-payment, gratuity.)*

competition—*n.* emulation, race, rivalry, contention, two of a trade, conflict. *(colleagueship, confederation, association, copartnership, collaboration, alliance, teamwork.)*

complacement—*adj.* kind, mannerly, pleased, amiable, acquiescent, affable, easygoing, satisfied, content, pleasant. *(morose, austere, grudging, dissatisfied, sullen, irritated, unmannerly, churlish.)*

complaint—*n.* repining, disease, murmur, lamentation, criticism, discontent, expostulation, sickness, annoyance, grievance. *(boon, sanity, benefit, congratulation, complacency, rejoicing, approbation, salve, applause, jubilee, health.)*

complement—*n.* totality, counterpart, completion, supply, fulfilment, correlative, supplement. *(defalcation, abatement, insufficiency, drawback, lessening, deficiency, diminution, deficit, detraction.)*

complete—*adj.* perfect, thorough, accomplished, full, exhaustive, intact, finished, total, consummate, adequate, entire. *(partial, imperfect, incomplete, inadequate, deficient, unfinished.)*

complexion—*n.* feature, indication, face, interpretation, makeup, aspect, hue, color, look, appearance, character. *(reticence, heart, unindicativeness, inexpression, core, concealment, reserve.)*

complicated—*adj.* involved, entangled, confused, perplexed, intricate, complex. *(simple, lucid, uninvolved, obvious, clear, unraveled.)*

compliment—*n.* courtesy, praise, homage, flattery, tribute. *(discourtesy, contempt, insolence, insult.)*

complimentary—*adj.* ecomiastic, lavish of praise, flattering, commendatory, laudatory, panegyrical, eulogistic. *(vituperative, condemnatory, disparaging, abusive, insulting, objurgatory, damnatory, reproachful, defamatory, denunciatory.)*

composition—*n.* combination, adjustment, commutation, mixture, settlement, compound, creation, conformation, compromise, structure. *(perpetuation, analysis, aggravation, criticism, segregation, discussion, examination, disturbance.)*

comprehend—*v.* embody, understand, apprehend, include, perceive, embrace, grasp, involve, enclose, comprise, conceive. *(misunderstand, reject, except, exclude.)*

comprehensive—*adj.* general, large, capacious, pregnant, embracing, inclusive, wide, extensive, all, universal, compendious, ample, significant, generic, brood. *(shallow, narrow, exceptive, exclusive, limited, restricted, adversative.)*

compromise—*v.* adjust, settle, implicate, involve, arbitrate, reconcile, compose, endanger. *(disengage exempt, exonerate, enfranchise, aggravate, extricate, excite, foster, perpetuate, arbitrate.)*

conceal—*v.* keep secret, screen, hide, disguise, suppress, shield, dissemble, secrete, camouflage. *(divulge, manifest, publish, reveal, promulgate, disclose, expose, exhibit, avow, confess.)*

concentrate—*v.* muster, convene, centralize, conglomerate, assemble, converge, cluster, localize, condense, draw, congregate. *(dismiss, disperse, scatter, decentralize, dissipate.)*

concerning—*prep.* relating, about, touching, with respect to, relative to, of, with regard to, apropos of, with reference to, respecting, in relation to, regarding. *(disregarding, omitting, neglecting.)*

concert—*n.* combination, union, co-operation, concord, agreement, collaboration, association, harmony. *(counteraction, dissociation, disconnection, opposition.)*

conciliate—*v.* appease, disarm, placate, mollify, soothe, pacify, arbitrate. *(arouse, stir up, antagonize, alienate.)*

concrete—*adj.* explicit, precise, specific, actual, tangible, definite, material. *(general, vague, abstract, intangible, immaterial.)*

condescension—*n.* graciousness, stooping, affability, favor, humility. *(pride, haughtiness, superciliousness, scorn, arrogance, superiority, disdain.)*

condition—*n.* mood, qualification, situation, plight, requisite, state, circumstances, proviso, case, mode, stipulation, predicament, term, shape. *(fulfilment, relation, circumstances, adaptation, dependence, connection, situation, concession.)*

conducive—*adj.* promotive, effective, contributive, caustive, calculated, subsidiary, productive. *(contrariant, destructive, counteractive, repugnant, hindering, preventive.)*

conduct—*v.* transfer, manage, guide, administer, lead, control, bring, behavior, carry, direct. *(misconduct, mislead, follow, miscarry, misadminister, mismanage.)*

confer—*v.* deliberate, present, compare, give, palaver, collate, discuss, consult, converse. *(contrast, withhold, hazard, withdraw, dissociate, deny, conjecture.)*

confession—*n.* catechism, tenets, subscription, creed, articles, doctrine, declaration, revelation, profession. *(renunciation, refutation, heresy, protest, concealment, apostasy, index, abjuration, condemnation.)*

confidant—*n.* advisor, confederate, confessor, trusty companion. *(betrayer, rival, traitor, turncoat.)*

confident—*adj.* assured, bold, certain, impudent, sure, positive, undaunted, sanguine. *(diffident, apprehensive, despondent, dubious, uncertain.)*

confidential—*adj.* trustworthy, private, intimate, secret, honorable. *(open, official, treacherous, insidious, disloyal, public, patent.)*

confirm—*v.* stabilitate, settle, substantiate, perpetuate, verify, strengthen, sanction, ratify, establish, corroborate, prove, fix. *(annul, refute, upset, weaken, abrogate, confute, nullify, shake, cancel, repeal.)*

conform—*v.* fit, harmonize, reconcile, correspond, adapt, comply, agree, acquiesce, submit. *(diverge, deviate, disagree, oppose, differ.)*

confront—*v.* face, resist, encounter, menace, challenge, intimidate, oppose. *(encourage, abet, evade, countenance, rally.)*

confused—*adj.* perplexed, dazed, disordered, promiscuous, abashed, chaotic, disarranged, embarrassed, involved, disconcerted, complex, disorganized. *(unembarrassed, unconfused, unabashed, systematic, arranged, organized.)*

congregate—*v.* get together, flock, assemble, collect, convene, rally, meet, throng. *(scatter, part, disperse, separate, spread out.)*

congress—*n.* parliament, convention, synod, conclave, assembly, conference, council, legislature. *(conclave, cabal, mob, session.)*

conjecture—*v.* divination, guess, supposition, notion, estimate, hypothesis, surmise, theory. *(calculation, proof, computation, certainty, inference, deduction, reckoning.)*

connection—*n.* relation, kindred, union, junction, relationship, conjunction, kinsman, association, coherence, communication, concatenation, affinity, relevance, intercourse. *(irrelevance, disunion, disconnection, separation, disjunction, independence, dissociation.)*

conquer—*v.* vanquish, master, prevail over, subdue, surmount, subjugate, quell, crush, defeat, overthrow, overcome, overpower. *(forfeit, fail, cede, fall, resign, retreat, sacrifice, succumb, lose, capitulate, fly, submit, surrender.)*

conscious—*adj.* cognizant, alert, aware, sensible. *(unconscious, insensible, asleep, unaware.)*

consecutive—*adj.* coherent, continuous, orderly, subsequent, arranged. *(undigested, discursive, rambling, disordered, simultaneous, inconsecutive, inconsequent, incoherent.)*

consent—*v.* agree, concur, acquiesce, submit. *(disagree, refuse, dissent, disapprove, resist, decline.)*

consequence—*n.* dignity, effect, moment, issue, note, result, importance, inference, sequel, coherence, outcome, deduction, conclusion. *(paltriness, cause, meanness, antecedence, causation, irrelevance, inconsecutiveness, premise, inconse-*

quence, precursor, origin, insignificance, unimportance, axiom, postulate, datum.)

consider—*v.* revolve, think, deem, weigh, attend, ponder, judge, deliberate, mediate, cogitate, deduce, infer, investigate, reflect, opine, observe, regard, contemplate. *(hazard, disregard, conjecture, ignore, guess, pretermit, despise, omit.)*

considerate—*adj.* cautious, patient, thoughtful, careful, attentive, reflective, forbearing, circumspect, prudent, unselfish, judicious, serious. *(careless, rash, thoughtless, inconsiderate, injudicious, inattentive, rude, overbearing, heedless, selfish.)*

consistency—*n.* proportion, mass, consistence, analogy, congruity, harmony, composition, uniformity, substance, coherence, material, compactness, amalgamation, compound, density, closeness, compatibility, solidity. *(contrariety, volatility, subtility, contradiction, vaporousness, disproportion, incongruity, tenuity, variance, sublimation, incoherence, inconsistency.)*

consistent—*adj.* harmonious, congruous, compatible, accordant, agreeing, consonant, congenial. *(not agreeing with, incongruous, inharmonious, at variance with, incompatible, illogical.)*

conspicuous—*adj.* magnified, uniform, noticeable, visible, seen, observable, easily, prominent, salient, noted, eminent, famous, manifest, distinguished, evident. *(microscopic, invisible, unobservable, inconspicuous, noticeable, shrouded.)*

constant—*adj.* regular, trustworthy, true, uniform, faithful, perpetual, immutable, firm, continuous, stalwart, fixed, steady, invariable. *(exceptional, false, irregular, treacherous, variable, untrustworthy, faithless, fickle, vacillating, casual, incidental, accidental, broke, interrupted, inconsistent.)*

constitution—*n.* frame, regulation, temperament, law, structure, habit, temper, organization, texture, character, substance, nature, government, composition, state, consistence, policy. *(destruction, accident, demolition, habituation, disorganization, modification, dissipation, interference, change, revolution, anarchy, depotism, rebellion, tyranny.)*

construction—*n.* view, composition, interpretation, fabrication, fabric, creation, explanation, reading, rendering, understanding, erection, edifice. *(misconception, dislocation, misinterpretation, dismemberment, razing, demolition, misunderstanding, displacement, misconstruction, misplacement.)*

consult—*v.* ask advice of, confer, promote, interrogate, care for, canvass, consider, question, advise, deliberate, regard, counsel. *(contravene, resolve, counteract, explain, dictate, expound, instruct, direct, bypass.)*

consumption—*n.* lessening, decay, decrease, decline, waste, decrement, expenditure, depletion. *(development, growth, augmentation, conservation, enlargement.)*

contact—*n.* continuity, adjunction, touch, contiguity, collision, apposition. *(adjacence, non-contact, proximity, isolation, distance, interruption, separation, disconnection.)*

contagious—*adj.* infectious, catching, epidemic, transmitted, pestilential, communicated, transferred, spreading. *(preventive, sporadic, antipathetic, endemic, noninfectious.)*

contaminate—*v.* taint, corrupt, soil, pollute, defile, sully, befoul. *(chasten, purify, sanctify, cleanse, clarify, lave, ameliorate.)*

contemplate—*v.* project, mediate, intend, behold, design, survey, observe, purpose, study, ponder. *(waive, overlook, ignore, disregard, abandon.)*

contemptible—*adj.* trivial, mean, despicable, vile, paltry, pitiful, disreputable, trifling, detestable. *(venerable, grave, important, weighty, respectable, honorable, laudable.)*

content—*adj.* satisfied, gratified, resigned, full, willing, pleased, contented, happy. *(reluctant, unwilling, unsatisfied, discontented, dissatisfied, restless.)*

contentious—*adj.* perverse, exceptious, litigious, wayward, guarrelsome, splenetic, cantankerous. *(obliging, easy, pacific, obsequious, considerate, accommodating, harmonious.)*

contingent—*adj.* incidental, conditional, dependent, uncertain, provisional, co- efficient, hypothetical. *(irrespective, positive, uncontrolled, absolute, unaffected, unmodified, independent, contrived.)*

continually—*adv.* persistently, ever, repeatedly, continuously, frequently, constantly, always, perpetually, incessantly, unceasingly. *(intermittently, casually, fitfully, occasionally, rarely, spasmodically, sometimes, contingently.)*

contract—*v.* lessen, curtail, form, retrench, abridge, compress, diminish, abbreviate, agree, decrease, reduce, narrow. *(dilate, elongate, cancel, abandon, magnify, expand, amplify, reverse.)*

contract—*n.* agreement, compact, bargain, pact, covenant, treaty, bond, stipulation. *(assurance, promise, parole, discourse.)*

contradict—*v.* negate, refute, contravene, oppose, controvert, impugn, dissent, deny, confute, disprove. *(propound, argue, affirm, state, maintain, endorse, corroborate, confirm.)*

contrary—*adj.* incompatible, opposed, inconsistent, repugnant, opposite, adverse, antagonistic, negative. *(coincident, agreeing, kindred, consentaneous, consistent, obstinate, compatible.)*

contribute—*v.* supply, add, give, assist, cooperate, tend, conduce, bestow, subscribe. *(misapply, refuse, contravene, withhold, deny, misconduce.)*

contrive—*v.* arrange, plan, adjust, scheme, design, intrigue, fabricate, concert, devise, manage, adapt. *(overdo, hazard, chance, over-vault, demolish, bungle, hit, venture, run.)*

control—*v.* administer, curb, coerce, govern, manipulate, check, manage, restrain, regulate, guide, moderate, repress. *(liberate, abandon, misconduct, neglect, mismanage, license, release.)*

convenient—*adj.* seasonable, apt, opportune, handy, timely, fitted, adapted, useful, helpful, commodious, suitable, beneficial. *(untimely, awkward, inopportune, inconvenient, useless, unseasonable, obstructive, superfluous, unsuitable.)*

conventional—*adj.* usual, prevalent, customary, social, ordinary, traditional, stipulated. *(unsocial, natural, invariable, unusual, innovative, legal, immutable, statutable, compulsory.)*

conversant—*adj.* proficient, learned, familiar, versed, experienced, acquainted. *(strange, unfamiliar, inconversant, unacquainted, unversed, ignorant, unlearned.)*

convertible—*adj.* identical, equivalent, commensurate, equipollent, conterminous, transformable. *(contradictory,* *variant, contrariant, incommensurate, contrary, unequivalent, converse.)*

conviction—*n.* persuasion, faith, assurance, belief. *(misgiving, doubt, skepticism, disbelief.)*

co-operate—*v.* abet, concur, work together, conspire, assist, collaborate, help, contribute. *(oppose, rival, thwart, nullify, counteract.)*

copy—*n.* portraiture, transcript, image, imitation, likeness, reproduction, duplicate, counterfeit, facsimile. *(example, original, prototype, pattern, model, creation.)*

cordial—*adj.* earnest, hearty, invigorating, warm, sincere, affectionate, reviving, genial. *(formal, cold, hostile, distant, ceremonious.)*

corner—*n.* hole, recess, retreat, nook, cavity, confound. *(protection, coin, convexity, abutment, prominence, angle, elbow, protrusion, salience.)*

corpulent—*adj.* lusty, stout, fat, gross, fleshy, obese, plethoric, portly, burly. *(attenuated, emaciated, lean, slight, thin, gaunt.)*

correct—*adj.* exact, accurate, decorous, true, right, faultess, proper, strict. *(untrue, wrong, falsify, imprecise, false, incorrect.)*

correct—*v.* rectify, amend, set right, chasten, remedy, punish, improve, redress, emend, reform. *(ruin, falsify, corrupt, spare.)*

correction—*n.* discipline, chastisement, amendment, punishment, emendation, reparation. *(retrogradation, deterioration, recompense, debasement, reward, compensation.)*

correspond—*v.* fit, harmonize, agree, match, answer, correlate, suit, tally. *(disagree, vary, clash, jar, differ, deviate.)*

correspondence—*n.* adaptation, match, fitness, answerableness, letter, correlation, depatches, agreement, congruity, congeniality, writing, communication. *(colloquy, reservation, difference, withholding, conversation, repugnance, withdrawal, confabulation, dissimilarity, nonintercourse.)*

corrupt—*adj.* polluted, depraved, tainted, contaminated, defiled, vitiated, wicked, decayed, putrid, profligate, infected, rotten. *(undefiled, pure, moral, uncorrupt.)*

corruption—*n.* putrescence, taint, putrefaction,

decomposition, evil, contamination, decay, debasement, adulteration, deterioration, depravity, rottenness, perversion, defilement. *(purification, vitality, amelioration, morality, organization, purity.)*

cost—*v.* absorb, amount to, consume, require. *(produce, return, afford, yield, fetch, bring, obtain.)*

cost—*n.* outlay, expense, payment, expenditure, worth, outgoings, precious, charge, price, compensation, disbursement, *(emolument, profit, revenue, return, income, resources, perquisite, receipt.)*

costly—*adj.* expensive, precious, high-priced, exorbitant, valuable, rich, sumptuous. *(cheap, beggarly, mean, valueless, paltry, worthless, reasonable, low-priced.)*

council—*n.* consultation, parliament, synod, convocation, cabinet, convention, bureau, company, conference, chamber, conclave, meeting, congress, assembly, legislature. *(conspiracy, mob, crowd, league, cabal, intrigue, multitude, alliance.)*

counsel—*n.* instruction, monition, warning, recommendation, advice, admonition, consultation. *(misinstruction, betrayal, subversion, misguidance.)*

count—*v.* enumerate, reckon, compute, calculate, estimate, sum, total, number. *(conjecture, confound, guess, exclude, hazard, lump.)*

countenance—*v.* favor, support, help, encourage, patronize, abet, sanction, tolerate, aid. *(discourage, confront, discountenance, oppose, browbeat, condemn.)*

countenance—*n.* encourage, aid, support, visage, abet. *(discountenance, disapproval, thwart.)*

counteract—*v.* counterfoil, baffle, thwart, hinder, neutralize, counterinfluence, foil, negate, rival, oppose. *(conserve, promote, co-operate, aid, subserve, help, encourage, abet.)*

counterpart—*n.* fellow, brother, correlative, supplement, match, parallel, tally, complement, twin, copy. *(reverse, opposite, contradiction, counter-agent, contrary, opponent, observe, antithesis, contrast.)*

countryman—*n.* husbandman, clown, compatriot, yeoman, native, inhabitant, swain, rustic, citizen, boor, subject, fellow-citizen, provincial, fellow-subject, peasant, fellow-countryman, laborer, agriculturist. *(townsman, alien, cockney, oppidan, foreigner, stranger, emigrant.)*

couple—*v.* conjoin, bracket, unite, button, brace, yoke, link, connect, tie, buckle, splice, clasp, amalgamate, pair. *(part, separate, untie, loosen, detach, divorce, sever, uncouple, unclasp, isolate.)*

courage—*n.* fortitude, gallantry, intrepidity, boldness, pluck, heroism, bravery, fearlessness, resolution, valor. *(poltroonery, timidity, pusillanimity, cowardice, faintheartedness, dastardliness.)*

course—*n.* sequence, direction, race, order, method, continuity, conduct, plain, trail, manner, line, progress, succession, series, passage, route, mode, career, way, round, road. *(solution, disorder, conjecture, caprice, deviation, interruption, speculation, error, discursion, hazard, hindrance, cogitation.)*

courtly—*adj.* polished, aristocratic, mannerly, dignified, refined, high-bred, elegant. *(rough, awkward, unrefined, rustic, unmannerly, vulgar, undignified, coarse, unpolished, plebeian, boorish.)*

covetous—*adj.* avaricious, greedy, rapacious, acquisitive, lustful, grasping. *(bountiful, unselfish, profuse, generous, liberal, charitable, self-sacrificing.)*

coward—*n.* dastard, poltroon, renegade, craven, recreant, milquetoast. *(daredevil, champion, desperado, hero, lion.)*

coxcomb—*n.* puppy, pedant, fop, prig, dandy, dude. *(philosopher, savant, genius, sage, celebrity, authority, prophet.)*

coy—*adj.* shrinking, modest, shy, bashful, sheepish, reserved, retreating. *(rompish, bold, hoydenish, saucy, forward.)*

crabbed—*adj.* morose, petulant, irritable, crusty, sour, complicated, churlish, cross-grained. *(conversable, hearty, pleasant, cordial, precise, warm, open, genial, easy.)*

craft—*n.* underhandedness, art, dodge, artifice, chicanery, guile, intrigue, ingenuity, cunning, stratagem, wiliness, maneuver, duplicity, trickery. *(ingenuousness, candor, openness, straightforwardness, fairness, reliability, honesty, frankness, sincerity, artlessness.)*

cram—*v.* squeeze, gorge, ram, compress, stuff, choke, pack. *(vent, empty, unload, eliminate, deplete, disgorge, eviscerate, discharge, unpack.)*

crash—*n.* clang, resonance, clash. *(babble, din, murmur, silence, reverberation, whisper, rumbling.)*

crave—*v.* pine for, desire, want, covet, require, need, yearn for, wish for. *(repudiate, spurn, detest, abominate, despise, scorn, abhor.)*

cream—*n.* pith, acme, gist, marrow. *(offal, dross, garbage, refuse, dregs.)*

credential or credentials—*n.* seal, diploma, vouchers, missive, recommendation, title, letter, testament, warrant, certificates, testimonials. *(self-appointment, self license, autocracy, self constitution, self-derived power.)*

credit—*n.* trustworthiness, faith, honor, relief, reputation, merit, reliance, confidence, praise, security. *(insecurity, disbelief, untrustworthiness, disgrace, skepticism, distrust, shame, censure.)*

creed—*n.* articles, subscription, catechism, belief, doctrine, confession. *(abjuration, disbelief, protest, recantation, non-subscription, retractation, rejection.)*

criminal—*adj.* felonious, wrong, sinful, nefarious, indictable, flagitious, guilty, illegal, vicious, iniquitous, immoral, culpable. *(virtuous, laudable, right, lawful, honorable, just, blameless, praise-worthy, innocent, meritorious, moral, creditable.)*

critical—*adj.* exact, censorious, momentous, precarious, severe, nice, hazardous, important, delicate, crucial, fastidious, accurate, discriminating, dubious, ticklish. *(settled, popular, redressed, inexact, retrieved, supportive, loose, easy, determined, undiscriminating, safe, decided.)*

criticism—*n.* censure, evaluation, animadversion, stricture. *(praise, approval, acclaim, rave.)*

cross-grained—*adj.* wayward, peevish, cantankerous, obdurate, perverse, morose, ill-conditioned. *(pleasant, jolly, accommodating, genial, obliging, agreeable, gratifying.)*

crude—*adj.* undigested, unrefined, raw, half-studied, unchastened, unfinished, unconsidered, harsh, ill-prepared, unshaped, churlish.

(well-digested, artistic, well-prepared, highly-wrought, ripe, classical, well-considered, elaborate, well-adapted, refined, finished, classical, well-expressed, elegant.)

cruel—*adj.* barbarous, truculent, malignant, inhuman, maleficent, sanguinary, savage, brutal, unmerciful, pitiless, ruthless, unrelenting, inexorable, hard-hearted, harsh. *(forbearing, beneficent, humane, generous, forgiving, benevolent, beneficial, merciful.)*

crush—*v.* pound, crumble, pulverize, demolish, granulate, triturate, bray, overpower. *(compact, aggrandize, consolidate, solidify, liberate, stabilitate, compress, upraise, amalgamate, cake.)*

cuff—*v.* box, punch, buffet, slap, smack, pummel, hustle, smite. *(flagellate, cane, lash, whip, cudgel, thrash, strap, maul.)*

cultivate—*v.* foster, improve, till, improve, nourish, advance, cherish, promote, study, nurture, civilize, refine, fertilize. *(desert, uproot, neglect, extirpate, abandon, prevent, paralyze, stifle, abolish, discourage, impair, blight, blast, eradicate.)*

cupidity—*n.* acquisitiviness, stinginess, avarice, repacity, covetousness. *(extravagance, prodigality, generosity, liberality.)*

cure—*n.* restorative, renovation, convalescence, medication, remedy, heal-all, alleviation, restoration, amelioration, reinstatement. *(confirmation, disease, inoculation, corruption, aggravation, inflamation, complaint, ailment, contagion.)*

curiosity—*n.* interest, marvel, lion, celebrity, prying, wonder, inquisitiveness, interrogativeness, phenomenon, oddity, rarity. *(heedlessness, drug, song, abstraction, disregard, dirt, apathy, bagatelle, indifference, cipher, absence, weed.)*

curious—*adj.* inquisitive, odd, inquiring, recondite, meddling, unique, questioning, scrutinizing, rare, prying, peering, searching, peeping, singular. *(uninquiring, trite, superficial, blasé, indifferent, incurious, common, uninterested.)*

current—*adj.* prevalent, exoteric, general, running, vulgar, floating, widespread, ordinary, popular, present. *(private, secret, confined, obsolete, rejected, previous, esoteric, exploded.)*

custody—*n.* guardianship, care, conservation, protection, keeping. *(betrayal, jeopardy, abandonment, liberation, release, neglect, discharge, desertion, exposure.)*

cynical—*adj.* snarling, sneering, currish, cross-grained, sarcastic, contemptuous, snappish, carping. *(complaisant, lenient, sanguine, urbane, genial.)*

D

daft—*adj.* innocent, silly, light-headed, lunatic, foolish, idiotic, cracked. *(sensible, sane, practical, shrewd, palpable, deft, sound.)*

dainty—*adj.* rare, tasty, epicurean, choice, refined, delicate, luxurious, exquisite. *(unrelishing, dirty, gluttonous, nasty, greedy, gross, common, omnivorous, coarse.)*

damage—*n.* harm, impairment, injury, defacement, mutilation, loss, ruin, destruction. *(reparation, mend, improvement, betterment, repair.)*

damp—*adj.* moist, drizzly, humid, dewy, wet, vaporous.

dapper—*adj.* neat, smart, dashing, spruce, natty. *(unwieldy, untidy, slovenly, sloppy, awkward.)*

daring—*adj.* fearless, valorous, adventurous, intrepid, dashing, brave, bold, imprudent, courageous, foolhardy, venturesome, dauntless. *(timid, prudent, cautious, inadventurous.)*

dark—*adj.* sable, obscure, recondite, blind, benighted, inexplicable, dismal, sombre, sorrowful, opaque, black, swarthy, abstruse, ignorant, dim, secret, nebulous, joyless, dingy, dusky, enigmatical, besotted, unintelligible, shadowy, mysterious, hidden, murky, cheerless, gloomy, mournful. *(fair, luminous, white, radiant, festive, illumined, light, dazzling, radiant, glaring, brilliant, enlightened, bright, intelligible, lucid, transparent, crystalline.)*

dash—*v.* throw, scatter, hurl, course, fly, cast, shatter, subvert, drive, send, strike, dart, speed, rush, detrude. *(erect, lag, raise, support, reinstate, creep, hobble, crawl.)*

daunt—*v.* scare, intimidate, terrify, confront, frighten, appall, alarm, dishearten, cow. *(encourage, inspirit, countenance, fortify, rally.)*

dawdle—*v.* dally, lag, loiter, idle, loaf. *(speed, rush, fag, hustle, work, haste, dash.)*

dead—*adj.* departed, inanimate, still, deserted, spiritless, heavy, defunct, inert, torpid, deceased, cheerless, dull, unconscious, insensible, gone, lifeless. *(thronged, living, susceptible, joyous, bustling, stirring, responsive, vivacious, vital, animate, alive.)*

deadly—*adj.* venomous, fatal, pernicious, destructive, murderous, mortal, implacable, malignant, destructive, noxious, baneful. *(healthful, vital, wholesome, nutritious, innocuous, life-giving.)*

deaf—*adj.* disinclined, averse, dead, inaudible, surd, heedless, hard of hearing, inexorable, rumbling, insensible, inattentive. *(interested, acute, disposed, susceptible, alive, listening, sensible, willing, attentive, penetrating.)*

dear—*adj.* costly, beloved, loved, precious, priceless, expensive, high-priced. *(inexpensive, vile, nominal, cheap, misliked.)*

death—*n.* decease, exit, fall, expiration, departure, release, demise, cessation, dissolution, mortality, failure, eradication, termination. *(life, auspices, rise, inauguration, commencement, vigor, birth, existence, spirit, operation, animation, activity, vitality, action, growth.)*

debatable—*adj.* problematical, unsettled, doubtful, disputable, undecided, dubious, floating, uncertain, inestimable. *(sure, incontestible, certain, unquestionable, self-evident, settled, indisputable.)*

debauch—*v.*, **debauchery**—*n.* revel, orgies, gluttony, riot, excess, boisterous. *(fast, meal, frugality, maceration, moderation, abstinence, asceticism, refraining.)*

debase—*v.* disgrace, corrupt, adulterate, desecrate, lower, degrade, defile, befowl, corrupt, deteriorate. *(elevate, heighten, enhance, improve, uplift.)*

debt—*n.* liability, obligation, something due, debit, score, default, claim, bill. *(assets, gift, grace, accommodation, gratuity, credit, liquidation, trust, favor, obligation, grant.)*

decay—*v.* sink, wither, decrease, perish, decline, waste, wane, dwindle, ebb, rot, shrivel. *(grow, enlarge, rise, expand, flourish, increase, luxuriate, vegetate.)*

decay—*n.* waning, decadence, wasting, declension, dry rot, decline, sinking, corruption, putrefaction, consumption, rottenness, decrease, collapse. *(growth, increase, exuberance, prosperity, rise, birth, fertility, luxuriance, vigor.)*

deceit—*n.* imposition, fraud, artifice, hypocrisy, cunning, cheat, sham, trick, duplicity, deception, guile, indirection, double-dealing, circumvention, insidiousness, treachery, beguilement, delusion. *(honesty, verity, reality, openness, instruction, guidance, fair dealing, enlightenment, candor.)*

deceitful—*adj.* delusive, fallacious, deceptive, dishonest, fraudulent. *(fair, veracious, open, honest, truthful, delude.)*

deceive—*v.* beguile, gull, entrap, take in, trick, circumvent, ensnare, overreach, mislead, betray, cheat, dupe, delude. *(advise, deliver, illumine, be honest to, enlighten, guide, undeceive, disabuse.)*

decide—*v.* settle, terminate, resolve, determine, fix, adjudicate, arbitrate. *(drop, misdetermine, waive, raise, misjudge, suspend, waver, vacillate, moot, doubt.)*

decipher—*v.* spell, solve, unravel, unfold, read, explain, interpret, translate. *(symbolize, mystify, enigmatize, cipher, impuzzle, illustrate.)*

decision—*n.* resolve, conviction, determination, firmness, will, strength, perseverance, certainty, decisiveness. *(vagueness, weakness, vacillation, uncertainty, evasion, indecisiveness.)*

declaration—*n.* exhibition, avowal, manifestation, ordinance, affirmation, profession, assertion, statement, testimony. *(concealment, denial, retraction, suppression.)*

decompose—*v.* individualize, dissolve, analyse, segregate, spoil, resolve. *(mix, organize, compound, concoct, compose, brew.)*

decorum—*n.* propriety, order, good manners, modesty, seemliness, respectability, dignity, good behavior. *(impropriety, disorder, rudeness, unseemliness, disturbance.)*

decrease—*v.* lessen, abate, decline, curtail, wane, diminish, abbreviate, subside, lower, retrench, reduce. *(grow, expand, extend, enlarge, increase, escalate, amplify, augment.)*

decrepit—*adj.* weak, enfeebled, aged, infirm, superannuated, broken down, dilapidated, effete, tottering, crippled. *(robust, agile, youthful, strong, active, in good shape.)*

dedicate—*v.* consecrate, assign, set, devote, set apart, separate, hallow, apportion, offer, apply. *(misconvert, alienate, misapply, misuse, devolve, misappropriate, desecrate.)*

deed—*n.* commission, instrument, muniment, act, feat, action, accomplishment, achievement, document, perpetration, exploit. *(failure, recall, undoing, omission, reversion, abortion, non-per formance, false-witness, innocent, disproof, cancelling, invalidation, retraction, impossiblity, collapse.)*

deep—*adj.* subterranean, thick, heartfelt, occult, obscure, penetrating, profound, abstruse, submerged, learned, designing, recondite, sagacious, mysterious, intense, subtle. *(superficial, familiar, commonplace, undesigning, shallow, artless, obvious.)*

deface—*v.* spoil, disfigure, mar, destroy, damage, injure, mutilate, deform. *(adorn, embellish, beautify, decorate.)*

defame—*v.* libel, disparage, vilify, insult, slander, discredit, malign, stigmatize, belittle. *(flatter, laud, applaud, extol, compliment, boost, praise.)*

default—*n.* forfeit, delinquency, want, lapse, failure, defect, absence, omission. *(appearance, supply, maintenance, presence, compliance, plea, forthcoming, satisfaction.)*

defeat—*n.* discomfiture, frustration, disaster, overthrow. *(triumph, success, killing, victory.)*

defeat—*v.* worst, foil, baffle, conquer, frustrate, rout, overcome, vanquish, overthrow, overpower. *(establish, promote, advance, secure, aid, speed, insure, strengthen.)*

defect—*n.* blemish, shortcoming, want, fault, flaw, omission, deficiency, imperfection. *(sufficiency, virtue, emendation, complement, supply, ornament, strength, compensation.)*

defective—*adj.* insufficient, short, faulty, wanting, inadequate, imperfect, deficient. *(complete, ample, perfect, satisfactory, correct, sufficient, abundant, full.)*

defense—*n.* protection, excuse, apology, resistance, rampart, preservation, vindication, plea, justification, shelter, bulwark. *(surrender,* *exposure, prosecution, abandonment, betrayal.)*

defer—*v.* postpone, adjourn, put off, prolong, delay, retard, waive, procrastinate, shelve, prorogue, hinder, protract. *(hasten, press, hurry, expedite, dispatch, urge, quicken, overdrive, facilitate.)*

deference—*n.* consideration, honor, allegiance, respect, condescension, homage, contention, obedience, esteem, regard, reverence, submission, veneration. *(contumacy, defiance, attention, disrespect, contumely, disregard, impudence, rudeness, non-allegiance, slight, disobedience.)*

defiant—*adj.* mutinous, fractious, rebellious, ungovernable, lawless, willful, audacious, bold, stubborn. *(obedient, dutiful, meek, submissive, timid, docile.)*

definite—*adj.* specified, certain, clear, positive, limited, exact, determined, precise, bounded, definitive, specific, fixed, concrete, ascertained, restricted. *(confused, vague, obscure, unspecified, ambiguous, undetermined, intermingled, indefinite.)*

definition—*n.* specification, determination, restriction, clarification, limitation. *(vagueness, misconception, confusion, misstatement, ambiguity, acceptation, explanation, description.)*

defray—*v.* liquidate, bear, quit, discharge, meet, settle, pay, dispose of. *(misappropriate, repudiate, embezzle, dishonor, dissatisfy, swindle.)*

defy—*v.* challenge, despite, brave, scorn, provoke, spurn. *(agree, comply, obey, cooperate, submit, yield.)*

degree—*n.* stage, amount, grade, quantity, rank, station, step, order, class, limit, extent, mark, position, quality, level, rate, measure, range. *(magnitude, numbers, space, size, mass, volume.)*

deliberate—*v.* meditate, perpend, ponder, consider, reflect, debate, consult, weigh, contemplate. *(discard, risk, shelve, hazard, burke, haphazard, chance.)*

deliberate—*adj.* intentional, resolute, unbiased, determined, grave, unprejudiced, thoughtful, earnest, designed, purposed. *(playful, biased, jocose, prejudiced, facetious, instigated, irresolute, dictated, spontaneous, suggested, dubious, unresolved, compulsory, undetermined.)*

delicious—*adj.* luxurious, choice, exquisite, dainty, savory, delightful. *(common, nauseous, loathsome, unpalatable, coarse, unsavory, inedible.)*

delight—*n.* pleasure, happiness, esctasy, bliss, gratification, enjoyment, rapture, joy, transport, gladness, felicity. *(suffering, trouble, discontent, dissatisfaction, pain, sorrow, melancholy, misery, distress, displeasure, depression, discomfort, disappointment, dejection, disgust.)*

delinquent—*n.* culprit, criminal, violator, offender. *(paragon, worthy, pattern, model.)*

deliver—*v.* free, utter, consign, liberate, entrust, save, give up, set free, hand, surrender, give, yield, pronounce, rescue, transmit, concede, distribute. *(misdeliver, confine, suppress, appropriate, retain, assume, betray, withdraw, conserve.)*

deluxe—*adj.* choice, prime, posh, grand, luxurious, select, costly, sumptuous, elegant, splendid. *(ordinary, everyday, common, run of the mill, mediocre, cheap.)*

democratic—*adj.* autonomous, popular, republican, leveling, destructive, radical, unlicensed, subversive, anarchical. *(despotic, regal, autocratic, imperial, tyrannical, conservative, oligarchical, dictatorial, constitutional, aristocratic.)*

demonstrate—*v.* show, manifest, illustrate, describe, prove, exhibit, evince. *(conceal, obscure, misexemplify, disprove, misdemonstrate.)*

demure—*adj.* grave, discreet, sedate, prudish, staid, dispassionate, modest, sober, downcast, retiring. *(vivacious, indiscreet, boisterous, lively, hoydenish, facetious, wanton, noisy, rompish, wild, aggressive.)*

denial—*n.* rejection, declination, negation, refusal, veto, repulsion, prohibition, rebuff. *(acceptance, approval, permission, allowance, yes, affirmation.)*

denomination—*n.* designation, appellation, class, name, order, description, category, kind. *(misnomer, pseudonym, non-description.)*

dense—*adj.* thick, solid, stout, consolidated, thick-set, slow, stupid, dull, compact, close, condensed, stolid. *(uncompacted, quick, sparse, intelligent, clever, rare, meager, rarefied.)*

deny—*v.* withhold, oppose, refuse, disclaim, disown, reject, disavow, contradict, nullify, gainsay, negative. *(accept, indulge, afford, yield, grant, concede, affirm, acquiesce, confirm, admit.)*

department—*n.* division, portion, line, section, province, dominion, branch, function, office. *(establishment, body, society, institution, community, art, organization, whole, service, science, state, literature, conformity.)*

dependent—*adj.* contingent, resting, relative, hanging, relying, trusting, subject, subordinate. *(irrelative, free, independent, absolute, autonomous, irrespective.)*

deplorable—*adj.* lamentable, sorry, calamitous, regrettable, distressing, unfortunate, grievous, ill-fated, miserable. *(happy, felicitious, cheering, fortunate, gratifying, pleasant, agreeable.)*

depression—*n.* degradation, valley, dip, discouragement, hollow, dejection, despondency. *(prominence, raising, mound, elevation, eminence, exaltation, rising, promotion, encouragement, amelioration, preferment, rallying, optimism.)*

deprive—*v.* bereave, rob, hinder, despoil, dispossess, prevent, depose, strip, divest, abridge, confiscate. *(indemnify, invest, present, compensate, reinstate, endow, supply, enrich, furnish.)*

derision—*n.* contempt, irony, disrespect, scorn, contumely, sarcasm, mockery, isdain. *(admiration, respect, reverence, regard, esteem.)*

descendant—*n.* progeny, lineage, branch, offspring, family, stock, house, scion, posterity, issue, seed. *(source, progenitor, parent, author, origin, root, founder, ancestor, stock, forebear.)*

describe—*v.* explain, draw, depict, delineate, recount, picture, narrate, illustrate, define, relate, portray, represent, chronicle. *(confuse, distort, confound, caricature, mystify, misrepresent, contort.)*

desert—*n.* wilderness, void, wild, waste, solitude. *(field, pasture, oasis, civilization, enclosure, garden.)*

design—*v.* purpose, plan, project, contemplate, intend, prepare, fashion. *(conjecture, miscontrive, risk, hit, fluke guess, misconceive, chance, peril.)*

design—*n.* intention, sketch, plan, artifice, scheme, contemplation, pattern, project, purpose, intent, preparation, contrivance, draft, delineation, guile, drawing, artfulness, cunning. *(performance, accident, execution, change, result, simplicity, sincerity, issue, artlessness, construction, openness, candor, structure, fairness, frankness.)*

desirable—*adj.* advisable, beneficial, valuable, expedient, judicious, profitable, acceptable, delightful, good, proper, enviable, worthwhile. *(unadvisable, evil, improper, undesirable, deplorable, injudicious, inexpedient, objectionable, unprofitable.)*

desire—*n.* affection, craving; appetency, yearning, concupiscence, longing, propension. *(abomination, loathing, reject, hate, repugnance, aversion, disgust, horror.)*

despair—*n.* despondency, alienation, desperation, hopelessness. *(expectation, hilarity, hopefulness, anticipation, elation, optimism, confidence, sanguineness.)*

desperate—*adj.* inextricable, audacious, frantic, irremediable, daring, hopeless, determined, mad, desponding, reckless, regardless, abandoned, furious, rash, despairing, heedless. *(propitious, cool, promising, calm, hopeful, shy, remediable, prudent, irresolute, timid, cautious.)*

despotic—*adj.* arbitrary, cruel, tyrannical, autocratic, self-willed, absolute, irresponsible, domineering, arrogant, dictatorial, imperious. *(constitutional, merciful, limited, yielding, humane.)*

destination—*n.* design, aim, end, purpose, goal, intention, location, design, point, consignment, scope, appointment, object, use, application, fate, doom, aspiration. *(effort, operation, project, tendency, initiation, exercise, design, action, movement, activity.)*

destiny—*n.* doom, fate, end, decree, necessity, fortune, lot, predestination, providence. *(volition, freedom, free will, choice, will, deliberation, selection.)*

destroy—*v.* annihilate, ruin, consume, demolish, waste, overthrow, subvert, undo, extinguish. *(construct, restore, repair, create, fabricate, make, reinstate, erect.)*

destructive—*adj.* hurtful, baleful, damaging, detrimental, subversive, deleterious, ruinous, injurious, baneful, noxious. *(conservative, restorative, constructive, wholesome, preservative, beneficial, subsidiary, reparatory.)*

determination—*n.* settlement, verdict, decision, arbitration, judgement, verification, corroboration, confirmation, resolution, authentication. *(uncertainty, vacillation, indecision, irresolution, hesitation, spinelessness.)*

detraction—*n.* backbiting, slander, diminution, depreciation, derogation, aspersion, deterioration. *(compliment, eulogy, augmentation, flattery, respect, improvement, enhancement.)*

detriment—*n.* prejudice, harm, inconvenience, loss, damage, hurt, disadvantage, deterioration, impairment, injury, disservice. *(improvement, remedy, augmentation, repair, benefit, reinstatement, enhancement.)*

detrimental—*adj.* hurtful, pernicious, prejudicial, injurious. *(profitable, augmentative, beneficial, advantageous.)*

develop—*v.* eliminate, expand, educe, enlarge, enucleate, amplify, lay open, enunciate, disclose, clear, unravel, unfold, mature. *(wrap, involve, narrow, envelop, conceal, obscure, compress, mystify, contract, restrict, condense, recede.)*

device—*n.* expedient, emblem, show, cognizance, invention, artifice, contrivance, design, implement, symbol, stratagem, project, plan. *(hazard, incognito, fair-dealing, abortion, openness, fortune, miscontrivance, hit, luck, camouflage.)*

devil—*n.* lucifer, arch-fiend, demon, satan, foul fiend, fiend, villain. *(angel, cherub, saint, archangel, seraph.)*

devise—*v.* plan, concert, manage, contrive, maneuver, create. *(mismanage, disorder, miscontrive.)*

devoid—*adj.* destitute, unprovided, void, unendowed, wanting, depleted. *(supplied, gifted, provided, furnished, replete, laden.)*

devotion—*n.* love, attachment, piety, self-sacrifice, devoutness, dedication, religiousness, loyalty, self-abandonment, ardor, consecration, self-surrender. *(apathy, impiety, indiference, profanity, alienation, selfishness, antipathy, coolness.)*

devour—*v.* consume, gorge, absorb, eat, bolt, swallow, gulp. *(vomit, regurgitate, disgorge.)*

dictate—*v.* suggest, order, decree, command, prompt, enjoin, rule, prescribe, instruct, direct, propose. *(obey, follow, answer, submit to, repeat, echo.)*

dictatorial—*adj.* domineering, autocratic, despotic, bossy. *(democratic, liberal, reasonable, tolerant, flexible, open-minded.)*

die—*v.* decay, cease, expire, perish, decrease, languish, sink, decline, disappear, wane, fade, wither, succumb. *(originate, regetate, begin, rise, luxuriate, live, strenghten, grow, blossom, flourish, develop.)*

difference—*n.* dissimilarity, dissent, variety, dissimilitude, separation, destruction, dissonance, estrangement, distinction, contrariety, unlikeness, discord, disagreement, individuality. *(consociation, identity, community, uniformity, condonation, reconciliation, similarity, harmony, consentaneousness, consonance, sympathy, likeness, agreement, resemblance.)*

difficult—*adj.* intricate, opposed, perplexing, reserved, hard, obscure, unamenable, complicated, involved, uphill, unmanageable, troublesome, enigmatical, arduous, trying. *(unreserved, plain, favorable, easy, amenable, lucid, tractable, categorical, straight, simple, complaisant.)*

digest—*v.* arrange, tabulate, sort, methodize, dispose, convert, order, incorporate, classify, ponder, prepare, assimilate, consider, study, recapitulate. *(disturb, discompose, displace, complicate, reject, eject, confound, derange, refuse, disorder, dislocate.)*

dignity—*n.* honor, loftiness, worth, stateliness, worthiness, grandeur, excellence, solemnity, behavior, decorum. *(disrepute, ignobility, shame, guilt, humility, lowness, unimportance.)*

dilemma—*n.* quandry, doubt, scrape, fix, difficulty, hobble, plight. *(rebutment, retort, superiority, solution, extrication, freedom, escape, solvent.)*

diligence—*n.* attention, industry, care, heed, assiduity, application, meticulousness. *(desultoriness, indifference, idleness, neglect, carelessness, inattention, inertness, heedlessness, lethargy.)*

dingy—*adj.* rusty, sombre, bright, dull, bedimmed, soiled, dusky, obscure, tarnished, colorless, dead, dirty, shabby. *(gleaming, burnished, lustrous, bright, luminous, high-colored, glossy, radiant, sparkling.)*

diplomacy—*n.* circumvention, tact, ministry, contrivance, negotiation, out- witting, ambassadorship, management, discretion, savoir-faire. *(recall, miscontrivance, self-defeat, mismanagement, cancel, ineptness, crassness, self-entanglement, mal-administration, over vaulting.)*

diplomatic—*adj.* sagacious, wise, well-managed, judicious, prudent, politic, astute, clever, well- contrived, discreet, delicate, knowing, well-planned. *(bungling, rude, ill-managed, injudicious, stultifying, undiplomatic, tactless.)*

direction—*n.* tendency, line, order, course, superscription, address, command, control, inclination, bearing, charge, trend. *(miscontrol, deviation, misinstruction, aberration, departure, alteration.)*

directly—*adv.* immediately, at once, quickly, straightaway, soon, promptly, instantly, speedily, precisely. *(by-and-by, indirectly, eventually, there-after, later.)*

dirty—*adj.* soiled, stained, foul, contaminated, polluted, unclean, filthy, grimy, tarnished, messy. *(spotless, clean, immaculate, pure, decent, respectable, washed.)*

disability—*n.* impotency, forfeiture, incompetency, infirmity, defect, incapacity, disqualification. *(fitness, merit, qualification, recommendation, capacity, deserving, strength.)*

disappoint—*v.* defeat, frustrate, foil, deluxe, betray, delude, baffle, mortify, vex, deceive, thwart. *(justify, fulfil, gratify, encourage, realize, satisfy, please, delight, verify.)*

discern—*v.* understand, discover, notice, behold, ascertain, note, recognize, apprehend, observe, perceive, distinguish. *(disregard, slight, neglect, overlook, pass by, fail to see.)*

discharge—*v.* remove, unburden, debark, unload, activate, explode, detonate, launch, propel, project. *(detain, keep, hire, load, maintain, fill, stow, burden.)*

discipline—*n.* strictness, drilling, coercion, organization, order, government, chastisement, rule, training, punishment, control. *(confusion, reward, disorganization, mutiny, disorder, chaos, turbulence, encouragement, rebellion.)*

discomfort—*n.* vexation, trouble, disagreeableness, disquiet, ache, annoyance, anguish, unpleasantness. *(ease, pleasure, agreeableness, comfort, pleasantness.)*

disconcert—*v.* confuse, derange, thwart, defeat, interrupt, ruffle, embarrass, frustrate, disorder, vex, abash, confound, upset, perplex, disturb, fret, unsettle, baffle, discompose. *(scheme, design, rally, encourage, prepare, order, hatch, reassure, countenance, pacify, aid, arrange, contrive, concoct.)*

discourtesy—*n.* incivility, rudeness, impoliteness, brusqueness, insolence, surliness, impudence, boorishness. *(civility, refinement, politeness, graciousness.)*

discreet—*adj.* wise, circumspect, wary, sensible, discerning, prudent, judicious, regulative, cautious, tactful, guarded. *(injudicious, blind, silly, foolish, indiscreet, reckless, undiscerning, insensitive, imprudent, unrestrained.)*

discrimination—*n.* discernment, sagacity, distinction, penetration, judgement, insight, acuteness, shrewdness, perception, acumen. *(hebetude, dullness, shortsightedness, carelessness, fairness, insensitivity, indescernment, confusedness.)*

disease—*n.* malady, complaint, sickness, affliction, disorder, ailment, illness, distemper, indisposition. *(sanity, health, vitality, convalescence, salubrity, strength.)*

disgrace—*n.* discredit, dishonor, disfavor, reproach, debase, infamy, degradation, tarnish, embarrassment, blemish. *(credit, glory, pride, reverence, honor, distinguish.)*

disgust—*n.* loathing, abhorrence, repugnance, nausea, dislike, irritate, abomination, aversion, distaste, revolt. *(liking, relish, fondness, avidity, desire, partiality, delight, longing, please, affection.)*

dismal—*adj.* tragic, dreary, sad, lonesome, melancholy, blank, funereal, somber, gloomy, depressed, foreboding, cheerless, doleful, pessimistic, sorrowful. *(ridiculous, gay, lively, promising, comic, elated, propitious, cheerful, exhilarating, joyous, pleasing.)*

dispatch—*v.* send, execute, conclude, hasten, expedite, accelerate, settle, push. *(obstruct, retard, stall, impede, detain, delay.)*

dispel—*v.* scatter, dissipate, dismiss, disperse, banish, drive away, disseminate, rout. *(mass, summon, congregate, recall, convene, assemble, collect, accumulate, conglomerate.)*

disperse—*v.* separate, dispel, distribute, dealout, disseminate, dissipate, scatter, dissolve, break up, spread abroad. *(summon, gather, meet, collect, concentrate, recall, congregate.)*

dispute—*v.* question, contest, quarrel, difference, argue, canvass, debate, altercation, controvert, challenge, squabble, contend, controversy, gainsay, impugn. *(forego, waive, allow, acquiesce, concede, agree.)*

dissemble—*v.* feign, repress, cloak, smother, disguise, restrain, conceal, pretend. *(manifest, feign, proclaim, pretend, exhibit, protrude, expose, evidence, vaunt, simulate, assume, profess, show.)*

dissiminate—*v.* propagate, claim, circulate, spread, promulgate, distribute, scatter, preach. *(suppress, extirpate, repress, eradicate, discountenance, stifle, quell, annihilate.)*

dissolute—*adj.* profligate, wanton, abandoned, loose, vicious, libertine, licentious, rakish. *(self-controlled, upright, correct, virtuous, strict, conscientious.)*

distance—*n.* absence, removal, remoteness, length, interspace, interval, aloofness, separation, space, gap. *(neighborhood, contact, proximity, adjacency, presence, nearness, propinquity, closeness, warmth, contiguity.)*

distinct—*adj.* independent, unlike, conspicuous, perspicuous, plain, separate, unconnected, disjoined, clear, obvious, dissimilar, detached, definite, different, transparent. *(confused, united, conjoined, indistinct, dim, one, consolidated, obscure, blurred, indefinite.)*

distinction—*n.* separation, dignity, eminence, characteristic, mark, difference. *(debasement, unity, insignificance, identity, degradation, anonymity.)*

distinguish—*v.* perceive, know, separate, discern, discriminate, divide, make famous, differentiate, descry, dissimilate, see, discover, characterize, isolate. *(confound, miss, overlook, confuse, oversee.)*

distinguished—*adj.* noted, famous, illustrious, celebrated, eminent, conspicuous, marked, dignified. *(inconspicuous, hidden, obscure, not famous, mediocre.)*

distress—*v.* embarrass, worry, disturb, afflict, harass, trouble, pain, vex, annoy, mortify, grieve, perturb, sadden. *(gratify, console, comfort, soothe, please, gladden,* *elate, compose, solace, sustain.)*

disturb—*v.* discompose, disquiet, derange, molest, disorder, vex, discommode, worry, plague, confuse, interrupt, rouse, trouble, agitate, annoy, upset, distract. *(collocate, soothe, leave, order, pacify, compose, arrange, quiet, organize.)*

diversion—*n.* divergence, detour, enjoyment, pastime, sport, deviation, recreation, amusement, entertainment. *(procedure, task, avocation, study, continuity, directness, labor, work, business, drudgery.)*

divide—*v.* dissect, portion, part, segregate, sunder, disunite, allot, keep apart, distribute, part among, multiply, separate, bisect, divorce, sever, deal out, partition. *(consociate, unite, join, collocate, convene, conglomerate, classify, congregate, conglutinate, co-ordinate, commingle, cement, splice.)*

divorce—*n.* divert, separate, alienate, dissever, disconnect, dissolution. *(unite, apply, reunite, conjoin, connect, reconcile, fusion.)*

do—*v.* accomplish, work, achieve, complete, finish, act, execute, perform, transact, enact, produce. *(mar, omit, neglect, undo, fail.)*

docile—*adj.* amenable, managed, yielding, quiet, tractable, tame, teachable, pliant, gentle, easily, compliant, submissive. *(obstinate, intractable, self-willed, dogged, stubborn, defiant.)*

dogmatic—*adj.* theological, arrogant, positive, magisterial, doctrinal, imperious, dictatorial, settled, authoritative, self-opinionated. *(active, diffident, vacillating, modest, practical, moderate, uncertain.)*

doleful—*adj.* rueful, piteous, somber, sorrowful, dismal, dolorous, melancholy, woebegone, mournful. *(joyful, blithe, gay, merry, beaming, cheerful.)*

dominion—*n.* tyranny, power, rule, government, empire, realm, jurisdiction, supremacy, territory, sway, control, despotism, authority. *(inferiority, weakness, servitude, subjugation, submission, docility.)*

dormant—*adj.* slumbering, quiescent, sleeping, latent, inert, oblivious, undeveloped. *(wakeful, energetic, vigilant, active, developed, operative, functioning.)*

doubt—*n.* scruple, suspense, distrust, indecision,

dubiousness, hesitation, suspicion, difficulty, uncertainty, ambiguity, perplexity, challenge, demur. *(clearness, determination, satisfaction, certainty, precision, conviction, decision, belief, trust.)*

dowdy—*adj.* shabby, slovenly, unfashionable, seedy, frumpy, unfashionable, sloppy, drab, bedraggled, unattractive. *(smart, stylish, chic, elegant, fashionable, modish, tidy, trim.)*

drain—*v.* percolate, exhaust, dry, draw, drip, strain, drop, empty, withdraw, discharge. *(supply, moisten, fill, inundate, swill, replenish, pour, energize, drown, drench, stimulate.)*

dramatize—*v.* intensify, highlight, punctuate, exaggerate, rant, embroider, spout, embellish, emote, color, interpret. *(play down, minimize, understate.)*

draw—*v.* pull, induce, sketch, entice, describe, delineate, rouse, inhale, drag, haul, attract, solicit. *(propel, drive, thrust, push, throw, carry, compel, repel, impel, shove, disperse.)*

dreadful—*adj.* monstrous, terrible, awful, horrible, fearful, dire, shocking, alarming, frightful, terrific, distressing, tragic. *(assuring, hopeful, promising, encouraging, suitable, inspiriting, cheerful.)*

dreamy—*adj.* visionary, absent, fanciful, speculative, foggy, abstracted, fabulous, rapt. *(earnest, practical, collected, attentive, awake, energetic, active, vigilant, aware.)*

dregs—*n.* sediment, lees, trash, refuse, offal, dross, outcasts, off-scouring, debris. *(pickings, flower, cream, sample, pink, bouquet, exemplification.)*

dress—*n.* preparation, accoutrements, garniture, vestments, clothing, don, lively, habiliments, uniform, apparel, raiment, investiture, garb, costume, array, arrangement, garments, drape, ornament. *(disorder, undress, nudity, disarrangement, deshabille, disrobe, divest.)*

drift—*n.* direction, tenor, scope, issue, conclusion, course, aim, tendency, motion, meaning, design, purport, intention, object, purpose, result, end, inference, vein. *(vagueness, indefiniteness, pointlessness, aberrancy, unmeaningness, confusedness, aimlessness, motionlessness, inertia.)*

drink—*v.* guaff, absorb, draught, imbibe, drain, guzzle, swallow, gulp. *(replenish, ex-*

ude, water, disgorge, moisten, pour, dampen.)

drivel—*n.* nonsense, snivel, fatuity, trifling, babble, rambling. *(coherence, solidity, soundness, substance, essence.)*

droll—*adj.* queer, funny, comic, farcical, whimsical, odd, quaint, fantastic, amusing, comical, laughable. *(lugubrious, sad, funereal, lamentable, ordinary, tragic.)*

drop—*v.* emanate, percolate, fall, faint, decline, descend, ooze, droop, trickle, distil. *(rise, recover, soar, rally, evaporate, climb, ascend.)*

drown—*v.* overwhelm, submerge, deluge, sink, swamp, engulf, perish, inundate, immerse, overflow. *(drain, ventilate, dry, expose, air, rescue, perserve.)*

dry—*adj.* parched, monotonous, dull, arid, juiceless, sarcastic, tame, moistureless, uninteresting, vapid, evaporated, barren, lifeless, tedious, withered. *(fresh, lively, damp, entertaining, juicy, soaked, moist.)*

due—*adj.* unpaid, payable, mature, accrued, owed, owing, outstanding, in arrears, demandable. *(unsuitable, inapt, wrong, undeserved, inappropriate.)*

dull—*adj.* stolid, insensible, heavy, dismal, turbid, dowdy, sad, commonplace, stupid, dead, doltish, callous, gloomy, clowdy, opaque, sluggish, tiresome, faded, muted. *(clever, animated, bright, burnished, exhilarating, sharp, lively, sensible, transparent, brilliant, cheerful, keen, intense.)*

durable—*adj.* permanent, firm, abiding, continuing, lasting, stable, sturdy, persistent, constant. *(transient, unstable, impermanent, perishable, evanescent.)*

duty—*n.* part, responsiblity, function, province, trust, service, liability, obligation, business, allegiance, office, calling, commission, task. *(exemption, license, desertion, freedom, direliction, dispensation, immunity, liberation.)*

dwindle—*v.* diminish, fall off, melt, pine, decline, waste, decrease, lessen, degenerate. *(enlarge, grow, flourish, expand, develop, augment, strenghten, increase, multiply.)*

dynamic—*adj.* vigorous, energetic, vital, forceful, active, oscillating, impelling, powerful. *(fixed, still, inert, stable, dead, passive, weak, enverated.)*

E

early—*adj.* forward, quickly, anon, beforehand, soon, first, betimes, matutinal, shortly, premature. *(backward, belated, late, vespertinal, tardily, retarded.)*

earn—*v. acquire, obtain, gain, realize, merit, achieve, win, deserve, collect. (forego, lose, squander, forfeit, waste, spend, exhaust, dissipate.)*

earnest—*adj.* serious, determined, solemn, warm, ardent, eager, fervent, intent, strenuous, grave, intense, devoted. *(playful, unearnest, jesting, indifferent, flippant, idle, desultory, irresolute, sportive, superficial.)*

easy—*adj.* comfortable, indulgent, lenient, gentle, self-possessed, not difficult, unconcerned, quiet, manageable, facile, unpretentious. *(disturbed, difficult, hard, embarrassed, uneasy, exacting, anxious, painful, unmanageable, awkward, uncomfortable.)*

ebb—*v.* recede, fall, decline, wane, lessen, shrink, dwindle, sink, diminish, weaken, decrease. *(grow, wax, enlarge, increase, swell, prosper, flowish, build.)*

economical—*adj.* thrifty, spare, frugal, saving, prudent, chary, careful, parsimonious, cheap, scrimping. *(prodigal, lavish, improvident, spendthrift, elaborate, ample, generous, liberal.)*

economy—*n.* dispensation, rule, administration, management, distribution, arrangement, frugality, thrift. *(waste, mismanagement, prodigality, misrule, disorder, maladministration, imprudence, extravagance.)*

ecstasy—*n.* inspiration, frenzy, emotion, delight, happiness, rapture, fervor, enthusiasm, joy, transport, exhilaration. *(coolness, weariness, tedium, fidget, misery, bore, dullness, indifference, sorrow.)*

edifice—*n.* building, tenement, structure, house, fabric, institute. *(heap, dismantlement, ruin, demolition, devastation.)*

educate—*v.* nurture, train, develop, school, initiate, teach, instruct, discipline, ground, enlighten, cultivate. *(misinstruct, misnurture, miseducate, mistrain.)*

effective—*adj.* conducive, cogent, able, powerful, telling, talented, efficient, effectual, serviceable, operative, patent, efficacious, competent. *(futile, nugatory, ineffective, inoperative, weak, inconducive, inadequate, useless.)*

effete—*adj.* barren, sterile, exhausted, worn-out, sere, unproductive, decadent, morally, decayed, spent, deteriorated. *(fruitful, inventive, prolific, creative, teeming, vital, vigorous, youthful.)*

effort—*n.* attempt, exertion, trial, endeavor, struggle, stress. *(misadventure, facility, spontaneity, ease, failure, unsuccess, futility, inactivity, frustration, collapse.)*

egotism—*n.*vanity, self-assertion, conceit, self-exaltation, pride, self-praise, narcissism, arrogance. *(deference, modesty, self-abnegation, considerateness.)*

ejaculation—*n.* utterance, cry, exclamation, vaciferation. *(silence, speech, dumbfoundedness, obmutescence, speechlessness, drawl, oration, address.)*

elastic—*adj.* extensile, resilient, flexible, springy, modifiable, buoyant, ductile, alterable, supple. *(unchangeable, inert, tough, brittle, rigid, inflexible, obstinate, dull, crystallized.)*

elated—*adj.* inspirited, proud, cheered, inflated, joyed, gleeful, jubilant. *(dispirited, dejected, disappointed, depressed, sad, humiliated, gloomy, abashed, confounded.)*

elegance—*n.* refinement, taste, grandeur, beauty, symmetry, gracefulness, luxuriousness. *(awkwardness, rudeness, ungracefulness, plainness, deformity, coarseness, crudeness, disproportion.)*

elegant—*adj.* lovely, well made, accomplished, refined, graceful, handsome, symetrical, polished, luxurious, well formed, graud. *(deformed, coarse, rude, unsymmetrical, plain, ungraceful, inelegant, crude.)*

elementary—*adj.* material, simple, ultimate, physical, constituent, primary, physical, basic, natural, component, inchoate, fundamental. *(incorporeal, compound, aggregate, organized, complicated, immaterial, collective, impalpable, developed, complex.)*

elevate—*v.* basic, fundamental, elemental, rudimentary, primary, original, initial, simple, primitive. *(debase, belittle, degrade, reduce, weaken, impair, depreciate.)*

eligible—*adj.* suitable, desirable, choice, preferable, capable, prime, worthy, chosen, proper. *(worthless, ordinary, indifferent, unprofitable, undesirable, unacceptable, ineligible, unsuitable.)*

eloquent—*adj.* forceful, fluent, articulate, inspired, passionate, persuasive, cogent, inspired, vivid, emphatic. *(inarticulate, dull, hesitant, clumsy, routine, commonplace, prosaic, weak.)*

elude—*v.* avoid, baffle, parry, frustrate, wade, eschew, shun, escape, fence, dodge, mock, flee. *(court, defy, encounter, confront, dare, meet, challenge.)*

emaciated—*adj.* wasted, thin, scrawny, famished, gaunt, haggard, frail, atrophied, wizened, skeletal. *(well-fed, fat, corpulent, plump, obese, hardy, robust.)*

embarrass—*v.* desconcert, confuse, clog, entangle, puzzle, encumber, distress, trouble, hamper, perplex, mortify. *(expedite, assist, extricate, disencumber, liberate, facilitate, accelerate, put at ease.)*

embezzle—*v.* confuse, piculate, appropriate, falsify, misappropriate, pilfer, steal. *(balance, square, recompense, clear, remunerate.)*

embody—*v.* methodize, codify, aggregate, compact, enlist, express, systematize, incorporate, integrate, introduce, combine, consolidate. *(segregate, dissipate, dismember, disband, eliminate, analyse, disintegrate, colliquate, disembody, divide, disunite.)*

embrace—*v.* comprehend, hug, contain, incorporate, clasp, close, encompass, include, comprise, embody. *(reject, except, repudiate, exclude, decline.)*

emergency—*n.* conjuncture, strait, exigency, difficulty, crisis, casualty, pitch, necessity, embarrassment, tension. *(solution, provision, arrangement, rescue, anticipation, subsidence, deliverance, stability.)*

eminent—*adj.* excellent, foremost, outstanding, esteemed, celebrated, noted, renowned, distinguished, honored, famous, laureate, paramount. *(obscure, humble, mediocre, undistinguished, unknown, modest, unpretentious, petty.)*

emotion—*n.* feeling, agitation, trepidation, passion, excitement, tremor, perturbation, worry, turmoil. *(impassiveness, peace, stoicism, in-*

difference, harmony, insensibility, imperturbability.)

emphatic—*adj.* forceable, energetic, positive, special, consummate, earnest, strong, impressive, important, egregious, decisive. *(cool, ordinary, commonplace, mild, unnoticeable, unimpassoned, unimportant, hesitant.)*

employ—*v.* apply, occupy, engross, use, economize, engage, hire, enlist. *(dismiss, misemploy, discard, misuse, discharge, fire.)*

empower—*v.* commission, qualify, warrant, direct, enable, encourage, delegate, sanction, authorize, permit. *(prevent, disable, disqualify, hinder, discourage, forbid, disbar.)*

empty—*adj.* void, unobstructed, waste, unfrequented, vacuous, unfilled, untenanted, deficient, silly, senseless, vacant, idle, unencumbered, unoccupied, devoid, uninhabited, destitute, unfurnished, evacuated, weak, frivolous. *(occupied, obstructed, substantial, colonized, informed, experienced, significant, important, full, encumbered, abundant, sensible, cultivated, inhabited, well-instructed, forcible.)*

enamor—*v.* fascinate, charm, bewitch, captivate, enchain, enslave, endear, infatuate. *(disgust, disenchant, repel, horrify, estrange, revolt.)*

enclose—*v.* encircle, afforest, include, envelop, shut, circumscribe, wrap, surround. *(disclose, bare, develop, open, exclude, expose, disencircle, boycott, disenclose.)*

encourage—*v.* rally, abet, inspirit, embolden, enhearten, incite, urge, foster, promote, advance, impel, forward, animate, prompt, reassure, countenance, cherish, stimulate, cheer, advocate. *(discourage, dispirit, deter, dissuade, dishearten, daunt.)*

end—*n.* stop, terminus, limit, tip, boundary, point, finish, close, conclusion, finale, cessation, point, expiration, aftermath. *(origin, beginning, source, start, commencement, infancy, inception, outset.)*

endanger—*v.* risk, imperil, jeopardize, peril, commit, expose, hazard, compromise. *(defend, screen, cover, protect, safeguard, shield.)*

endear—*v.* gain, attach, make dear, conciliate, idolize, treasure. *(alienate, embitter, estrange, provoke.)*

endless—*adj.* illimitable, eternal, uncensing, deathless, infinite, everlasting, interminable, unending, perpetual, boundless, imperishable, immortal. *(temporary, transient, ephemeral, finite, terminable, limited, brief, periodic, fugitive, measured.)*

endowment—*n.* provision, capacity, qualification, gift, benefaction, donation, benefit, attainment, grant. *(incapacity, impoverishment, lack, loss, poverty, detriment, drawback, harm.)*

enforce—*v.* compel, exact, strain, urge, require, exert, administer, impose. *(forego, abandon, relax, disregard, waive, remit, default.)*

engage—*v.* vouch, promise, buy, involve, undertake, employ, occupy, attract, adopt, agree, hire, gain, stipulate, commit, pledge, enlist. *(refuse, dismiss, extricate, disengage, decline, withdraw, discard, fire, cancel.)*

enhance—*v.* magnify, intensify, heighten, elevate, lift, boast, embellish, augment, fortify, escalate. *(diminish, detract, undermine, reduce, lessen, depreciate, minimize, weaken.)*

enigmatical—*adj.* perplexing, elusive, mystic, puzzling, obscure, cryptic. *(explanatory, self-evident, lucid, plain, candid, frank.)*

enlarge—*v.* expand, broaden, stretch out, dilate, augment, swell, increase, extend, amplify, magnify, widen. *(lessen, restrict, curtail, narrow, reduce, contract, diminish, dwindle, condense.)*

enlighten—*v.* edify, illuminate, teach, illumine, instruct, inform, educate, apprise. *(darken, obscure, perplex, mislead, mystify, confound, delude, deceive.)*

enlist—*v.* register, embody, enroll, enter, incorporate, recruit, obtain. *(erase, dismiss, retire, disembody, withdraw, expunge, disband, resign.)*

enmity—*n.* asperity, bitterness, animosity, malignity, maliciousness, hostility, discord, hate, malevolence, aversion, ill-feeling, opposition, acrimony, malice, antipathy. *(love, esteem, cordiality, friendship, affection, friendliness, harmony, amicability.)*

enormous—*adj.* immense, gross, colossal, vast, monstrous, huge, prodigious, elephantine, gigantic, astronomic. *(insignificant, venial, ordinary, trivial, diminutive, regular, average, puny, undersized.)*

enough—*adj.* ample, abundance, plenty, sufficient, adequate. *(scant, inadequate, short, bare, insufficient, deficient.)*

ensue—*v.* accrue, befall, follow, supervene, result. *(threaten, forewarn, precede, herald, premonish.)*

ensure—*v.* determine, seal, secure, fix, guarantee. *(hazard, forfeit, imperil, jeopardize, endanger.)*

enterprising—*adj.* bold, dashing, active, adventurous, forceful, speculative, venturesome, daring. *(inadventurous, inactive, cautious, timid, apathetic.)*

entertain—*v.* maintain, foster, recreate, harbor, amuse, receive, conceive, engross. *(exclude, debar, tire, weary, eject, deny, bore, annoy, ignore.)*

enthusiasm—*n.* frenzy, passion, fervor, devotion, excitement, sensation, transport, warmth, vehemence, ardor, inspiration, zeal, rapture, fervency, ebullience. *(callousness, disaffection, alienation, coldness, contempt, repugnance, indifference, apathy.)*

entire—*adj.* complete, total, all, undiminished, solid, whole, integral, unimpaired, full, perfect, intact. *(impaired, partial, broken, incomplete, fragmentary.)*

entitle—*v.* empower, characterize, denominate, qualify, fit, name, designate, style, enable, permit. *(disable, disqualify, not characterize, desentitle, not designate, unfit.)*

entreat—*v.* obsecrate, beseech, crave, supplicate, ask, petition, implore, beg, importune, solicit, pray, urge, plead with. *(insist, enjoin, bid, command, demand.)*

enumerate—*v.* name, recount, reckon, calculate, over, specify, number, detail, compute, call, list. *(miscount, miscalculate, misreckon, confound.)*

ephemeral—*adj.* evanescent, fugacious, momentary, transient, fleeting, fugitive, temporary. *(persistent, perpetual, perennial, abiding, immortal, external, permanent, lasting.)*

equable—*adj.* regular, even, easy, smooth, uniform, tranquil, proportionate. *(uneasy, desultory, fitful, irregular, agitated, variable, disjointed.)*

equal—*adj.* commensurate, alike, even, sufficient, co- extensive, uniform, smooth, impartial, co-ordinate, identical, adequate, equivalent, equable. *(incommensurate, inadequate, unequal, partial, incoordinate, variable, disparate.)*

equitable—*adj.* proportionate, fair, honest, reasonable, just, proper, even- handed, impartial, upright honorable. *(disproportionate, unfair, partial, biased, unjust.)*

erase—*v.* efface, blot, eradicate, cancel, expunge, obliterate. *(write, stamp, delineate, mark.)*

erect—*v.* institute, establish, set up, elevate, manufacture, raise, build plant, found, construct, uplift. *(supplant, remove, demolish, raze, subvert, destroy, depress, lower.)*

erratic—*adj.* aberrant, capricious, desultory, abnormal, changeful, unpredictable, flighty. *(normal, calculable, undeviating, regular, predictable, methodical, steady, unalterable.)*

error—*n.* mistake, deception, untruth, fault, hallucination, blunder, misunderstanding, falsity, fallacy. *(correctness, soundness, truth, rectification, correction, flawlessness, accuracy.)*

escape—*v.* decamp, avoid, fly, elude, evade, shun, flee, abscond. *(meet, confront, suffer, trap, incur, encounter.)*

esoteric—*adj.* cryptic, obscure, arcane, abstruese, inscrutable, mysterious, private, veiled, occult, hidden. *(clear, simple, open, exoteric, obvious, plain.)*

essential—*adj.* inherent, leading, immanent, innate, requisite, crucial, necessary, indispensable, vital, key, main. *(qualitative, option, promotive, induced, ascititious, superfluous, adventitious, minimal, accidental, quantitative, regulative, imported, redundant.)*

establish—*v.* settle, substantiate, plant, found, prove, organize, inaugurate, confirm, fix, demonstrate, institute. *(presume, surmise, guess, supplant, break-up, misstate, refute, subvert, conjecture, suppose, unsettle, disestablish, upset, confute, invalidate.)*

esteem—*n.* value, deem, believe, think, affect, revere, respect, venerate, love, price, consider, admiration, like, admire, honor, appreciate, regard, judge, estimate, prize, treasure. *(disconsider, dislike, underrate, deprecate, disregard, disaffect, undervalue, decry, contempt.)*

eternal—*adj.* endless, deathless, never-dying, everliving, undying, infinite, unceasing, immortal, perpetual, ceaseless, everlasting, imperishable, constant. *(temporal, fleeting, ephemeral, evanescent, mortal, transient, perishable.)*

etiquette—*n.* fashion, manners, conventionality, protocal, breeding, decorum. *(rudeness, singularity, nonconformance, boorishness, vulgarity, misobservance.)*

evaporate—*v.* exhale, colliquate, distil, melt, liquefy, dissolve, vaporize, dehydrate, disappear. *(crystallize, solidify, consolidate, indurate, condense, compact.)*

even—*adj.* level, smooth, flush, regular, straight, flat, uniform, tranquil, serene, calm. *(jagged, askew, unfair, uneven, rough, lumpy, jumpy, unstable, biased.)*

event—*n.* circumstance, adventure, accident, fact, occurence, incident, happening, issue, episode, result. *(predisposition, cause, tendency, antecedent, union, convergence, contribution, operation, inducement.)*

eventful—*adj.* memorable, marked, critical, notable, remarkable, signal, active, stirring, noted, important. *(unmarked, trivial, ordinary, unimportant, empty, characterless, uninteresting, eventless.)*

evidence—*n.* attraction, testimony, declaration, sign, proof, exemplification, token, illustration, manifestation, averment, disposition, appearance, corroboration, indication. *(conjecture, fallacy, surmise, counter-evidence, refutation, suppression, disproof, concealment, misindication, disguising.)*

evident—*adj.* visible, manifest, obvious, palpable, plain, clear, incontrovertible, indisputable, conspicuous, apparent. *(questionable, doubtful, dubious, obscure, uncertain, unsure.)*

evil—*adj.* deleterious, bad, hurtful, unhappy, unpropitious, corrupt, unfair, miserable, ill, sorrowful, noxious, wrong, mischievous, sinful, adverse, wicked, harmful, notorious, immoral. *(beneficial, virtuous, pure, fortunate, joyous, grateful, welcome, good, wholesome, right, holy, happy, felicitous, noble.)*

exactly—*adv.* correspondently, truly, precisely, accurately, literally. *(inadequately, loosely, otherwise, approximately, differently, incorrectly.)*

exaggerate—*v.* enlarge, magnify, overdraw, over-paint, strain, overestimate, embellishment, amplify, heighten, overstate, inflate. *(attenuate, lenify, soften, modify, disparage, palliate, mitigate, qualify, understate, minimize, underestimate.)*

examine—*v.* ponder, perpend, scrutinize, prove, discuss, search, explore, weigh, inspect, overhaul, inquire, study, test, criticize, investigate, survey. *(conjecture, slur, guess, discard, misinvestigate, misconsider, ignore.)*

example—*n.* specimen, model, copy, illustration, issue, development, sample, pattern, instance, standard. *(material, law, stock, character, substance, rule, case, principle, quality, system, anomaly.)*

excellent—*adj.* superior, great, fine, splendid, exceptional, superb, remarkable, outstanding, magnificent, choice. *(average, inadequate, mediocre, deficient, rotten, worthless, so-so, inferior.)*

except—*v.* save, segregate, exclude, bar, negate, omit, ignore. *(include, state, propound, admit, count, reckon, classify, affirm, attest.)*

exceptional—*adj.* peculiar, unusual, rare, uncommon, irregular, abnormal, outstanding. *(regular, ordinary, common, normal, usual, typical.)*

excessive—*adj.* undue, overmuch, extravagant, immoderate, enormous, inordinate, exorbitant, unreasonable, superfluous, superabundant, extreme. *(scant, inadequate, insufficient, want, shortage.)*

excuse—*v.* pardon, exculpate, condone, exonerate, release, absolve, extenuate, defend, forgive, vindicate, overlook, remit, mitigate, indulge, free, justify, acquit, exempt, alibi. *(inculpate, sentence, strain, charge, condemn, exact, accuse, blame, criticize.)*

exemplary—*adj.* praiseworthy, honorable, meritorious, excellent, laudable, conspicuous, wary, worthy, commendable. *(objectionable, regrettable, exceptionable, detestable, worthless.)*

exempt—*adj.* irresponsible, free, clear, privileged, unamenable, absolved, liberated, special, responsible, liable, amenable, subject, accountable.

exercise—*n.* use, application, drill, employment, exertion, training, practice, discipline, preparation. *(idleness, ease, recreation, relaxation, inactivity, rest.)*

exhaust—*v.* spend, weaken, void, drain, debilitate, deplete, weary, waste, empty, consume. *(replenish, refresh, obtain, fill, invigorate, augment.)*

existence—*n.* entity, creature, being, subsistence, life. *(non-existence, chimera, nothingness, nonenity.)*

expand—*v.* dilate, open, spread, amplify, unfold, distend, swell, enlarge, diffuse, extend, develop. *(curtail, restrict, contract, diminish, condense, attenuate, deflate.)*

expect—*v.* await, forebode, anticipate, wait for, foresee, forecast, contemplate, hope, rely on, predict. *(recognize, realize, welcome, fear, greet, hail, dread.)*

expediency—*n.* advantage, aptness, utility, interest, usefulness. *(disadvantage, inutility, idealism, detriment, inexpediency.)*

expend—*v.* disburse, waste, use, exhaust, spend, lay out, consume, dissipate. *(economize, preserve, husband, save, hoard.)*

expense—*n.* cost, payment, outlay, price, amount, charge, expenditure. *(receipt, income, proceeds, profit, gain.)*

experience—*v.* feel, encounter, suffer, try, undergo, endure, perceive. *(miss, evade, foil, escape, lose, baffle.)*

experience—*n.* test, proof, habit, knowledge, experiment trial, observation. *(theory, surmise, inexperience.)*

explain—*v.* teach, decipher, interpret, expound, elucidate, illustrate, demonstrate, clear up, describe. *(obscure, bewilder, mystify, confuse, misinterpret, darken.)*

explanation—*n.* interpretation, description, explication, sense, exposition, reason, analysis. *(obscuration, misinterpretation, mystification, confusion, complication.)*

explicit—*adj.* detailed, declaratory, stated, determinate, express, plain, precise, inobscure, categorical, distinctly, definite. *(implied, vague, obscure, implicit, hinted, suggestive.)*

expression—*n.* indication, term, lineament, phrase, delivery, countenance, feature, look, face. *(enigma, suppression, falsification, solecism, restraint, misstatement.)*

exquisite—*adj.* refined, perfect, intense, delicious, choice, elegant, rare, consummate, matchless, delicate. *(coarse, ordinary, gross, common, uncouth.)*

extend—*v.* expand, increase, reach, apply, spread, avail, prolong, augment, unfurl, stretch, amplify, enlarge. *(contract, narrow, fail, return, curtail, constrict, miss, restrict, limit, recur, shorten.)*

extinguish—*v.* quench, put out, abolish, extirpate, annihilate, destroy, eradicate, kill, douse, smother. *(replenish, promote, propagate, confirm, implant, secure, establish, ignite, cherish, invigorate, light*

extraneous—*adj.* irrelevant, extra, immaterial, incidental, external, accidental, superfluous, nonessential, peripheral. *(apropos, apt, inherent, germane, pertinent, relevant, essential.)*

extraordinary—*adj.* uncommon, preposterous, unwonted, wonderful, strange, monstrous, unprecedented, peculiar, marvelous, prodigious, amazing, unusual, remarkable. *(unimportant, frequent, wonted, usual customary, common, ordinary, unremarkable, expected.)*

extravagant—*adj.* abnormal, wild, profuse, monstrous, lavish, wasteful, profligate, reckless, prodigal, absurd, preposterous, excessive. *(usual, frugal, sound, consistent, fair, sober careful, thrifty, economical, regular, rational.)*

extreme—*adj.* ultimate, final, distant, immoderate, severe, terminal, remote, extravagant, last, utmost, farthest, most violent. *(moderate, judicious, initial, primal, average, mild.)*

F

fable—*n.* fiction, falsehood, romance, fabrication, romance, parable, apologue, fantasy, allegory, untruth, novel, invention. *(narrative, truth, history, fact, authenticity.)*

fabrication—*n.* deceit, fiction, forgery, lie, deception, fib, untruth, prevarication, creation. *(fact, verity, destruction, truth, reality, actuality.)*

facetious—*adj.* jocular, droll, pungent, comical, jesting, humorous, clever, flippant, witty, funny. *(matter-of-fact, saturnine, lugubrious, grave, heavy, sombre, dull, serious, sedate, sad.)*

facile—*adj.* tractable, indulgent, irrisolute, affable, pliable, docile, characterless, easy, weak, flexible, manageable, dexterous. *(obstinate, crusty, self-willed, self-reliant, sturdy, determined, inflexible, resolue, independent, pig-headed, arduous.)*

facility—*n.* address, quickness, dexterity, adroitness, proficiency, ease, readiness, pliancy, skill. *(awkwardness, labor, ineptness, difficulty, exertion.)*

fact—*n.* deed, certainty, event, truth, reality, incident, occurence, circumstance. *(supposition, unreality, delusion, romance, fiction, opinion, falsehood, invention, lie, chimera.)*

fade—*v.* decline, etiolate, pale, vanish, fall, droop, dissolve, set, fail, bleach, dwindle, change, blur, taper. *(increase, endure, bloom, stand, rise, brighten, grown, flourish, last, abide.)*

failure—*n.* lapse, miscarriage, decline, disappointment, collapse, ruin, insolvency, defeat, bankruptcy. *(victory, conquest, prosperity, luck, success, hit, fortune.)*

faint—*adj.* languid, inconspicious, weak, fatigued, irresolute, exhausted, obscure, faded, collapse, unenergetic, feeble, timid, pale, half-hearted, dim. *(glaring, strong, fresh, vigorous, conspicuous, energetic, marked, resolute, daring, courageous, prominent.)*

fair—*adj.* clear, unspotted, reasonable, serene, just, equitable, open, impartial, attractive, spotless, untarnished, unblemished, beautiful, honorable. *(fraudulent, dull, disfigured, lowering, fowl, inclement, unfair, ugly, dishonorable.)*

faithful—*adj.* firm, loyal, close, correspondent, equivalent, incorruptible, true, staunch, attached, accurate, consistent, exact, trustworthy. *(fickle, inexact, false, capricious, faithless, treacherous, untrue, wavering, inaccurate.)*

fallacy—*n.* error, misconception, chimera, fiction, saphistry, blunder, delusion, bugbear, deception. *(verity, logic, proof, axiom, truth, certainty, fact, argument, postulate, soundness.)*

false—*adj.* faithless, untrue, fiction, fallacious, spurious, fabrication, mendacious, mock, unfaithful, falsity, dishonorable, fib, bagus, sham, counterfeit, deceptive, sophistical, hypocritical, erroneous. *(correct, faith-*

ful, true, sound, authentic, genuine, real, honorable, candid, conclusive, staunch.)

falsify—*v.* misinterpret, cook, mistake, garble, misrepresent, betray, distort, belie. *(correct, declare, verify, expose, rectify, publicate, confirm, exhibit, check, justify, certify.)*

falter—*v.* hesitate, slip, flinch, halt, vacillate, fluctuate, hobble, dubitate, demur, stammer, waver. *(career, proceed, resolve, run, persevere, speed, persist, flow, determine, discourse.)*

fame—*n.* renown, eminence, repute, notice, reputation, prominence, notability, esteem, notoriety. *(anonymity, seclusion, retirement, oblivion, dishonor, infamy.)*

familiar—*adj.* common, intimate, household, conversant, free, apprised, accustomed, frank, well- acquainted, affable, every- day. *(rare, unfamiliar, new, unaccustomed, uncommon, extraordinary, strange, ignorant, unacquainted, inconversant.)*

famous—*adj.* glorious, eminent, celebrated, prominent, illustrious. *(obscure, unknown, unsung, inglorious, humble.)*

fanciful—*adj.* chimerical, fitful, grotesque, unreal, quaint, absurd, whimsical, erroneous, imaginary, eccentric, humorous, freakish, capricious, erratic, fantastic. *(literal, calculable, natural, regular, sober, real, truthful, correct, ordinary, accurate, orderly, prosaic.)*

fancy—*n.* belief, supposition, idea, caprice, conceit, inclination, humor, desire, thought, illusion, imagination, notion, vagary, whim, predilection. *(horror, object, fact, aversion, subject, verity, reality, unadorned, system, order, law, truth.)*

far—*adj.* remote, removed, long-distant, estranged, alienated, faraway, separated, yonder. *(close, adjacent, near, familiar, neighboring, contiguous, handy, convenient.)*

fashion—*n.* mold, shape, ceremony, form, vague, way, guise, manner, style, usage, appearance, figure, practice, character, custom, mode. *(strangeness, work, outlandishness, person, speech, eccentricity, dress, derangement, shapelessness, formlessness.)*

fast—*adj.* gay, firm, dissipated, secure, reckless, fixed, wild, constant, accelerated, steadfast, rapid, stable, unswerving, unyielding, immovable. *(virtuous, loose, slow, sober, insecure, tardy, steady, tenuous, wavering.)*

fastidious—*adj.* dainty, critical, squeamish, over-nice, particular, censorious, punctilious, over-refined, meticulous. *(omnivorous, easy, uncritical, neglectful, coarse, indulgent.)*

fat—*adj.* oleaginous, corpulent, obese, fleshy, unctuous, brawny, pursy, fertile, rich, stout, luxuriant, portly, rotund. *(anatomical, lean, exsanguineous, slender, scant, attenuated, poor, emacinated, barren, marrowless, gaunt, cadaverous.)*

fatal—*adj.* lethal, calamitous, mortal, deadly, destructive, terminal, pernicious. *(harmful, beneficial, superficial, wholesome, slight, nutritious, restorative, salubrious, vitalizing, nonlethal.)*

fate—*n.* doom, necessity, fortune, lot, destiny, end, providence. *(independence, choice, freedom, will, chance, decision.)*

fault—*n.* error, drawback, flow, defect, want, imperfection, misdeed, omission, failure. *(perfection, sufficiency, goodness, completeness, correctness.)*

favor—*n.* patronage, permission, countenance, grace, boon, gift, concession, preference, civility, accomodation, condescension, goodwill, regard, predilection, benefit, kindness. *(discountenance, refusal, withholding, injury, denial, frown, prohibition, disfavor, withdrawal, malice, disapproval.)*

favorable—*adj.* friendly, fond, permissive, auspicious, partial, indulgent, liberal, propitious, concessive, advantageous, beneficial. *(unpropitious, impartial, contrary, unsatisfactory, reluctant, unfavorable.)*

fear—*n.* solicitude, awe, fright, apprehension, timidity, alarm, dread, trepidation, horror, dismay, panic, terror, consternation, misgiving. *(boldness, fearlessness, assurance, bravery, confidence, trust, courage.)*

feasible—*adj.* practicable, attainable, possible, suitable, practical, operable, reasonable, expedient, desirable. *(impractical, unworkable, unsuitable, impossible, unfeasible.)*

feeble—*adj.* scanty, weak, vain, pitiable, wretched, fruitless, poor, frail, incomplete, infirm, debilitated, dull, invalid, forceless, faint, puny, enervated, enfeebled, nerveless. *(robust, effective, abundant, vigorous, strong, active, successful.)*

feeling—*n.* sensation, passion, touch, sensitiveness, pathos, sentiment, contact, emotion, tenderness, impression, sensibility, awareness, consiousness. *(insensateness, callousness, coldness, apathy, insensibility, inexcitability, imperturbability, numbness.)*

felicitous—*adj.* timely, opportune, happy, successful, joyous, appropriate, apropos. *(unhappy, sad, unsuccessful, unfortunate, inopportune, irrelevant, disastrous, untimely.)*

feminine—*adj.* womanly, modest, delicate, soft,tender, gentle, ladylike. *(manly, rude, unfeminine, robust, indelicate, rough, masculine.)*

ferment—*v.* stir up, incite, agitate, trouble, disturb, rouse, shake, seethe, fester, perturb, provoke, effervesce, foam. *(soothe, relax, calm, compose, allay, still, quiet.)*

fertile—*adj.* inventive, rich, copious, ingenious, luxuriant, fruitful, teeming, fecund, productive, prolific, exuberant, causative, pregnant, fraught, conducive. *(unimaginative, poor, uninventive, sterile, inoperative, barren, fruitless, inconducive, ineffective, unproductive, unyielding.)*

fickle—*adj.* unstable, fanciful, inconstant, fitful, restless, capricious, variable, irresolute, shifting, unpredicitable, changeable, veering, unrealiable, vacillating, mutable. *(uniform, sober, steady, orderly, trustworthy, reliable, calculable, well-regulated, faithful.)*

fiction—*n.* myth, invention, romance, fabrication, falsehood, creation, fable, fantasy, figment. *(truth, reality, accuracy, fact, verity.)*

fidelity—*n.* attachment, loyalty, truthfulness, integrity, fealty, honesty, allegiance, faithfulness, devotion, accuracy, exactness, closeness. *(disloyalty, infidelity, treachery, inexactness, disaffection, inaccuracy, untruthfulness, unrealiability.)*

fierce—*adj.* furious, cruel, enraged, violent, ravenous, extreme, savage, ferocious, brutal. *(gentle, docile, mild, harmless, moderate, meek, calm, submissive, placid, domesticated.)*

fiery—*adj.* hot-brained, vehement, irritable, hot, impassioned, ardent, fervid, fervent, glowing, fierce, smoldering, enkindled, passionate, excited, irascible, choleric. *(tame, cold, quenched, icy, extinguished, indifferent, mild, apathetic, unimpassioned, passionless, phlegmatic.)*

fight—*n.* engagement, battle, action, struggle, encounter, contention, skirmish, conflict, combat, contest. *(reconciliation, compromise, pacification, appeasement.)*

figure—*n.* illustration, aspect, delineation, shape, likeness, emblem, metaphor, type, symbol, imagine, form, appearance, condition, silhouette. *(deformity, defigurement, malformation, misrepresentation.)*

fill—*v.* content, expand, replenish, increase, glow, supply, swell, satisfy, rise, gorge, store, glut, appoint, occupy, stuff, saturate. *(diminish, exhaust, evaporate, deprive, ebb, drain, shrink, dissatisfy, subside, stint, misappoint, vacate, empty.)*

filthy—*adj.* polluted, foul, dirty, putrid, sordid, stained, unclean, unwashed, slimy, piggish, squalid. *(washed, hygienic, cleansed, purified, sanitary, decent, virtuous, pure.)*

final—*adj.* terminal, last, decisive, ultimate, latest, irrevocable, definite, conclusive, extreme, developed. *(rudimental, open, nascent, initiative, inchoate, unconcluded, inaugural, dynamic, incipient, current, continuous, progressive.)*

find—*v.* confront, furnish, meet, invent, ascertain, discover, experience, observe, perceive. *(elude, miscontrive, overlook, miss, withdraw, lose, withhold, misplace.)*

fine—*adj.* minute, casuistical, thin, subtle, slender, nice, delicate, high, presumptuous, pure, ostentatious, grand, elegant, noble, showy, pretty, sensitive, beautiful, refined, generous, handsome, honorable, dull, exemplary, pretentious, excellent, superior, finished, smooth, choice, filmy, artistic, gauzy, keen, pulverized. *(indissective, coarse, unreflective, large, unanalytical, rough, plainspoken, blunt, rude, categorical, unfinished, affable, mean, unaffected, petty, modest, illiberal, unimposing, paltry, mediocre.)*

finesse—*n.* tact, savior faire, discretion, skill, polish, artfulness, cleverness, diplomacy, adroitness, delicacy. *(clumsiness, stupidy, ineptitude, crudeness, tactlessness, maladroitness.)*

finical—*adj.* dandyish, euphuistic, affected, factitious, over nice, foppish, spruce, dallying, over-fastidious. *(coarse, genuine, unaffected, rude, outspoken, effective, blunt, practical, real, natural, energetic, competent.)*

finish—*v.* terminate, complete, shape, perfect, end, accomplish, achieve, conclude, cease, desist. *(commence, botch, miscontrive, begin, mar, start, mismanage. undertake, fail, launch.)*

first—*adj.* onmost, leading, chief, primary, highest, pristine, primeval, original, principal, foremost, primitive, earliest. *(secondary, hindmost, subsequent, last, subordinate, unimportant, subservient, lowest, terminating, concluding.)*

fit—*adj.* befitting, proper, decent, ripe, expedient, meet, contrived, apt, calculated, fitting, adequate, adapted, prepared, seemly, suitable, appropriate, particular, becoming, peculiar, decorous, congruous, qualified, germane. *(improper, awkward, unfit, ungainly, inexpedient, misfitting, miscontrived, ill-suited, miscalculated, unseemly, inadequate, inappropriate, unprepared, amiss, unsuitable, out of place.)*

fix—*v.* fasten, secure, attach, plant, decide, place, determine, settle, position, link, root, locate, establish, tie, immobilize. *(unsettle, change, shake, remove, transfer, disestablish, unfix, displace, uproot, disconnect, reverse, disarrange, transplant, weaken, disturb.)*

flagrant—*adj.* brazen, scandalous, outrageous, glaring, indecent, blatant, disgraceful, shocking, shameless, notorious, infamous, audacious. *(clandestine, sneaky, concealed, hidden, surreptitious, undercover.)*

flat—*adj.* insipid, mawkish, dull, level, lifeless, tame, vapid, tasteless, downright, horizontal, even, spiritless, absolute, uniform. *(rugged, interesting, sensational, exciting, thrilling, animated.)*

flexible—*adj.* lithe, yielding, elastic, ductile, pliable, easy, pliant, indulgent, rubbery, supple. *(hard, inelastic, inexorable, rigid, tough, inflexible, brittle.)*

flimsy—*adj.* thin, superficial, gauzy, shallow, poor, weak, fragile, transparent, trifling, puerile, trivial, inane, slight. *(substantial, sound, irrefragable, cogent, durable, solid.)*

flippant—*adj.* forward, malapert, thoughtless, pert, saucy, brazen, superficial. *(deferential, servile, accurate, complimentary, flattering, respectful, polite, obsequious, considerate.)*

flood—*n.* abundance, drench, inundation, deluge, shower. *(ebb, subsidence, drought, scarcity, drain, shortage.)*

florid—*adj.* sanguine, overwrought, rubicund, meretricious, flowery, embellished, ornate. *(exsanguineous, unadorned, sober, pallid, nude, understated, chaste, bare.)*

flounder—*v.* blunder, wallow, roll, bungle, tumble, struggle, boggle. *(career, rise, emerge, skim, course, flow, emanate, speed, flourish.)*

flourish—*v.* thrive, triumph, wave, flower, prosper, speed, brandish. *(decline, ground, arrest, fail, miscarry, sheathe, wither, fade, founder.)*

flow—*v.* issue, course, run, surge, stream, career, glide, progress. *(stick, hesitate, halt, recoil, abate, regurgitate, stint, ebb, stickle, stop, fail, beat.)*

fluent—*adj.* facile, flowing, glib, graceful, articulate, smooth, ready, effusive, uninterrupted, expert, constrained. *(halting, hesitant, limping, constrained, stammering, uneven.)*

flurry—*v.* ruffle, excite, fluster, agitate, disturbance, worry. *(compose, calm, soothe, tranquilize, mesmerize, quiet.)*

foible—*n.* failing, weakness, peccadillo, infirmity, defect, fault. *(atrocity, sin, crime, strength, enormity.)*

follow—*v.* accompany, succeed, attend, copy, pursue, observe, chase, shadow, ensue, supplant, obey, imitate, result. *(elude, abandon, quit, produce, forerun, shun, cause avoid, disobey, precede.)*

folly—*n.* nonsense, imbecility, absurdity, madness, silliness, misconduct, weakness, irrationality, foolishness, imprudence. *(wisdom, judgment, sobriety, sense prudence, allay, rationality.)*

foment—*v.* cherish, propagate, fan, agitate, encourage, excite. *(extinguish, extirpate, allay, quench, discourage, hinder.)*

fond—*adj.* attached, foolish, weak, empty, devoted, silly, loving, doting, enamored, affectionate, friendly. *(sensible, unloving, undemonstrative, averse, hostile, well-*

groomed, unaffectionate, rational, strong-minded, austere.)

foolish—*adj.* idiotic, shallow, simple, ridiculous, senseless, crazed, weak, asinine, nonsensical, injudicious, contemptible, absurd, brainless, witless, preposterous, silly, imbecile, objectionable, irrational. *(sane, advisable, deep, sensible, eligible, clearsighted, wise, calculating, sagacious, intelligent, strongminded, judicious, prudent, sound.)*

forbearance—*n.* restraint, sympathy, meekness, mildness, temperance, gentleness, mercy, clemency, patience, tolerance, self-control. *(vindictiveness, rancor, ruthlessness, impatience, intolerance, vengefulness.)*

forbidding—*adj.* deterrent, offensive, repulsive, prohibitory, menacing. *(encouraging, permissive, attractive, cordial, alluring, seductive.)*

force—*n.* strength, instrumentality, cogency, violent, coercion, power, agency, validity, compulsion, army duress, host, vehemence, pressure, dint, might, vigor. *(counteraction, inefficiency, pointlessness, inconclusiveness, weakness, debility, feebleness, impotence, neutralization.)*

foreign—*adj.* outlandish, strange, extraneous, exotic, alien, imported, irrelevant. *(native, pertinent, domestic, germane, indigenous, congenial.)*

forfeit—*n.* mulct, loss, penalty, damages, transgress, amercement, fine. *(reward, douceur, compensation, gratuity, entice, premium, remuneration, bribe.)*

forget—*v.* unlearn, overlook, lose, oblivate, pretermit, unintentionally. *(learn, recollect, mind, treasure, reminisce, retain, acquire, remember.)*

form—*v.* mould, constitue, frame, devise, produce, create, shape, fashion, contrive, make, scheme, arrange, construct. *(analyze, deform, distort, disorganize, disintegrate, dislocate, dissipate, derange, dismember, subvert.)*

formal—*adj.* complete, sufficient, stately, ceremonious, stiff, explicit, affected, systematic, methodical, exact, regular, shapely, precise, pompous, dignified, correct. *(incomplete, easy, unceremonious, irregular, informal, nonconformist, inadequate, unassuming, incorrect.)*

formality—*n.* parade, stateliness, ritualism, punctiliousness, ceremony, etiquette, affectation. *(casualness, ease, nonconformism, eccentricity, informality.)*

former—*adj.* antecedent, ancient, anterior, foregoing, preceding, previous, preliminary, bygone, first- mentioned, prior, earlier. *(subsequent, latter, succeeding, future, modern, ensuing, posterior, coming.)*

fortunate—*adj.* propitious, happy, felicitous, auspicious, successful, blessed, lucky, prosperous, providental. *(unhappy, disastrous, unlucky, infelicitous, unfortunate.)*

forthright—*adj.* direct, candid, blunt, honest, frank, sincere, explicit, plain, straightforward, truthful. *(guarded, equivocal, misleading, devious, indirect, circuitous.)*

forward—*adj.* ready, anxious, bold, self-assertive, presumptuous, advanced, eager, brash, obtrusive, impertinent, confident, progressive, onward. *(reluctant, slow, modest, timid, backward, tardy, retiring, indifferent.)*

found—*v.* institute,fix, root, ground, establish, set, endow, plant, originate, build, base, setup, rest. *(supplant, uproot, disestablish, annihilate, subvert.)*

foundation—*n.* establishment, basis, ground, rudiments, underlying, institution, footing, skeleton, base, origin, groundwork, principle, substratum. *(superstructure, pinnacle, disestablishment, summit.)*

fragrant—*adj.* scented, balmy, aromatic, odoriferous, redolent, odorous, perfumed, sweet-smelling, sweet-scented, spicy. *(scentless, fetid, malodorous, inodorous, mephitic.)*

frail—*adj.* erring, delicate, mutable, irresolute, wispy. *(virtuous, robust, lasting, resolute, vigorous.)*

frank—*adj.* candid, unreserved, free, honest, sincere, plain, evident, ingenious, open, artless, familiar, easy, outspoken. *(close, guarded, disingenious, reserved, devious.)*

freakish—*adj.* whimsical, erratic, sportful, capricious, grotesque, frisky, fanciful, strange. *(sober, unwhimsical, reliable, uniform, temperate, equable, demure, consistent, unfanciful, steady.)*

free—*adj.* playing, open, unoccupied, unimpeded, unhindered, gratuitous, at liberty, liberal, unconfined, loose, munificent, frank, gratis, generous, detached, operating, unobstructed, permitted, exempt, unconditional, bounteous, clear, untrammelled, careless, easy, unreserved, bountiful. *(stingy, qualified, intern, amenable, unlawful, impeded, occupied, restricted, bound, biased, enslaved, subservient, shocked, clogged, obstructed, compulsory, liable, conditional, niggardly.)*

frequent—*adj.* repeated, recurrent, continual, common, many, numerous, usual, habitual, general. *(solitary, scanty, few, sporadic, casual, rare.)*

fresh—*adj.* young, cool, renewed, untarnished, blooming, novel, modern, flourishing, unskilled, untried, ruddy, unfaded, new, unimpaired, recent, vigorous. *(stale, weary, stagnant, original, tarnished, decayed, sickly, mouldy, fusty, polluted, musty, putrid, pallid, faded, impaired, ordinary, former, old, jaded.)*

fretful—*adj.* fractious, impatient, waspish, cranky, petulant, peevish, irritable. *(forbearing, meek, unmurmuring, agreeable, patient, contented, resigned.)*

friction—*n.* grating, abrasion, rubbing, attrition, contact, grinding. *(detachment, harmony, lubrication, isolation, compatibility.)*

friend—*n.* companion, familiar, chum, coadjutor, adherent, ally, intimate, confidant, messmate, acquaintance, associate. *(foe, antagonist, rival, opponent, adversary, enemy, competitor.)*

friendly—*adj.* well-disposed, kindly, neighborly, affectionate, cordial, comradely, well-inclined, amicable, social, sociable, favorable. *(ill-disposed, inimical, distant, antagonistic, averse, hostile, aloof, ill- inclined.)*

frightful—*adj.* horrible, ugly, monstrous direful, shockful, terrific, horrendous, horrid, awful, dreadful, hideous, grim, alarming, terrible. *(attractive, fair, lovely, charming, encouraging, beautiful, pleasing.)*

frivolous—*adj.* silly, petty, worthless, flighty, trifling, trivial, giddy. *(earnest, grave, significant, important, serious.)*

frolic—*n.* game, festivity, gambol, lark, merry-making, play, sport, entertainment, gayety, spree, prank, outing. *(undertaking, engagement,* *obligation, study, occupation, purpose.)*

frugal—*adj.* economical, abstinent, temperate, thrifty, sparing, provident, parsimonious, abstemious, saving, cautious. *(luxurious, prodigal, intemperate, generous, self-indulgent, extravagant, profuse.)*

fruitful—*adj.* prolific, fraught, effectual, successful, abundant, fecund, productive, pregnant, causative, useful, fertile, plenteous, plentiful, valuable. *(sterile, fruitless, useless, futile, abortive, ineffectual, barren, unproductive.)*

fulfill—*v.* complete, verify, achieve, effect, consummate, execute, fill, accomplish, discharge. *(sober, delicate, nice, chaste, abandon.)*

fulsome—*adj.* gross, nauseous, fawning, extravagant, offensive, sickening, loathsome, excessive. *(sober, delicate, tempered, chaste, nice.)*

function—*n.* part, capacity, duty, administration, operation, power, office, character, business, role, discharge, exercise, employment, pursuit. *(maladministration, misdemeanor, misconduct, misdeed.)*

fundamental—*adj.* important, essential, primary, foremost, indispensable. *(unimportant, ascititious, secondary, superficial, nonessential, adventitious.)*

funny—*adj.* droll, laughable, jocose, ludicrous, ridiculous, amusing, diverting, humorous, comical, sportive. *(tedious, lugubrious, grave, sad, sober, lamentable, serious, dismal, mournful, dull.)*

furnish—*v.* provide, afford, bestow, give, provide, purvey, yield, equip, supply. *(withdraw, demolish, dismantle, withhold.)*

fuss—*n.* excitement, worry, ado, bustle, fidget, flurry, tumult, stir, agitation. *(peace, tranquility, silence, calm, quiet, composure, sedateness.)*

future—*n.* coming, destiny, advenient, forthcoming, forecast. *(bygone, previous, past, gone, prior.)*

G

gabby—*adj.* loquacious, wordy, chatty, talkative, garrulous, windy, talky, glib, talkative, voluble. *(terse, quiet, taciturn, reticent, laconic, reserved.)*

gain—*v.* get, procure, reach, profit, earn, realize, reap, acquire, win, accomplish, obtain, benefit, attain, achieve. *(suffer, deplete, forfeit, lose, squander.)*

gallant—*adj.* chivalrous, courteous, fearless, valiant, splendid, gay, undaunted, showy, bold, courageous, heroic, intrepid, brave. *(discourteous, timid, churlish, cowardly, fearful.)*

game—*n.* recreation, amusement, diversion, contest, play, frolic, pastime, sport. *(labor, duty, flagging, weariness, study, trust, toil, business, occupation.)*

garble—*v.* misquote, cook, color, pervert, misstate, distort, falsify, dress, misrepresent, mutilate. *(recite, quote, cite, clarify, extract.)*

gather—*v.* assemble, mass, store, accumulate, muster, collect, marshal, congregate, group, deduce, pile. *(disperse, scatter, separate, distribute, spread, dissipate, allot.)*

gaudy—*adj.* fine, bespangled, gay, showy, garish, ostentatious, showy, tawdry, meretricious. *(simple, chaste, fine, subtle, rich, handsome.)*

gauge—*v.* fathom, probe, assess, measure, evaluate, appraise, calculate. *(conjecture, scan, observe, survey, view, guess, mismeasure, analyze.)*

gawky—*adj.* ungainly, clumsy, awkward, foolish, uncouth, clownish. *(handy, handsome, polished, neat, graceful.)*

gay—*adj.* merry, lively, sportive, smart, gladsome, cheerful, blithe, joyous, jolly, sprightly, festive, pleasuresome. *(melancholy, sad, sombre, dowdy, miserable, heavy, grave, dull.)*

general—*adj.* universal, comprehensive, broad, prevalent, common, impartial, collective, generic, panoramic, vague, categorical. *(exclusive, limited, individual, local, specific, precise, explicit.)*

generous—*adj.* chivalrous, honorable, disinterested, magnanimous, munificent, noble, benevolent, liberal, bountiful, open-hearted. *(ignoble, selfish, mean, illiberal, churlish, stingy, petty.)*

genial—*adj.* cordial, cheering, festive, hearty, restorative, warm, balmy, merry, joyous, revivifying, affable. *(cutting, deleterious, deadly, destructive, lethal, cold, surly, harsh, noxious, blighting, uncongenial.)*

genteel—*adj.* well-bred, courteous, elegant, polished, cultured, polite, refined, aristocratic, graceful, fashionable. *(boorish, clownish, unpolished, plebeian, rude, ill-bred, churlish, unfashionable, inelegant.)*

gentle—*adj.* polite, mild, tame, amiable, soft, tender, serene, placid, meek, docile, bland, high-bred, courteous. *(rude, fierce, heartless, savage, coarse, rough.)*

geniune—*adj.* true, pure, natural, sincere, veritable, proven, real, authentic, unalloyed, unaffected, sound, unadulterated. *(apocryphal, fictitious, counterfeit, spurious, adulterated, fake.)*

get—*v.* procure, earn, attain, achieve, acquire, secure, obtain, gain, receive. *(forfeit, forego, lose, avoid, surrender.)*

ghastly—*adj.* wan, cadaverous, pallid, shocking, hideous, spectral, grim, deathlike, appalling. *(blooming, buxom, ruddy, seemly, fresh, comely, beautiful.)*

giddy—*adj.* vertiginous, inconstant, lofty, dizzy, flighty, whirling, thoughtless, unsteady, faint, beetling, harebrained. *(slow, thoughtful, steady, unelevated, circumspect, serious, wary, low, earnest, ponderous, stationary.)*

gift—*n.* present, boon, benefaction, talent, alms, donation, douceur, faculty, endowment, gratuity, grant, contribution. *(refusal, purchase, compensation, inanity, forfeit, fine, penalty, reservation, wages, earnings, remuneration, stupidy, surrender, confiscation.)*

gigantic—*adj.* huge, enormous, mammoth, collosal, tremendous, immense, gargantuan, vast, stupendous, prodigious. *(miniature, tiny, dwarfish, small, microscopic, infinitesimal.)*

gist—*n.* pith, substance, force, essence, main point, marrow, kernel, core, meaning. *(redundancy, environment, garb, surplusage, additament, accessories, clothing, excess.)*

give—*v.* grant, impart, produce, concede, afford, furnish, donate, bestow, confer, yield, surrender, present, communicate. *(withdraw, retain, fail, deny, accept, withhold, refuse, grasp, restrain.)*

glad—*adj.* joyous, gratified, gleeful, delighted, elated, happy, merry, joyful, cheerful, gladsome, blithesome, pleased. *(sorrowful, disap-*

pointed, tearful, dismal, sorry, unhappy, disastrous.)

glare—*v.* shine, ray, glow, stare, dazzle, beam, gleam, radiate. *(scintillate, smoulder, glisten, sparkle, flicker, glance, shimmer, glitter, glimmer, glister, flash.)*

glassy—*adj.* smooth, glacial, brittle, crystalline, limpid, silken, expressionless, glossy, pellucid, transparent, glabrous, polished, vitreous. *(scabrous, muddy, opaque, pliant, uneven, bright, rough, rugged, tough, luteous, turbid.)*

gloom—*n.* depression, despair, woe, melancholy, despondency, sorrow, pessimism, misery, sadness, dejection. *(glee, happiness, joy, delight, mirth, frivolity, cheerfulness.)*

glory—*n.* radiance, honor, fame, pomp, magnificence, renown, prestige, splendor, luster, celebrity, brightness, effulgence. *(igonominy, dishonor, obscurity, cloud, degradation, infamy.)*

glut—*v.* fill, cram, cloy, gorge, satiate, surfeit, stuff, devour. *(empty, disgorge, vacant, void.)*

glut—*n.* redundancy, overstock, surplus, deluge, superfluity, saturation. *(drainage, dearth, scantiness, exhaustion, deficiency, scarcity, failure.)*

go—*v.* depart, travel, reach, evaporate, move, budge, pass, vanish, extend, stir, set out. *(stay, remain, abide, endure, fail, approach, lack, stand, come, persist, rest.)*

good—*adj.* complete, sound, pious, propitious, suitable, sufficient, valid, actual, honorable, righteous, true, just, efficient, excellent, right, virtuous, benevolent, serviceable, admirable, competent, real, considerable, reputable, proper, upright. *(imperfect, vicious, evil, niggardly, unserviceable, inefficient, incompetent, fictitious, inconsiderable, disgraceful, bad, mediocre, disreputable, mean, supposititious, invalid, inadequate, unsuitable, unpropitious, profane, unsound, wrong.)*

good—*n.* benefit, gain, mercy, prosperity, profit, welfare, enjoyment, interest, boon, weal, advantage, blessing, virtue. *(loss, disadvantage, calamity, hurt, catastrophe, curse, ill, injury, infliction, evil, detriment.)*

goodly—*adj.* desirable, fair, fine, personable, pleasant, excellent, comely, graceful, considerable. *(uncomely,* *unpleasant, inconsiderable, disagreeable, undesirable.)*

goodness—*n.* honesty, integrity, morality, virtue, righteousness, merit, innocence, benevolence, worth, quality. *(dishonesty, vice, evil, wickedness, corruption, malice, imperfection, cruelty, spite.)*

gorgeous—*adj.* splendid, rich, grand, magnificent, glorious, costly, superb, strong, beautiful. *(naked, bare, dingy, poor, homely, threadbare, cheap.)*

govern—*v.* direct, moderate, conduct, manage, rule, influence, control, guide, sway, command, supervise. *(misdirect, misrule, submit, comply, miscontrol, follow.)*

grace—*n.* beauty, kindness, charm, pardon, favor, refinement, condescension, elegance, mercy, excellence. *(deformity, pride, awkwardness, ugliness, gawkiness, inelegance, unkindness, disfavor.)*

gracious—*adj.* courteous, kind, condescending, friendly, gentle, affable, beneficent, compassionate, benignant, civil, merciful, tender. *(discourteous, churlish, uncivil, haughty, illdisposed, ungracious, austere.)*

gradual—*adj.*step by step, slow, progressive, continuous, steady, gradational, unintermittent, successive. *(instantaneous, recurrent, disconnected, abrupt, sudden, broken, intermittent, momentary, periodic, hasty, discontinuous.)*

grand—*adj.* dignified, important, magnificent, majestic, exalted, impressive, splendid, elevated, gorgeous, superb, large, imposing, eventful, grandly, august, stately, lofty, pompous, sublime. *(undignified, secondary, unimportant, little, ignoble, insignificant, mean, paltry, unimposing, inferior, petty, beggarly, common.)*

grant—*v.* award, accord, bestow, donate, impart, confer, allow, give, yield, concede, apportion, allocate. *(refuse, deny, reject, renounce, forbid, despite, repel, withdraw, disclaim, withhold.)*

graphic—*adj.* illustrative, pictorial, vivid, described, striking, forcible, picturesque, descriptive, emphatic, comprehensible. *(unrealistic, dull, undescriptive, unpicturesque, hazy, unillustrative, dubious.)*

grateful—*adj.* acceptable, thankful, welcome, pleasant, appreciative, agreeable, obliged. *(disagreeable, rude, disobliged, unpleasant, careless, ungrateful.)*

gratify—*v.* satisfy, humor, charm, please, delight, indulge, regale, exhilarate. *(dissatisfy, stint, curb, inure, deprive, displease, deny, disappoint, discipline, harden, frustrate.)*

gratitude—*n.* gratefulness, obligation, thankfulness, acknowledgment, thanks, recognition. *(resentment, ingratitude, indignation, unthankfulness, beholdenness, thanklessness.)*

grave—*adj.* serious, weighty, sedate, thoughtful, sombre, important, heavy, sad, cogent, subdued, momentous, pressing, demure, sober, solemn, aggravated. *(merry, unimportant, trivial, frivolous, joyous, inconsequential, futile, light, ridiculous, facetious.)*

great—*adj.* huge, protracted, large, bulky, gigantic, grand, august, magnanimous, powerful, noticeable, stupendous, big, numerous, wide, excellent, immense, majestic, vast, sublime, eminent, noble, exalted. *(narrow, scanty, short, ignoble, unimportant, little, few, diminutive, puny, mean, weak.)*

greedy—*adj.* voracious, desirous, gluttonous, mercenary, avaricious, hungry. *(abstinent, contented, philanthropic, abstemious, indifferent.)*

grief—*n.* tribulation, mourning, affliction, sadness, heartbreak, trouble, woe, regret, sorrow. *(exultation, elation, bliss, joy, hilarity, solace, delight.)*

grieve—*v.* burden, distress, wound, sorrow, affict, lament, deplore, weep, trouble, annoy, bewail, pain, hurt, mourn, complain. *(console, please, exult, alleviate, gladden, ease, soothe, rejoice, gratify.)*

grim—*adj.* ferocious, hideous, ghastly, stern, fierce, terrible, savage, ugly, sullen. *(docile, placid, mild., amiable, benign, attractive.)*

groan—*v.* whine, grumble, moan, lament, growl, complain. *(cackle, titter, chuckle, laugh, giggle, snicker.)*

gross—*adj.* flagrant, deplorable, grievous, shocking, glaring, dreadful, outrageous, obvious, unmitigated. *(minor, trivial, small, graceful, elegant, refined, cultivated, inoffensive.)*

groundless—*adj.* suppositious, baseless, gratuitous, false, unwarranted, vain, unfounded, fanciful, chimerical. *(substantial, actual, authentic, well-founded, logical, authoritative, justified.)*

group—*n.* bunch, assemblage, class, clump, assembly, order, cluster, knot, collection, congregation, collocation. *(individual, confusion, isolation, crowd, medley, disperse.)*

grudge—*v.* retain, envy, spare, resent, covet, withhold, stint. *(welcome, spend, impart, gratify, please, satisfy.)*

grudge—*n.* grievance, rancor, pique, discontent, spite, aversion, resentment, refusal, dissatisfaction, hatred. *(satisfaction, bestowal, approval, benefaction, liberality, complacency, welcome, contentment.)*

gruff—*adj.* surly, harsh, blunt, impolite, rough, bearish, rude. *(mild, courteous, genial, affable, smooth.)*

guess—*v.* surmise, suppose, fancy, estimate, imagine, suspect, conjecture, divine. *(prove, establish, deduce, elaborate, examine, certainty, investigate, demonstrate.)*

guide—*v.* direct, pilot, superintend, train, lead, manage, shield, conduct, regulate, influence. *(misconduct, mismanage, misguide, betray, mislead, dupe, deceive, miseducate, misregulate, misdirect, ensore.)*

gush—*v.* stream, gush, rush, flow-out, burst, eject, flow, pour out, spout. *(drop, trickle, drain, filter, drip, dribble, ooze, percolate, strain, discharge.)*

guttural—*adj.* harsh, gruff, deep, hoarse, rasping, cracked, rough, gargling, throaty, inarticulate. *(high, ringing, musical, clear, pleasant, dulcet, nasal, squeaky.)*

H

habit—*n.* custom, association, usage, way, routine, manner, practice, inurement, familiarity, habituation. *(inexperience, desuetude, irregularity, dishabituation, inconversance.)*

habitual—*adj.* ordinary, customary, familiar, wonted, chronic, regular, perpetual, usual, accustomed. *(extraordinary, unusual, rare, sporadic, irregular, occasional, exceptional.)*

hail—*v.* salute, applaud, greet, acclaim, cheer, call, honor, signal, summon, accost, welcome. *(ignore, avoid,* *shun, neglect, pass over, disregard, rebuff, insult.)*

half—*n.* bisection, partial, dimidiation, moiety, divided. *(entirety, whole, total, integrity, totality, aggregate.)*

halt—*v.* rest, falter, stammer, dubitate, hold, still, restrain, stop, limp, hammer, demur, pause, stand still. *(decide, speed, career, continue, advance, determine, flow.)*

handsome—*adj.* good-looking, liberal, ample, graceful, elegant, stately, comely, generous, beautiful, pretty, lovely. *(ill-looking, illiberal, uncomely, unhandsome, repulsive, ungenerous.)*

handy—*adj.* convenient, helpful, dexterous, expert, accessible, near, useful, manageable, ready. *(inconvenient, useless, unwieldy, worthless, remote, awkward, cumbrous, unhandy.)*

haphazard—*adj.* aimless, random, accidental, purposeless, casual, fortuitous, incidental, arbitrary, unmethodical, unsystematic. *(controlled, planned, deliberate, intentional, designed, organized, thoughtful, premeditated, systematic.)*

happy—*adj.* fortunate, successful, joyous, blithesome, glad, ecstatic, lucky, felicitious, delighted, merry, prosperous, blissful. *(unfortunate, sorry, unsuccessful, unlucky, unhappy, lugubrious, ecstatic, infelicitous, sorrowful, disappointed, dull, desponding.)*

hard—*adj.* dense, compact, impenetrable, difficult, distressing, oppressive, unfeeling, born, forced, inexplicable, severe, obdurate, callous, hardened, cruel, flinty, constrained, harsh, stubborn, exacting, rigorous, firm, grievous, arduous, unyielding, solid, formidable. *(fluid, elastic, penetrable, mild, tender, uninvolved, intelligible, soft, liquid, brittle, easy, pliable, lenient, ductile, simple, perspicuous, resilient.)*

hardship—*n.* burden, grievance, infliction, affliction, ordeal, endurance, calamity, annoyance, trouble. *(amusement, recreation, relief, facilitation, treat, pleasure, happiness, alleviation, boon, gratification, assuagement.)*

hardy—*adj.* robust, resolute, stout-hearted, intrepid, manly, sturdy, valiant, brave, vigorous, inured, strong. *(uninured, irresolute, debilitated, fragile, weak, delicate, enervated, tender, dainty.)*

harm—*n.* mischief, detriment, evil, misfortune, mishap, injury, hurt, trauma, damage, wrong, ill. *(boon, improvement, compensation, remedy, benefit, amelioration, reparation, healing, welfare, cure.)*

harmonious—*adj.* accordant, uniform, musical, tuneful, peaceful, amicable, concordant, compatible, congruous, proportioned, melodious, dulcet, consistent, agreeable, friendly. *(discordant, unshapely, unmelodious, grating, riotous, quarrelsome, conflicting, incongruous, disproportioned, harsh, sharp, unfriendly, unpeaceful.)*

hasty—*adj.* rapid, hurried, impetuous, head-long, incomplete, immature, precipitate, passionate, quick, rash, prompt, speedy, superficial, irascible, reckless, crude, undeveloped, swift, fiery, slight, excitable, cursory. *(leisurely, close, developed, complete, thoughtful, meticulous, slow, careful, reflective, matured, deliberate, elaborate.)*

hateful—*adj.* detestable, odious, execrable, repulsive, offensive, abominable, vile, heinous, loathsome. *(lovely, delightful, enticing, tempting, agreeable, pleasant, lovable, desirable, attractive, enjoyable.)*

have—*v.* possess, entertain, bear, keep, acquire, own, feel, accept, enjoy. *(need, forego, reject, desiderate, desire, crave, want, lose, discard, miss, covet.)*

hazard—*n.* risk, danger, imperil, venture, dare, peril, jeopardy, chance. *(security, warrant, calculation, safety, assurance, protection, certainty, law.)*

hazy—*adj.* nebulous, filmy, cloudy, caliginous, smoky, murky, gauzy, misty, foggy. *(clear, transparent, distinct, crystalline, diaphanous.)*

head—*n.* crown, leader, mind, section, topic, culmination, leadership, commander, summit, superior, top, chief, ruler, source, division, gathering, crisis, guide, acme. *(bottom, servant, tail, subordinate, inferiority, bulk, continuation, worker, follower, retainer, subordination, body, subject.)*

healthy—*adj.* hale, sound, hearty, vigorous, in the pink, robust, virile, strong, hygienic, healing, lusty. *(sickly, ill, weak, delicate, feeble, emaciated, ailing, infirm, debilitated, unsound.)*

hearty—*adj.* robust, sound, honest, genuine, sincere, hale, generous, healthy, cordial, warm, earnest, well, heart felt. *(delicate, cold, frail, insincere, infirm, unhealthy.)*

heat—*n.* ardor, excitement, ebullition, temperature, intensity, fever, passion, warmth. *(indifference, calmness, reflection, tranquillity, composure, subsidence, coolness.)*

heavy—*adj.* ponderous, slow, inert, stupid, impenetrable, cumbrous, afflictive, burdensome, laborious, weighty, dull, stolid, grievous, oppressive, sluggish, depressed, substantial. *(trifling, agile, light, quick, alleviative, skimpy, buoyant, weightless, trivial, active, joyous, consolatory, animating.)*

heighten—*v.* increase, intensify, vivify, raise, lift up, strengthen, amplify, exalt, enhance, color, aggravate, exaggerate. *(depress, deteriorate, temper, extenuate, qualify, abate, lower, diminish, abase, tone, modify.)*

heinous—*adj.* hateful, detestable, atrocious, abominable, enormous, repugnant, flagrant, flágitious, odious, execrable. *(laudable, praiseworthy, justifiable, palliable, creditable, excellent, meritorious, distinguished, excusable.)*

help—*v.* succor, prevent, assist, co-operate, second, befriend, aid, remedy, avoid, promote, relieve. *(obstruct, incur, hinder, aggravate, oppose.)*

herculean—*adj.* formidable, mighty, prodigious, heroic, titanic, exhausting, difficult, arduous, overwhelming, stupendous. *(feeble, delicate, weak, restful, effortless, frail, easy.)*

hereditary—*adj.* ancestral, inbred, lineal, inherited, congenital. *(won, conferred, acquired, earned.)*

heroism—*n.* bravery, valor, courage, daring, gallantry, prowess, boldness, chivalry. *(cowardice, timidity, meanness, weakness, baseness, cravenness.)*

hesitate—*v.* waver, scruple, stammer, doubt, tentative, dubitate, demur, falter, pause. *(determine, flow, positive, career, run, decide.)*

hide—*v.* secrete, dissemble, protect, ensconce, cover, camouflage, burrow, screen, disguise, store, mask, conceal. *(discover, manifest, strip, reveal, expose, exhibit, betray.)*

hideous—*adj.* unshapely, horrid, ugly, grim, repulsive, ghastly, grisly, horrible, monstrous, frightful. *(beautiful, charming, attractive, graceful, captivating.)*

high—*adj.* lofty, eminent, noble, violent, exalted, prominent, elevated, tall, excellent, haughty, proud. *(low, ignoble, mean, affable, insignificant, depressed, stunted, base.)*

hilarious—*adj.* laughable, comical, uproarious, riotous, gleeful, mirthful, boisterous, funny. *(serious, depressed, miserable, melancholy, sad, woebegone.)*

hinder—*v.* interrupt, retard, embarrass, thwart, stop, delay, block, impede, debar, obstruct, prevent. *(expedite, promote, accelerate, enable, support, facilitate, encourage.)*

hoarse—*adj.* grating, raucous, gruff, guttural, rough, harsh, husky. *(mellow, sweet, full, mellifluous, rich, melodious.)*

hold—*v.* grasp, support, defend, occupy, sustain, consider, have, continue, occupy, keep, retain, restrain, maintain, possess, regard, cohere. *(abandon, fail, desert, vacate, break, relinquish, cease, drop, surrender, release, forego, concede.)*

hollow—*adj.* concave, weak, insincere, unsubstantial, flimsy, senseless, unsound, empty, foolish, faithless, artificial, void, transparent, vacant, false, sunken. *(solid, strong, sincere, genuine, sound, cogent, full, well-stored, firm, true, substantial.)*

homely—*adj.* coarse, modest, uncomely, plain. *(beautiful, courtly, ostentatious, handsome, refined.)*

honest—*adj.* upright, proper, sincere, reliable, conscientious, honorable, virtuous, right. *(dishonorable, improper, wrong, deceitful, dishonest, vicious, insincere.)*

honor—*n.* reverence, dignity, reputation, high-mindedness, self-respect, grandeur, glory, esteem, respect, nobility, eminence, fame, spirit, renown. *(contempt, slight, degradation, abasement, cowardice, infamy, humiliation, disrespect, irreverence, obscurity, disgrace, demoralization, dishonor.)*

honorary—*adj.* unofficial, nominal, titular, complimentary, gratuitous, unremuneration. *(remuneration, jurisdictional, official, professional, skilled.)*

hope—*n.* prospect, longing, desire, trust, contemplation, anticipation, vision, confidence, expectation. *(despondency, disbelief, abjuration, doubt, abandonment, distrust, despair.)*

horrible—*adj.* destestable, fearful, ghastly, hateful, horrid, frightful, shocking, abominable, dreadful, hideous, terrific, direful, awful. *(desirable, attractive, fair, amiable, lovely, enjoyable, beautiful, pleasant, delightful.)*

hostility—*n.* enmity, will, dislike, animosity, defiance, spite, hatred, contempt, abhorrence, antagonism. *(goodwill, warmth, benevolence, cordiality, friendliness, affability.)*

huge—*adj.* monstrous, vast, large, prodigious, stupendous, mammoth, gigantic, immense, enormous, colossal, bulky, great. *(undersized, puny, petty, pigny, microscopic.)*

humane—*adj.* kind, merciful, compassionate, charitable, benign, tender, benevolent. *(cruel, inhuman, unkind, brutal, unmerciful.)*

humble—*adj.* lowly, meek, low, unassuming, submissive, obscure, modest, unpretending, insignificant. *(lofty, proud, high, arrogant, pretentious, eminent, boastful, assuming, haughty.)*

humor—*n.* temper, caprice, pleasantry, drollery, disposition, nonsense, fun, frame, jocoseness, mood. *(personality, will, purpose, nature, mind, seriousness, sadness.)*

hurt—*v.* bruise, injure, pain, ache, grieve, damage, wound, harm. *(soothe, repair, reinstate, benefit, alleviate, compensate, heal, console.)*

hurt—*n.* injury, wound, detriment, harm, laceration, mischief, damage. *(pleasure, benefit, content, comfort.)*

hurtful—*adj.* injurious, baleful, baneful, detrimental, harmful, mischievous, pernicious, deleterious, noxious, moleficent. *(remedial, good, advantageous, helpful.)*

hypocritical—*adj.* sanctimonious, smooth, unctuous, pharisaical, faultfinding, mincing, mealy, smug. *(candid, sincere, transparent, plainspoken, lenient, genuine, truthful.)*

hysterical—*adj.* distraught, crazed, frenzied, overwrought, distracted, ludicrous, droll. *(composed, poised, grave, sad, calm, somber, serious.)*

I

idea—*n.* notion, belief, supposition, fiction, thought, fantasy, image, sentiment, opinion, fancy, doctrine, understanding, conception, impression. *(form, thing, fact, reality, subject, object, weight.)*

ideal—*adj.* notional, intellectual, spiritual, supposititious, unreal, chimerical, imaginative, visionary, mental, conception, creative, poetical, fictitious, fanciful, imaginary. *(visible, tangible, real, palpable, factual, substantial, physical, material, historical, actual.)*

identical—*adj.* same, uniform, twin, equal, duplicate, alike, one, synonymous, equivalent, substitute, indistinguishable. *(separate, diverse, contrary, different, divergent, opposite, unlike, distinct.)*

idle—*adj.* unoccupied, vain, empty, useless, lazy, jobless, indolent, void, waste, unemployed, inactive. *(occupied, filled, helpful, assiduous, industrious, tilled, populated, employed.)*

ignoble—*adj.* base, humble, lowly, unworthy, mean, dishonorable, plebeian, inferior. *(noble, exalted, grand, illustrious, admirable, honorable, eminent, lordly, notable.)*

ignominious—*adj.* scandalous, infamous, humiliating, shameful, dishonorable. *(reputable, honorable, worthy, creditable, estimable.)*

ignorant—*adj.* uneducated, stupid, unlearned, unlettered, untaught, uninformed, illiterate. *(learned, cultivated, intelligent, well-informed, wise, cultured.)*

illegal—*adj.* illicit, banned, wrong, unlawful, prohibited, criminal, felonious, unconstitutional, illegitimate. *(lawful, sanctioned, permitted, legal, authorized, permissible, licit.)*

illegible—*adj.* cramped, obscure, scribbled, unreadable, indecipherable, unintelligible. *(clear, plain, legible, readable, intelligible.)*

illusion—*n.* mockery, delusion, phantasm, myth, show, fallacy, mirage, dream, deception, error, hallucination, vision, false. *(reality, substance, actuality, form, body, truth.)*

illustrious—*adj.* glorious, exalted, eminent, celebrated, noble, famous, remarkable, renowned, brillant, conspicuous, splendid. *(disgraceful, inglorious, obscure, ignominious, infamous, notorious, disreputable.)*

ill-will—*n.* hatred, dislike, spite, antipathy, malevolence, malice, aversion. *(bene-*

ficence, favor, congeniality, good-will.)

imaginative—*adj.* conceptive, poetical, inventive, enterprising, original, creative, ideal, romantic. *(practical, unpoetical, prosaic, unromantic, uninventive, matter-of-fact, realistic.)*

imagine—*v.* suppose, understand, fabricate, presume, apprehend, think, create, conceive, deem, surmise, fancy, envision. *(exhibit, prove, verify, validate, depict, represent, demonstrate, substantiate.)*

imitate—*v.* copy, follow, depict, pattern, mock, counterfeit, after duplicate, mimic, represent, ape, resemble, portray, repeat, echo. *(caricature, vary, differentiate, remodel, change, distort, misrepresent, alter, dissimilate, modify.)*

immaculate—*adj.* spotless, clean, unsoiled, untarnished, stainless, untainted, spic-and-span. *(unclean, soiled, tarnished, dirty, spotted, stained.)*

immediate—*adj.* contigious, direct, next, closest, proximate, present, instant. *(remote, mediate, indirect, distant, future.)*

immoral—*adj.* bad, wicked, unprincipled, corrupt, evil, heinous, obscene, indecent, unethical. *(good, ethical, honest, moral, decent, noble, virtuous, honorable, chaste.)*

impair—*v.* injure, damage, vitiate, lessen, obstruct, deteriorate, reduce, enfeeble, diminish. *(improve, repair, amend, enhance, augment, facilitate.)*

impassive—*adj.* phlegmatic, calm, insensible, reserved, unmoved, unemotional, aloof, sedate, apathetic, indifferent. *(theatrical, expressive, demonstrative, responsive, dramatic, emotional, perturbed.)*

impediment—*n.* obstacle, barrier, stumbling block, hinderance, obstruction, delay. *(help, succor, furthermore, relief, furtherance, support, assistance, aid, encouragement.)*

imperative—*adj.* irresistable, inexorable, compulsory, mandatory, obligatory, urgent, dictatorial, peremptorily. *(lenient, entreative, optional, voluntary, indulgent, mild, supplicatory, discretional.)*

imperious—*adj.* exacting, haughty, authoritative, arrogant, lordly, insolent, domineering, dictatorial. *(submissive, docile, lenient, subservient, mild, yielding, compliant, ductile, gentle.)*

Implement—*n.* utensil, appliance, instrument, tool, apparatus. *(work, art, labor, agriculture, manufacture, science.)*

Implicate—*v.* associate, criminate, entangle, compromise, embroil, connect, charge, involve, infold. *(dissociate, extricate, exclude, acquit, disconnect.)*

Imply—*v.* mean, suggest, denote, import, include, connote, hint, involve, indicate. *(pronounce, declare, express, describe, state.)*

Importance—*n.* moment, significance, avail, import, concern, signification,weight, consequence. *(insignificance, immateriality, triviality, unimportance, nothingness.)*

Important—*adj.* expressive, main, considerable, dignified, weighty, material, essential, serious, significant, relevant, leading, great, influential, momentous, grave. *(trivial, irrelevant, petty, uninfluential, negligible, unimportant, insignificant, minor, inexpressive, inconsiderable, mean, secondary.)*

Impotent—*adj.* powerless, feeble, nerveless, Incapacitated, enfeebled, weak, useless, helpless. *(vigorous, virile, forceful, strong, powerful.)*

Impractical—*adj.* unfeasible, inoperable, unrealistic, ideal, unintelligent, careless, speculative, quixotic, romantic. *(practical, viable, prosaic, pragmatic, realistic, sensible, systematic.)*

Impressive—*adj.* solemn, grand, imposing, magnificent, important, forcible, affecting, effective. *(unimpressive, tame, dry, unimportant, ordinary, insignificant, weak, feeble, jejune, vapid.)*

Improvement—*n.* amendment, increase, proficiency, enrichment, advancement, progress, correction, beneficial. *(degeneration, debasement, retrogression, ruination, degeneracy, deterioration, retrogradation.)*

Impudent—*adj.* insolent, shameless, rude, immodest, presumptuous, impertinent, saucy, brazen, bold. *(obsequious, bashful, diffident, modest, timid, servile, sycophantic, retiring, deferential.)*

Impulse—*n.* push, force, instigation, motive, stimulus, incentive, incitement, thought, feeling. *(repulse, denial, deliberation, premeditation, rebuff, rejection.)*

Inactive—*adj.* inert, stationary, inoperative, dormant, dilatory, idle, languid, indolent, dull, sedentary. *(operative, active, functional, dynamic, vigorous, energetic, busy, industrious.)*

Inadequate—*adj.* deficient, lacking, unequal, unqualified, unfit, imperfect, meager, scant, slight, incapable, inept. *(adequate, fit, abundant, enough, sufficient, competent, capable, ample, equal.)*

Inadvertent—*adj.* accidental, fortuitous, chance, thoughtless, unobservant, inconsiderate, careless, involuntary, unpremeditated. *(deliberate, careful, intentional, aware, premeditated, calculated, planned, studied.)*

Inaudible—*adj.* inarticulate, muttering, stifled, silent, low, muffled, suppressed, mumbling. *(outspoken, loud, articulate, ringing, clear, audible, sonorous, candid.)*

Incapable—*adj.* unable, weak, feeble, insufficient, inadequate, unqualified, unfitted, disqualified, incompetent. *(able, clever, fitted, qualified, skilled, strong.)*

Incidental—*adj.* occasional, concomitant, accidental, casual, subordinate, appertinent, concurrent, fortuitous. *(regular, disconnected, essential, inherent, invariable, fundamental, systematic, independent, irrelative, imminent, uniform.)*

Incivility—*n.* ill-breeding, uncourteousness, ill-manners, discourtesy, rudeness, impudence. *(urbanity, politeness, good-manners, civility, respect.)*

Inclement—*adj.* tyrannical, raw, unmerciful, stormy, rigorous, tempestuous, harsh, cruel, severe, rough. *(benign, genial, pleasant, merciful, clement, mild.)*

Inclination—*n.* slope, disposition, aptness, bias, attachment, liking, leaning, tendency, wish, proneness, predelection, bent, affection, desire. *(inaptness, disinclination, dislike, distate, inaptitude, repulsion.)*

Incoherent—*adj.* incongruous, loose, illogical, unconnected, inconsequential. *(connected, plain, coherent, articulate, clear.)*

Incomparable—*adj.* unique, transcendent, matchless, superlative, consummate. *(ordinary, mediocre, average, common.)*

Inconsistent—*adj.* incompatible, incoherent, contrary, opposed, careless, remiss, thoughtless, vacillating, volatile, changing. *(coherent, uniform, steady, reliable, homogeneous, orderly, suitable, constant.)*

Inconsolable—*adj.* joyless, melancholy, disconsolate, forlorn, heartbroken, cheerless, spiritless, gloomy, comfortless, heartsick. *(hopeful, consolable, enthusiastic, cheerful.)*

Inconstant—*adj.* mutable, fitful, unsteadfast, erractic, fickle, changeable, variable, unstable. *(reliable, steady, constant, steadfast, loyal.)*

Incontestable—*adj.* impregnable, indisputable, unassailable, undeniable, unquestionable, irrefutable. *(questionable, supposititious, dubious, problematical, hypothetical, arbitrary, assumptive, unctuous.)*

Inconvenient—*adj.* annoying, awkward, cumbersome, bothersome, troublesome, tiresome, inopportune, untimely, unwieldy. *(opportune, helpful, convenient, handy, advantageous, timely.)*

Increase—*n.* advance, development, augmentation, extension, addition, expansion, grouth, enlargement, spread, benefit. *(diminution, loss, decrease, reduction, drop, contraction.)*

Incredible—*adj.* belief, marvelous, remarkable, surpassing, fabulous, preposterous. *(believable, usual, ordinary, credible, common, unremarkable.)*

Inculcate—*v.* urge, infuse, instill, implant, teach, impart, press, impress, enforce. *(suggest, disavow, denounce, intimate, insinuate, abjure.)*

Incumbent—*adj.* binding, urgent, indispensable, devolvent, imperative, pressing, coercive, obligatory, persistent. *(discretional, exempt, optional, privileged.)*

Incurable—*adj.* irredeemable, terminal, cureless, irremediable, hopeless. *(remediable, tractable, curable, removable, correctable.)*

Indecent—*adj.* immodest, improper, distasteful, indelicate, lewd. *(proper, delicate, modest, virtuous, ethical.)*

Ineffable— *adj.* inconceivable, indeclarable, exquisite, perfect, unutterable, inexpressible, insurpassable, indescribable. *(trivial, vulgar, colloquial, commonplace, frivolous, common, superficial, conversational, obvious.)*

Ineffectual—*adj.* useless, idle, abortive, ineffective, unsuccessful, fruitless, vain, unavailing, inoperative. *(successful, effective, profitable, effectual, useful.)*

Inexcusable—*adj.* unpardonable, unjustifiable, outrageous, unmitigated, indefensible, unforgiving. *(pliable, vindicable, pardonable, forgivable, mitigable, justifiable, defensible.)*

Inexhaustible—*adj.* unwearied, perennial, unlimited, illimitable, incessant, indefatigable. *(poor, measured, limited, scant, wearied.)*

Inexpedient—*adj.* inadvisable, imprudent, disadvantagious, undesirable, indiscreet. *(expedient, advisable, judicious, profitable.)*

Infallible—*adj.* perfect, sure, reliable, foolproof, dependable, all-wise, incontestable, tested, unimpeachable, certain. *(errant, dubious, refutable, uncertain, unsure, doubtful, unsure, contestable, unreliable.)*

Infamy—*n.* degradation, ignominy, extreme, dishonor, corruption, despair, disgrace, obloquy, vileness. *(reputation, glory, integrity, renown, honor, celebrity.)*

Inference—*n.* corollary, deduction, consequence, assumption, conclusion. *(enunciation, anticipation, proposition, statement.)*

Inferiority—*n.* minority, mediocrity, servitude, insignificance, poverty, subordination, subjection, depression, inadequacy. *(majority, edge, eminence, mastery, elevation, advantage, superiority, excellence, independence, exaltation.)*

Infidel—*n.* unbeliever, heretic, freethinker, pagan, skeptic. *(pietist, Christian, religionist,believer, devotee.)*

Infinitesimal—*adj.* tiny, wee, microscopic, diminutive, insignificant, imperceptible, minute. *(vast, colossal, huge, enormous, tremendous, gargantuan, great.)*

Inflame—*v.* kindle, rouse, fire, incense, infuriate, irritate, fan, anger, ignite, enrage, excite, madden, exasperate, imbitter. *(extinguish, cool, quiet, soothe, quench, allay, pacify.)*

Inflexible—*adj.* firm, steadfast, determined, rigid, mulish, resolute, adamant, stubborn, obstinate, stringent. *(elastic, resilient, pliable, supple, flexible, springy, malleable, fluid.)*

Influence—*n.* control, affection, power, character, weight, prestige, supremacy, authority, effect, causation, impulse, credit, sway, ascendancy. *(ineffectiveness, nullity, inefficacy, aloafness, inefficiency, inoperativeness, neutrality.)*

Influential—*adj.* powerful, forcible, controlling, considerable, inspiring, potent, efficacious, persuasive, guiding. *(ineffective, weak, inconsiderable, unpersuasive, impede, inoperative.)*

Information—*n.* advice, notice, knowledge, evidence, counsel, instruction, notification. *(occulatation, ignorance, unawareness, concealment, mystification, hiding.)*

Infringe—*v.* violate, contravene, intrude, break, trangress. *(conserve, satisfy, keep within bounds, observe, preserve.)*

Ingenious—*adj.* adept, inventive, frank, creative, skillful, clever, ready, sincere, imaginative. *(slow, unready, unskillful, clumsy, inept, uninventive.)*

Ingenuous—*adj.* candid, frank, straightforward, open, honest, unsophisticated, noble, generous, sincere, honorable, artless. *(reserved, subtle, disingenuous, insincere, sly, mean.)*

Ingrained—*adj.* innate, inborn, inherent, intrinsic, rooted, organic, inbred, implanted. *(surface, alien, external, superficial, learned, superimposed, acquired.)*

Ingredient—*n.* component, factor, constituent, element, module, section. *(refuse, counter-agent, non-ingredient, incongruity, residuum.)*

Inherent—*adj.* congenial, ingrained, intrinsic, inbred, essential, innate, immanent, inborn, natural. *(ascititious, separable, foreign, extraneous, superficial, temporary.)*

Initiative—*n.* leadership, start, example, independence, commencement, enterprise. *(termination, wake, prosecution, rear.)*

Injunction—*n.* order, exhortation, requirement, mandate, precept, command. (insubordination, infraction, nonobservance, non-compliance, disobedience.)

Injurious—*adj.* deleterious, noxious, baleful, wrongful, damaging, abusive, baneful, hurtful, prejudicial, detrimental, pernicious, mischievous. *(advantageous, helpful, constructive, healing, beneficial.)*

Innocence—*n.* inoffensiveness, guiltlessness, purity, sinlessness, innocuousness, guilelessness, simplicity, harmlessness. *(offensiveness, guilt, corruption, sinfulness, reprehensibility, hurtfullness, guile, contamination, impurity.)*

Innocent—*adj.* blameless, pure, spotless, harmless, sinless, guiltless, naive, unsophisticated, unwordly, ingenuous, honest, chaste, virginal. *(sinful, guilty, corrupt, impure, wily, evil, culpable, immoral, nefarious, tainted, dishonest.)*

Innocuous—*adj.* harmless, moderate, wholesome, bland, inoffensive. *(deleterious, obnoxious, insidious, hurtful, pernicious.)*

Inquiry—*n.* question, investigation, examination, scrutiny, probe, exploration, interrogation, asking, search, research, analysis. *(supposition, hypothesis, guess, theory, conjecture, intuition, assumption.)*

Insatiable—*adj.* unappeasable, ravenous, greedy, unlimited, voracious, omnivorous, rapacious. *(delicate, dainty, appeasable, moderate, fastidious, squeamish, limited.)*

Insidious—*adj.* treacherous, dangerous, sly, artful, wily, underhanded, designing, deceitful, crafty. *(undesigning, straightforward, innocuous, overt, sincere, frank.)*

Insincere—*adj.* false, deceitful, fraudulent, hollow, perfidious, hypocritical, dishonest, guileful, double-dealing, devious. *(earnest, honest, sincere, direct, truthful, genuine, candid, straightforward.)*

Insinuate—*v.* insert, ingratiate, suggest, hint, convey, introduce, worm, intimate, infuse. *(retract, extract, withdraw, remove, alienate.)*

Insipid—*adj.* vapid, uninteresting, flavorless, pointless, prosy, monotonous, stupid, tasteless, characterless, flat, lifeless, dull. *(savory, tasty, flavorful, delicious, pungent, stimulating, piquant, lively, provocative, spirited.)*

insist—*v.* demand, contend, persist, urge, vouch, stand, maintain, persevere, assert. *(waive, yield, plead, abandon, forego, concede, surrender.)*

insolent—*adj.* overbearing, abusive, impertinent, offensive, surly, outrageous, rude, insulting, haughty, contemptuous, saucy, opprobrious, pert, scurrilous. *(courteous, civil, polite, obedient, deferential, respectful.)*

insolvent—*adj.* ruined, penniless, overextended, beggared, bankrupt. *(flourishing, solid, thriving, flush, monied, sound.)*

inspire—*v.* inspirit, imbue, encourage, enliven, breathe in, exhilarate, influence, animate, inflame, impel, inhale, cheer, infuse. *(dispirit, deter, discourage, stifle, depress, squelch.)*

inspiring—*adj.* encouraging, inspirational, moving, eloquent, lofty, motivating, heartening, stimulating, uplifting. *(depressing, dull, boring, uninspiring, dispiriting, discouraging.)*

instance—*n.* request, persuasion, solicitation, illustration, entreaty, occurrence, precedence, specimen, prompting, example, case, exemplification, point. *(warning, statement, misexemplification, breach, dissuassion, rule, depreciation, principle.)*

instill—*v.* infuse, import, insinuate, indoctrinate, pour, inculcate, introduce, implant. *(strain, eradicate, remove, discard, drain, extract, extirpation, eliminate.)*

instinctive—*adj.* voluntary, intuitive, innate, impulsive, natural, spontaneous. *(forced, willed, rationalistic, premeditated, cultivated, reasoning.)*

instruction—*n.* education, counsel, direction, command, guidance, teaching, information, advice, order. *(misinformation, misdirection, obedience, pupilage, misteaching, misguidance, misinstruction.)*

insufferable—*adj.* unpermissible, unendurable, outrageous, unbearable, unallowable, intolerable. *(allowable, supportable, bearable, tolerable, endurable.)*

insupportable—*adj.* intolerable, unendurable, obnoxious, unbearable, insufferable. *(comfortable, to be borne, tolerable, endurable.)*

integrity—*n.* honor, probity, candor, conscientiousness, rectitude, parity, virtue, uprightness, honesty, truthfulness, single-mindedness, entireness, completeness. *(sleight, meanness, duplicity, roguery, immorality, rascality, unfairness, underhandedness, chicanery, fraud.)*

Intellectual—*adj.* metaphysical, inventive, cultured, mental, psychological, learned, knowledgeable. *(unlearned, unintellectual, illiterate, unmetaphysical.)*

Intelligence—*n.* apprenhension, conception, report, tidings, information, rumor, intellectual, capacity, knowledge, news, notice, intellect, perception, publication, understanding, comphrension, mind, announcement, advice, instruction. *(misinformation, stupidy, suppression, darkness, silence, misguidance, misrepart, dullness, ineptitude, misapprehension, misunderstanding, misconception, ignorance, concealment, nonpublication, misintelligence.)*

Intensity—*n.* force, strain, energy, eagerness, strength, tension, concentration, attention, ardor. *(debility, languor, coolness, diminution, decrease, laxity, relaxative, indifference, coolness, hebetude.)*

Intentional—*adj.* designed, intended, contemplated, studied, planned, purposed, deliberate, done on purpose, premeditated. *(casual, accidental, haphazard, undersigned, unintentional, fortuitous.)*

Intercourse—*n.* dealing, intimacy, commerce, conversation, connection, correspondence, intercommunication. *(suspension, disconnection, interpellation, restraint, reticence, cessation, interception.)*

Interest—*n.* business, profit, share, curiosity, cause, consequence, concern, advantage, attention, behalf. *(disconnection, disadvantage, inattention, loss, indifference, boredom, unconcern, repudiation, incuriosity.)*

Interior—*adj.* inside, inner, proximal, enclosed, internal, encapsulated, remote, inland. *(exterior, outer, external, outside,exposed, distal, surface.)*

Intermediate—*adj.* included, comprised, moderate, transitional, interjacent, intervening, interposed, middle. *(surrounding, embracing, extreme, exclusive, advanced, circumjacent, enclosing, outside, excluded.)*

interpret—*v.* render, explain, expone, declare, elucidate, solve, unravel, translate, construe, expound, represent, understand, decipher. *(misunderstand, misconceive, distort, misrepresent, confuse, misinterpret, mistake, falsify, misdeclare.)*

interrupt—*v.* disconnect, obstruct, intersect, stop, hinder, break, discontinue, distrub. *(prosecute, resume, expedite, continue.)*

interval—*n.* meantime, gap, interspace, space between, pause, season, interim, period, intermission, cessation. *(perpetuity, uninterruptedness, continuity, simultaneousness.)*

intimate—*v.* communicate, declare, suggest, insinuate, allude, mention briefly, impart, announce, tell, hint. *(repress, withhold, proclaim, reserve, conceal.)*

intoxication—*n.* poison, bewilderment, hallucination, ecstasy, alcoholism, drunkenness, venom, obfuscation, delirium, ravishment, inebriation, inebriety. *(clarification, sanity, melancholy, antidote, temperance, depression, sobriety, ebriety.)*

intricate—*adj.* involved, labyrenthine, tortuous, perplexing, complicated, mazy, entangled. *(uninvolved, direct, plain, unadorned, obvious, simple.)*

introduction—*n.* importation, taking, insertion, preliminary, initiative, vestibule, gate, prelude, conducting, induction, leading, presentation, commencement, preface, portico, entrance, preamble. *(extraction, elimination, estrangement, completion, egress, withdrawal, education, exportation, ejection, conclusion, end.)*

introductory—*adj.* initatory, precursary, preparatory, beginning, prefatory, commendatory, preliminary. *(final, alienative, terminal, ultimate, valedictory, completive, conclusive, supplemental.)*

intuition—*n.* apprehension, insight, clairvoyance, instinct, recognition. *(learning, elaboration, induction, reasoning, information, instruction, acquirement, experience.)*

invalid—*adj.* sick, frail, incapacitated, infirm, wealthy, feeble. *(healthy, strong, hearty, well, vigorous.)*

invent—*v.* contrive, imagine, conceive, devise, originate, frame, feign, create, discover, concoct, elaborate, design, fabricate, find out, forge. *(copy, reproduce, simulate, imitate, execute.)*

invincible—*adj.* immovable, unsubduable, indomitable, insupirable, impregnable, unyielding, inexpugnable, irresistible, unconquerable, insurmountable. *(spiritless, weak, puny, vulnerable, effortless, powerless.)*

invisible—*adj.* ultimate, minute, concealed, atomic, mysterious. *(separable, obvious, divisible, discerptible, visible.)*

involve—*v.* confound, envelop, include, entangle, contain, implicate, mingle, compromise, complicate. *(extricate, liberate, disconnect, separate.)*

irreligious—*adj.* ungodly, profane, blasphemous, impious, godless, undevout. *(godly, reverential, devout, worshipful, religious, reverent, pious.)*

irrepressible—*adj.* ungovernable, insuppressible, unconfined, vibrant, excitable, unrepressible, uncontrollable, free. *(governable, calm, depressed, bound down, repressible, controllable.)*

irresponsible—*adj.* unencumbered, not answerable, lawless, despotic, unreliable. *(obligatory, imperative, under obligation, legal, trustworthy, legitimate, responsible, binding, chargeable on, lawful.)*

irritate—*v.* annoy, exasperate, anger, provoke, agitate, irk, trouble, pester, offend. *(calm, soothe, appease, please, placate, pacify, comfort.)*

isolate—*v.* segregate, insulate, quarantine, sequester, detach, separate, exile, set apart. *(unite, mix, join, combine, blend, merge, coordinate.)*

J

jealous—*adj.* self-anxious, invidious, resentful, suspicious, envious, covetous. *(liberal, self-denying, unjealous, tolerant, unenvious, genial, indifferent.)*

jejune—*adj.* deficient, inadequate, lacking, wanting, inane, dull, insubstantial, insipid, prosaic. *(invigorating, vital, nourishing, solubrious, exciting, mature, inspired.)*

jeopardy—*n.* danger, exposure, risk, hazard, peril, insecurity, precariousness, liability. *(safety, security, certainty.)*

jingle—*n.* tinkle, jangle, ring, clink, rattle. *(harmony, melody, euphony, consonance, chord.)*

jocular—*adj.* humorous, witty, funny, whimsical, droll, jovial, frolicsome, amusing, jolly, comical. *(solemn, earnest, grave, sober, serious, sedate, humorless.)*

join—*v.* adhere, add, connect, annex, combine, accompany, splice, confederate, unite, link, adjoin, couple, associate, append. *(disjoin, disconnect, sever, separate, subtract, deviate, quit, disassociate.)*

jollification—*n.* festivity, fun, merry-making, jubilation, revelry, conviviality, carnival. *(tediousness, tedium, weariness, monotony, soberness, redundance.)*

jolly—*adj.* joyful, mirthful, jovial, robust, plump, gay, cheerful, merry, gladsome, genial, jubilant, lively. *(mournful, cheerless, lugubrious, gloomy, saturnine, lean, sad, joyless, unmirthful, morose.)*

jostle—*n.* push, jog, hustle, thrust, shake, tremor, jolt, collison. *(lead, guidance, convoy, escort, squire, pilot.)*

jovial—*adj.* gay, gleeful, blithe, cheerful, jocular, delightful, humorous, merry, animated, buoyant. *(dour, gloomy, melancholy, saturnine, somber, pensive, sober, cheerless, morose.)*

joy—*n.* pleasure, happiness, transport, ecstasy, bliss, mirth, festivity, charm, delight, blessedness, gladness, elation, exultation, felicity, rapture, gaiety, merriment, hilarity. *(pain, misery, grief, tears, despondency, distress, despair, sorrow, trouble, melancholy, affliction, depression.)*

jubilant—*adj.* triumphant, glad, congratulatory, joyous, exultant, elated, festive, ecstatic, radiant. *(mournful, wailing, penitential, remorseful, dejected, doleful, sorrowful, penitent, lugubrious, forlorn.)*

judgement—*n.* determination, sagacity, judiciousness, intellect, estimation, verdict, discernment, intelligence, award, arbitration, condemnation, decision, adjudication, penetration, sense, belief, opinion, sentence, discrimination, prudence. *(consideration, inquiry, speculation, investigation, insagacity, evidence, obtuseness, pronunciation, argument, proposition, pleading, injudiciousness.)*

judicious—*adj.* sagacious, wise, sensible, discriet, well-advised, discerning, cautious, thoughtful, expedient, prudent, well-judged, polite. *(unwise, foolish, imprudent, ill-judged, silly, impolitic, rash, injurious, unreasonable, indiscreet, ill-advised, inexpedient, blind.)*

juggle—*v.* cheat, shuffle, beguile, swindle, mystify, manipulate, mislead, conjure, bamboozle, trick, circumvent, overreach. *(correct, guide, undeceive, detect, direct, expose, enlighten, lead, disillusionize.)*

junior—*adj.* secondary, younger, subordinate, minor, inferior, youthful, immature, juvenile, adolescent. *(superior, older, advanced, elder, senior, primary, mature, adult.)*

just—*adj.* fitting, fair, harmonious, reasonable, honorable, impartial, upright, orderly, right, proper, decent, exact, true, proportioned, honest, sound, normal, equitable, regular, lawful, righteous. *(misfitted, ill-proportioned, inharmonious, unreasonable, biased, dishonorable, unequitable, irregular, disorderly, inexact, disproportioned, untrue, unfair, unsound, partial, unjust, abnormal.)*

justice—*n.* impartiality, right, propriety, desert, virtue, integrity, equity, fairness, reasonableness, uprightness. *(wrong, unfairness, unlawfulness, dishonor, inadequateness, injustice, partiality, unreasonableness.)*

justify—*v.* defend, vindicate, excuse, exonerate, acquit, warrant, advocate, plead for, varnish, clear. *(incriminate, tax, accuse, blame, censure, denounce, indict, implicate, condemn.)*

juvenile—*adj.* young, boyish, early, adolescent, childish, unsophisticated, puerile, youthful, infantine, girlish, immature, pubescent. *(later, womanly, aged, anile, adult, developed, superannuated, mature, manly, elderly, senile.)*

K

keen—*adj.* vehement, piercing, acute, biting, sarcastic, ardent, shrewd, knife-like, eager, sharp, penetrating, cutting, severe, satirical, prompt. *(languid, dull, flat, obtuse, blind, indifferent.)*

keep—*v.* restrain, detain, guard, suppress, conceal,

support, tend, conduct, obey, observe, celebrate, adhere to, hinder, possess, hold, retain, preserve, repress, maintain, continue, haunt, frequent, sustain, protect, practice. *(acquit, send, betray, divulge, abandon, disobey, transgress, desert, ignore, release, liberate, dismiss, neglect, discard, intermit, disregard, obviate, forsake.)*

key—*adj.* crucial, salient, decisive, vital, essential, basic, chief, fundamental, indispensable, material. *(immaterial, secondary, insignificant, minor, peripheral.)*

kind—*n.* character, designation, genus, sort, nature, breed, progeny, style, description, denomination, species, class, set. *(dissimilarity, unlikeness,variety.)*

kind—*adj.* benign, indulgent, clement, compassionate, good, forbearing, charitable, benevolent, tender, humane, lenient, gentle, gracious, kind-hearted. *(harsh, cruel, illiberal, bitter, unkind, severe, hard, ruthless.)*

kindle—*v.* light, ignite, provoke, inflame, arouse, excite, stir, enkindle, awaken, set fire to. *(douse, smother, quench, stifle, extinguish.)*

kindness—*n.* goodness, benevolence, philanthropy, humanity, tolerance, compassion, tenderness, mercy, generosity, goodwill, charity. *(meanness, cruelty, inhumanity, coldness, severity, unkindness, malevolence.)*

kindred—*adj.* akin, fraternal, familial, allied, harmonious, congenial, related, united, germane. *(uncongenial, dissimilar, different, unlike, alien, unrelated.)*

king—*n.* sovereign, lord, czar, tycoon, master, potentate, leader, monarch, chief. *(subject, slave, serf, follower, dependent, vassal, servant.)*

knack—*n.* skill, ability, gift, genius, aptitude, facility, flair, dexterity, cleverness. *(ineptitude, gaucherie, clumsiness, awkwardness, disability.)*

knit—*v.* join, fasten, affix, link, attach, connect, unite, secure, weave, bind. *(part, divide, separate, split.)*

knot—*n.* bond, difficulty, twist, cluster, band, protuberance, joint, . tie, intricacy, perplexity, collection, group. *(unfastening, solution, unraveling, multitude, untie, indentation, smoothness, cavity, loosening, dissolution, crowd, explication, dispersion, evenness.)*

knotty—*adj.* gnarled, bumpy, knotted, rough, lumpy, uneven, nodular, coarse, rugged. *(flat, level, smooth, plane, obvious, clear.)*

knowing—*adj.* astute, sharp, sagacious, proficient, acute, intelligent, well-informed, perceptive, accomplished, shrewd, discerning, penetrating, skillful, experienced. *(dull, gullible, stolid, unwise, silly, simple, innocent, undiscerning.)*

knowledge—*n.* comprehension, understanding, experience, familiarity, notice, instruction, enlightenment, attainments, erudition, apprehension, recognition, conversance, acquaintance, cognizance, information, learning, scholarship, ability, wisdom. *(inobservance, deception, misunderstanding, inconversance, ignorance, incognizance, rudeness, uneducatedness, illiterateness, incapacity, misapprehension, incomprehension, misconception, inexperience, unfamiliarity, misinformation, misinstruction, untutoredness.)*

L

laborious—*adj.* diligent, indefatigable, burdensome, wearisome, hard-working, difficult, tedious, strenuous, assiduous, painstaking, arduous, toilsome, industrious, active. *(indiligent, easy, indolent, facile, simple, idle, dainty, lazy, light, feasible.)*

lack—*n.* deficiency, absence, shortcoming, want, gap, failure, insufficiency, dearth,omission. *(surplus, extra, excess, sufficiency, plethora, adequacy, amplitude.)*

laconic—*adj.* curt, epigrammatic, concise, terse, concentrated, summary. *(wordy, prosy, circumlocutory, prolix, tedious, talkative, garrulous, laquacious.)*

laggardly—*adv.* tardily, slowly, belatedly, dilatorily, hesitantly, languidly, sluggishly, slackly, backwardly. *(quickly, speedily, willingly, smartly, readily, briskly.)*

lame—*adj.* faltering, hesitating, impotent, halt, imperfect, crippled, weak, hobbling, ineffective, deformed, defective. *(agile, efficient, cogent, telling, nimble, robust, potent, satisfactory, convincing, effective.)*

language—*n.* talk, dialect, tongue, phraseology, accents, expression, verbalization, speech, conversation, discourse, diction, articulation, vernacular. *(jabber, babel, cry, bark, roar, dumbness, jargon, inarticulateness, chatter, gabble, speechlessness, gibberish, whine, howl, obmutescence, muteness.)*

languid—*adj.* weary, unnerved, pining, enervated, flagging, apathetic, spiritless, faint, feeble, unbraced, drooping, exhausted. *(healthy, strong, vigorous, braced, fatigued, robust, active.)*

large—*adj.* bulky, abundant, ample, comprehensive, catholic, vast, substantial, wide, big, extensive, capacious, liberal, enlightened, great. *(mean, circumscribed, scanty, niggardly, petty, minute, sordid,small, narrow, contracted, illiberal, bigoted.)*

last—*v.* remain, endure, live, persevere, continue,hold, abide. *(fail, fly, depart, terminate, expire, cease, fade, wane, disappear.)*

last—*adj.* ending, concluding, past, lowest, ultimate, terminal, latest, final, hindmost, extreme, remotest. *(introductory, opening, ensuing, minor, nearest, temporary, first, initiatory, foremost, highest, next.)*

latent—*adj.* hidden, potential, dormant, quiescent, suspended, inactive, smoldering, passive, concealed, covert. *(evident, active, apparent, manifest, kinetic, patent, activated, developed.)*

laud—*v.* extol, glorify, honor, applaud, esteem, compliment, approve, acclaim, praise. *(denigrate, belittle, decry, censure, disparage, minimize.)*

laughter—*n.* glee, ridicule, contempt, mocking, merriment, derision, cachinnation. *(tears, sorrow, veneration, whimper, wailing, weeping, mourning, admiration, respect, whine.)*

law—*n.* edict, decree, order, enactment, method, principle, legislation, jurisdiction, ordinance, jurisprudence, rule, regulation, command, statute, mode, sequence, code, adjudication. *(disorder, rebellion, hazard, irregularity, casualty, chaos, accident, misrule, anarchy, insubordination, chance, caprice.)*

lawful—*adj.* permissible, right, fair, rightful, permitted, legitimate, legal, orderly, allowable, constitutional. *(impermissible, wrong, unfair, prohibited, illegal, unlawful, lawless.)*

lay—*v.* establish, allay, arrange, put, set down, repose, place, deposit, prostrate, dispose, spread. *(raise, excite, disorder, abrade, elevate, erect, lift, disarrange, scrape.)*

lead—*v.* guide, induce, pass, inaugurate, persuade, conduct, influence, accompany, precede, spend, commence, convoy, direct. *(mislead, dissuade, leave, depart, misguide, misconduct, follow, abandon.)*

lead—*n.* prominence, guidance, direction, control, priority. *(inferiority, followership, submission, subordination.)*

lean—*v.* rest, tend, depend, repose, slope, slant, incline, support, bend, hang, confide. *(re-erect, rise, reject, straighten, stabilitate, erect, raise.)*

lean—*adj.* lank, emaciated, bony, scraggy, slender, skeletal, scanty, meagre, tabid, shrivelled, thin, skinny. *(brawny, fleshy, well- conditioned, fat, plump.)*

learned—*adj.* erudite, skilled, literary, well-informed, profound, versed, conversant, read, scholarly, knowing. *(illiterate, unlearned, uneducated, unscholarly, inconversant, ignorant.)*

learning—*n.* erudition, lore, acquirements, scholarship, tuition, wisdom, knowledge, literature, letters, attainments, education, culture, skill. *(boorishness, emptiness, intuition, inspiration, nescience, ignorance, sciolism, illiterateness, revelation.)*

leave—*n.* permission, concession, sanction, liberty, license. *(prohibition, veto, inhibition, refusal, restriction, prevention.)*

leery—*adj.* wary, suspicious, cautious, dubious, skeptical, unsure, uncertain, shy, distrustful. *(credulous, gullible, confident, trustful, secure, assured.)*

legal—*adj.* legitimate, lawful, licit, rightful, legalistic, judiciary, statutory, juristic, permissible, legislative. *(illegal, unlawful, illicit, extrajudicial, invalid, illegitimate.)*

legend—*n.* fable, story, saga, myth, marvelous, fiction. *(fact, occurrence, event, history, actual.)*

lengthy—*adj.* prolix, long-drawn, diffuse, verbase, interminable, tedious, elongated. *(compendious, short, laconic, condensed, fleeting, suc-*

cinct, concise, curt, brief, compact.)

leniency—*n.* indulgence, patience, mercifulness, softness, pity, charity, benevolence, compassion, mildness, mercy, gentleness. *(roughness, severity, sternness, harshness, mercilessness, implacability.)*

lesson—*n.* warning, lecture, information, exercise, precept, instruction, homily. *(misguidance, misinstruction, deception, misinformation.)*

lethargic—*adj.* apathetic, lazy, sluggish, drowsy, languid, dull, comatose, slow, sleepy, slothful, indolent, idle. *(vigorous, vital, energetic, alert, animated, lively, strenuous, spirited.)*

level—*n.* surface, equality, plane, platform, coordinateness, floor, position, horizontalness, aim, ground. *(acclivity, inequality, verticality, elevation, declivity, unevenness, uncoordinateness.)*

level—*v.* smooth, flatten, raze, align, plane, roll, equalize. *(furrow, graduate, engrave, roughen, disequalize.)*

level—*adj.* plain, even, flat, uniform, smooth, horizontal. *(uneven, rolling, sloping, broken, rough.)*

libel—*n.* detraction, calumny, defamatory, lampoon, innuendo, defamation, traducement, slander, publication. *(vindication, eulogy, puff, encomium, retraction, cancellation, apology, panegyric, advocacy.)*

liberal—*adj.* gentle, polished, free, bountiful, enlarged, ample, large, munificent, noble-minded, tolerant, lavish, plentiful, refined, generous, catholic, capious, profuse, handsome, abundant, bounteous. *(low, boorish, illiberal, niggardly, greedy, narrow-minded, prejudiced, scanty, bigoted, mean, inadequate, churlish, ungenerous, grasping, avaricious, gainful, conservative, contracted.)*

liberty—*n.* leave, permission, license, immunity, impropriety, voluntariness, audacity, exemption, freedom, independence, privilege, franchise, insult, volition. *(servitude, constraint, dependence, compulsion, respect, necessity, predestination, bondage, slavery, restraint, submission, obligation, deference, considerateness, fatality.)*

licentious—*adj.* dissolute, lax, debauched, loose, libertine, unbridled, voluptuous, rakish, self-indulgent, profligate. *(strict, self-controlled, self-denying, rigid, puritanical, temperate, sober, ascetic.)*

lie—*n.* untruth, subterfuge, fib, falsity, deception, falsehood, fabrication, evasion, fiction. *(veracity, truth, reality, fact.)*

lie—*v.* repose, remain, lounge, be, rest. *(stir, change, rise, move.)*

life—*n.* duration, condition, spirit, animation, personality, society, history, vitality, career, existence, vigor, state, morals, activity, conduct, vivacity. *(decease, non-existence, torpor, lethargy, extinction, lifelessness, mortality, death, dullness, portraiture.)*

lift—*v.* elevate, upheave, hoist, erect, heighten, raise, upraise, exalt, elate. *(sink, crush, overwhelm, plunge, lower, depress, hurl, degrade, cast, dash.)*

light—*n.* radiance, gleam, scintillation, flash, brilliancy, splendor, candle, lantern, instruction, understanding, day, luster, life, luminosity, beam, phosphorescence, coruscation, brightness, effulgence, blaze, lamp, explanation, illumination, interpretation. *(dimness, shade, night, gloom, misinterpretation, dusk, misunderstanding, death, tenebrosity, mystification, extinguish, darkness, obscurity, duskiness, extinction, ignorance, confusion.)*

light—*adj.* portable, buoyant, easy, scanty, unencumbered, slight, unsteady, vain, characterless, unthoughtful, inadequate, unsubstantial, not difficult, bright, trifling, sparse, imponderous, unweighty, volatile, digestible, active, empty, gentle, capricious, frivolous, thoughtless, unconsidered, incompact, inconsiderable, whitish. *(dark-colored, heavy, weighty, leaden, hard, full, encumbered, oppressed, loaded, ballasted, serious, violent, firm, cautious, reliable, sensible, thoughtful, adequate, compact, ponderous, immovable, solid, indigestible, lazy, burdened, weighed, laden, grave, important, steady, principled, reflective, liable, earnest, well-considered, stiff, dark, substantial.)*

likeness—*n.* resemblance, similitude, copy, portrait, image, carte de visite, appearance, picture, similarity, correspondence, parity, imitation, representation, effigy. *(dissimilitude, inequality,* *original, difference, dissimilarity, disparity, unlikeness.)*

line—*n.* thread, outline, direction, course, succession, continuity, filament, cord, length, row, verse, method, sequence. *(contents, divergency, fluctuation, interruption, discontinuance, constancy, breath, space, deviation, variation, solution.)*

link—*v.* couple, combine, merge, attack, join, consolidate, fuse, fasten, splice, connect. *(untie, sever, divide, disconnect, part, detach, divorce, disengage, uncouple.)*

liquid—*adj.* liquescent, running, fluent, mellifluous, flowing, smooth, moist, fluid, melting, watery, soft, limpid, clear. *(solidified, congealed, dry, insoluble, discordant, hard, cohesive, solid, concrete, harsh, indissolvable.)*

listen—*v.* attend, incline, heed, eavesdrop, hear, hearken, give ear, overhear. *(ignore, repudiate, neglect, disregard, refuse.)*

literal—*adj.* grammatical, close, positive, plain, precise, exact, verbal, real, actual. *(substantial, free, allegorical, spiritual, general, metaphorical.)*

literary—*adj.* scholarly, bookish, studious, erudite, poetic. *(unstudious, untutored, unscholarly, illiterate.)*

literature—*n.* erudition, study, attainment, literary works, writings, lore, reading, learning, scholarship. *(genius, inspiration, creation, intuition.)*

little—*adj.* tiny, diminutive, brief, unimportant, slight, inconsiderable, illiberal, petty, dirty, dwarf, miniature, small, pigmy, short, scanty, insignificant, weak, trivial, mean, paltry, shabby. *(bulky, enormous, long, monstrous, big, developed, large, important, serious, liberal, huge, noble, handsome, magnanimous, full, full-sized, much, grave, momentous, generous, high-minded.)*

live—*v.* grow, continue, dwell, act, subsist, exist, prevail, vegetate, survive, abide, last, behave, breathe. *(perish, demise, vanish, fall, depart, decrease, expire, die, wither, migrate, fade, languish, drop.)*

live—*adj.* vital, animate, energetic. *(defunct, inert, inanimate.)*

load—*n.* lading, oppression, drag, encumbrance,

burden, weight, cargo, incubus. *(support, alleviation, lightness, consolation, solace, refreshment, emptiness.)*

load—*v.* charge, cargo, oppress, weight, burden, lade, cumber. *(unload, lighten, believe, liberate, disburden, disencumber, alleviate.)*

loan—*n.* mortgage, hypothecation, accommodation, advance, credit. *(foreclosure, recall, return, resumption.)*

loathsome—*adj.* detestable, evil, repulsive, abominable, obnoxious, disgusting, horrible, revolting, contemptible, nasty. *(delightful, sweet, beautiful, lovely, charming, engaging, alluring, attractive.)*

locate—*v.* establish, fix, lodge, detect, place, settle, dispose, discover, pinpoint. *(disestablish, remove, leave, displace, dislodge, conceal.)*

lofty—*adj.* towering, dignified, stately, majestic, tall, sublime, elevated, high, eminent, haughty, airy. *(low, undignified, unstately, unimposing, affable, dwarfed, depressed, stunted, ordinary, mean, unassuming.)*

logical—*adj.* argumentative, close, rational, sound, cogent. *(fallacious, inconclusive, confused, illogical.)*

lonesome—*adj.* dreary, wild, desolate, isolate, lonely, forlorn, forsaken, solitary. *(befriended, frequented, gay, bustling, cheerful, happy, festive, populous, animated.)*

long—*adj.* produced, lengthy, prolix, diffuse, interminable, protracted, dilatory, tedious, extensive, far-reaching. *(curt, brief, quick, condensed, small, short, curtailed, speedy, concise.)*

loose—*v.* unfasten, let go, free, untie. *(fasten, retain, hold, secure, tie.)*

loose—*adj.* detached, scattered, incompact, inexact, dissoluted, released, licentious, unbound, flowing, sparse, vague, rambling. *(tied, tight, lashed, thick, dense, pointed, exact, strict, conscientious, precise, bound, fastened, moored, close, secured, compact, accurate, consecutive, logical, scientific.)*

loquacious—*adj.* chatty, wordy, talkative, garrulous, verbose, vociferous, voluble, gushy, profuse. *(reticent, silent, reserved, taciturn, terse, quiet.)*

lose—*v.* drop, forfeit, vanish, miss, mislay, misplace, waste, flounder, fail. *(retain, recover, earn,* *treasure, utilize, abandon, reject, vanquish, keep, find, locate, guard, economize, preserve, discard.)*

loss—*n.* dropping, missing, waste, damage, depletion, mislaying, forfeiture, privation, detriment. *(recovery, satisfaction, economy, advantage, preservation, gain, profit, earning, restoration, augmentation.)*

lot—*n.* fortune, hazard, doom, destiny, chance, fate, ballot, heritage. *(provision, disposal, purpose, portion, grant, law, allotment, arrangement, design, plan.)*

loud—*adj.* sonorous, noisy, vociferous, obstreperous, tumultuous, sounding, resonant, audible, clamorous. *(gentle, whispering, murmuring, pattering, dulcet, quiet, peaceful, soft, subdued, rustling, babbling, tinkling, inaudible.)*

love—*n.* attachment, devotion, charity, fondness, kindness, affection, passion, benevolence. *(dislike, alienation, bitterness, indifference, infidelity, unkindness, uncharitableness, loathing, hatred, disaffection, estrangement, coldness, repugnance, desertion, malice.)*

lovely—*adj.* lovable, beautiful, delightful, gracious, charming, amiable, enchanting, pleasing. *(unamiable, hateful, plain, unattractive, distasteful, unlovely, unlovable, hideous, homely.)*

lover—*n.* wooer, swain, fiance, beau, suitor, sweetheart. *(wife, spouse, mate, husband.)*

low—*adj.* sunk, stunted, deep, inaudible, gentle, degraded, poor, abject, unworthy, feeble, frugal, subdued, insignificant, humble, abated, depressed, declining, cheap, subsided, dejected, mean, base, lowly, moderate, repressed, reduced. *(lofty, ascending, high, violent, excited, eminent, strong, influential, honorable, intensified, wealthy, ample, rich, elevated, tall, rising, exorbitant, loud, elated, considerable, high-minded, proud, aggravated, raised.)*

lower—*v.* decrease, bate, drop, sink, humble, submerge, diminish, depress, reduce, abate, humiliate, debase. *(raise, exalt, superior, aggrandize, elevate, hoist, heighten, increase.)*

lower—*adj.* secondary, inferior, subordinate. *(superior, elevate, higher.)*

loyal—*adj.* obedient, allegiant, true, constant,

staunch, submissive, faithful. *(insurgent, rebellious, unfaithful, untrue, disaffected, treacherous, insubmissive, malcontent, disobedient, unallegiant, inconstant.)*

lucid—*adj.* understandable, plain, transparent, pellucid, distinct, evident, comprehensible, clear, bright. *(dark, fuzzy, vague, confusing, unintelligible, gloomy, opaque, turgid.)*

lucky—*adj.* auspicious, successful, blessed, favorable, fortunate, prosperous. *(unfortunate, unprosperous, ill-fated, luckless, unpromising, unlucky, inauspicious, adverse, disastrous.)*

ludicrous—*adj.* farcical, comic, funny, preposterous, comical, ridiculous, laughable, droll. *(momentous, sad, mournful, lugubrious, sombre, solemn, doleful, serious, grave, sorrowful, tragic, melancholy.)*

lugubrious—*adj.* mournful, dismal, sad, doleful, melancholy, gloomy, woeful, depressed, downcast, sorrowful. *(happy, content, joyous, cheerful.)*

lunatic—*n.* maniac, psychopath, madman, schizophrenic. *(philosopher, genius, solon, luminary, rational.)*

lurid—*adj.* lowering, dismal, sensational, gloomy, murky, wan. *(luminous, bright, sunny.)*

luscious—*adj.* delicious, honied, toothsome, delectable, sweet, sugary, delightful, savory. *(sharp, bitter, unpalatable, sour, tart.)*

luxurious—*adj.* self- indulgent, sensual, voluptuous, epicurean, pampered, pleasurable. *(painful, ascetic, austere, hardy, hard, spartan, self-denying.)*

luxury—*n.* epicurism, wantonness, softness, delicacy, profuseness, wealth, effeminacy, voluptuousness, self-indulgence, animalism, dainty. *(asceticism, self-denial, penury, hardness, stoicism, hardship, need.)*

lying—*adj.* false, untruthful, deceit, mendacious, untrue. *(veracious, honesty, true.)*

M

macabre—*adj.* ghastly, gruesome, horrible, weird, grim, eerie, dreadful, deathly, horrid. *(lovely, delightful, appealing, pleasant, beautiful, inviting.)*

mad—*adj.* demented, lunatic, crazy, frantic, wild, unbalanced, distracted, insane, furious, infuriated, maniacal, rabid. *(sound, quiet, lucid, unexcited, sane, sober, sensible, composed.)*

madden—*v.* enrage, inflame, provoke, infuriate, exasperate. *(pacify, mesmerize, soothe, lay, calm, assuage.)*

magnanimous—*adj.* high-minded, high-souled, lofty, chivalrous, honorable, noble, exalted, liberal. *(petty, mean, selfish, vindictive.)*

magnetic—*adj.* captivating, alluring, tantalizing, entrancing, hypnotic, enthralling, fascinating, intriguing, dynamic. *(repulsive, offensive, repellent, forbidding, antimagnetic.)*

magnificent—*adj.* magnanimous, splendid, august, gorgeous, grand, majestic, sublime, exalted, noble, pompous, superb, imposing, stately, dignified. *(mean, paltry, beggarly, ordinary, unimposing, unpretentious, petty, little, flat, humble, tawdry, tame.)*

maid—*n.* girl, lass, virgin, maiden, damsel, miss. *(married woman, matron, dowager, matriarch.)*

maintain—*v.* carry on, protract, preserve, perpetuate, continue, extend, overhaul, fix, mend, secure. *(discontinue, refrain, cease, ruin, demolish, quit, wreck.)*

majority—*n.* predominance, priority, preponderance, bulk, minority, superiority, seniority, lion's share. *(juniority, childhood, minority, inferiority, little.)*

make—*v.* produce, frame, create, construct, do, execute, gain, find, establish, reach, shape, bring about, fashion, fabricate, effect, perform, compel, constitute, mould, form. *(unmake, dismember, destroy, miss, mar, dismantle, disestablish, annihilate, undo, disintegrate, defeat, lose.)*

malaise—*n.* disquiet, alienation, uneasiness, anxiety, apprehension, nervousness, discontent, qualm, exhaustion, fatigue. *(serenity, well-being, vim, contentment, restfulness, vigor, hardiness.)*

malevolent—*adj.* vicious, spiteful, hostile, pernicious, malign, mean, malignant, evil, hateful, antagonistic. *(kind, friendly, amicable, benevolent, cordial, compassionate.)*

manage—*v.* manipulate, conduct, mould, contrive,

husband, wield, operate, handle, control, administer, regulate, train, direct. *(impracticable, unmanageable, refractory, spoil, follow, difficult, impossible, intractable.)*

manageable—*adj.* feasible, docile, practicable, submissive, easy, possible, tractable. *(impracticable, unmanageable, refractory, contrary, difficult, impossible, intractable, unwieldy.)*

management—*n.* conduct, government, skill, skillful treatment, operation, treatment, administration, address, superintendence. *(misconduct, misgovernment, maladroitness, maltreatment, maladministration, mismanage.)*

manifest—*adj.* obvious, conspicuous, clear, plain, apparent, evident, open, candid, visible, distinct, indubitable, patent. *(dubious, indistinct, vague, invisible, inconspicuous.)*

manly—*adj.* courageous, open, frank, noble, fine, masculine, fearless, vigorous, manful, virile, dignified, bold, generous, chivalrous, firm, stately, mature, brave, hardy, manlike. *(childish, unmanly, weak, ungrown, cowardly, womanish, timid, dastardly, puny, boyish.)*

manner—*n.* method, form, kind, carriage, deportment, sort, practice, mode, style, fashion, behavior, habit. *(project, performance, action, appearance, creation, being, work, design, life, proceeding.)*

manners—*n.* behavior, courtesy, intercourse, refinement, demeanor, deportment, carriage, politeness. *(misbehavior, coarseness, unmannerliness, misdemeanor.)*

manufacture—*v.* production, make, composition, manipulation, devise, molding, fabrication, construction. *(employment, wear, destroy, use, consumption.)*

many—*adj.* abundant, manifold, sundry, myriad, multifarious, numerous, frequent, divers. *(scarce, infrequent, several, few, rare.)*

marginal—*adj.* insignificant, minor, unimportant, slight, trivial, expendable, borderline, indifferent replaceable. *(principal, capital, sovereign, crucial, primary, compelling.)*

mark—*n.* token, symptom, vestige, note, score, trace, sign, impression, indication. *(obliteration, plainness,* *erasure, deletion, effacement, unindicativeness.)*

mark—*v.* label, indicate, brand, signalize, observe, heed, specialize, identify, stamp, sign, decorate, stigmatize, note, regard, specify. *(overlook, mislabel, misindicate, misspecify, omit, obliterate, ignore, mismark, misobserve.)*

martial—*adj.* brave, warlike, belligerent, military. *(unmilitary, peaceful, conciliatory, unmartial.)*

marvel—*n.* prodigy, portent, wonder, astonishment, phenomenon, miracle, spectacle, admiration, amazement. *(unconcern, trifle, bagatelle, cipher, imposture, incuriosity, joke, farce, moonshine, drug.)*

masculine—*adj.* manly, hardy, virile, sturdy, male, manful, courageous. *(feminine, weak, womanly, effeminate, female, womanish.)*

mask—*n.* screen, ruse, hypocrisy, camouflage, pretext, pretense, cover. *(nakedness, exposure, verity, candor, unfolding, truth, detection, unmasking, openness.)*

mask—*v.* screen, cloak, shroud, disguise, hide, blink. *(unmask, divulge, detect, expose.)*

master—*n.* ruler, owner, proprietor, professor, chief, controller, adept, lord, governor, possessor, teacher. *(slave, property, tyro, pupil, subordinate, learner, servant, subject.)*

master—*v.* overcome, overpower, dominate, conquer, subdue. *(fail, succumb, capitulate to, yield, surrender.)*

masterful—*adj.* skillful, virtuoso, sharp, accomplished, commanding, able, authoritative, canny, wise, superb, deft. *(amateurish, inept, unable, incompetent, clumsy, unskillful, meek, spineless.)*

match—*n.* mate, contest, tally, pair, duplicate, equal, companion, competition, equality. *(inferior, oddity, inequality, unequal, superior, mismatched, disparity.)*

match—*v.* compare, pit, sort, mate, unite, equal, oppose, adapt, suit. *(exceed, surpass, dissociate, misfit, missort, divide, fail, predominate, mismatch, separate, misadapt.)*

matchless—*adj.* incomparable, surpassing, unrivaled, peerless, inimitable, consummate. *(ordinary, commonplace, undistinguished, common, every-day.)*

matter—*n.* stuff, body, material, substance, object, essence, gist, theme, content, sense. *(mind, intellect, moral, soul, ego, vision, thought, spirit.)*

mature—*adj.* grown, mellow, developed, full-grown, ripe, enriched, capable, complex, detailed, practiced. *(unripe, unfledged, raw, immature, tender, green, embryonic, young.)*

meagre—*adj.* lean, scanty, dry, paltry, thin, lank, barren, tame, sparse. *(fat, abundant, copious, generous, stout, brawny, fertile.)*

mean—*adj.* low, spiritless, contemptible, beggarly, vulgar, vile, intermediate, miserable, average, common, base, dishonorable, despicable, sordid, niggardly, middle. *(exalted, spirited, lordly, munificent, generous, excessive, superior, high, eminent, honorable, princely, liberal, extreme, exorbitant, deluxe.)*

mean—*n.* moderation, average, balance, medium, compromise, norm, rule. *(excess, disproportion, shortcoming, ultimate, inadequacy, extreme, preponderance, deficiency.)*

mean—*v.* purpose, signify, indicate, suggest, aim, intend, design, denote, hint. *(state, execute, declare, perform, say, enunciate, do.)*

means—*n.* instrument, media, resources, funds. *(object, end, purpose, point.)*

mechanical—*adj.* automatic, spontaneous, unimpassioned, routine, habitual, unreflective, effortless. *(self-conscious, forced, appreciative, lively, impassioned, manual, labored, feeling, spirited, lifelike, animated.)*

meddlesome—*adj.* obtrusive, officious, interfering, impertinent, intrusive. *(reserved, inobtrusive, unofficious, aloof.)*

mediocrity—*n.* commonplace, average, inferiority, sufficiency, mean, medium. *(superiority, rarity, distinction, brilliance, uniqueness, excellence.)*

meek—*adj.* gentle, modest, docile, unassuming, mild, submissive, yielding. *(arrogant, irritable, high-spirited, domineering, bold, self-asserting, proud.)*

melancholy—*adj.* sad, disconsolate, moody, cast down, unhappy, gloomy, dejected, dismal, hypochondriac. *(sprightly, merry, gleesome, happy, gamesome, vivacious, lively, gladsome, blithesome, cheerful, mirthful.)*

mellifluous—*adj.* harmonious, sweet, mellow, soft, smooth, full-toned, resonant, musical, dulcet, mellifluent, sweet-sounding. *(discordant, jarring, unmusical, grating, harsh, raucous, hoarse.)*

mellow—*adj.* rich, jovial, soft, velvety, ripe, full-flavored, mature. *(harsh, acid, crabbed, dry, gruff, unripe, sour, acrid, sober.)*

memorable—*adj.* striking, conspicuous, noticeable, extraordinary, eminent, distinguished, great, remarkable, prominent, illustrious, famous. *(trifling, trivial, insignificant, slight, ordinary, petty, prosaic, unnoticeable, mediocre.)*

memory—*n.* reminiscence, tribute, recollection, retrospect, fame, remembrance, perpetuation, retention. *(oblivion, amnesia, forgetfulness, blank.)*

mend—*v.* restore, promote, rectify, amend, better, recondition, repair, correct, improve, reform, ameliorate. *(impair, retard, falsify, corrupt, injure, damage, pervert, deteriorate, spoil.)*

mendacious—*adj.* dishonest, false, guileful, deceitful, untruthful, fraudulent, deceptive, double-dealing, lying, tricky. *(honest, true, creditable, sincere, veracious, truthful.)*

menial—*adj.* attendant, servile, lackey, drudge, domestic, dependent. *(sovereign, lordly, uncontrolled, dignified, autocratic, paramount, supreme, independent.)*

mental—*adj.* subjective, psychical, conscious, intellectual, psychological, metaphysical. *(objective, bodily, unconscious, corporal, physical.)*

mention—*n.* notice, observation, hint, indication, communication, declaration, announcement, remark. *(suppression, omission, disregard, silence, forgetfulness.)*

mercantile—*adj.* interchangeable, retail, business, marketable, commercial, wholesale. *(unmercantile, unmarketable, stagnant, inactive.)*

merchant—*n.* dealer, tradesman, trader, importer, shopkeeper, vendor. *(salesman, huckster, chandler, costermonger, shopman, hawker, peddler.)*

merciful—*adj.* kind-hearted, gracious, humane, kind, compassionate, clement. *(unrelenting, inex-*

orable, callous, pitiless, remorseless.)

mercurial—*adj.* flighty, volatile, capricious, fickle, unstable, changeable, erratic, impulsive, fluctuating, impetuous. *(steadfast, stable, predictable, constant, fixed, phlegmatic, callous.)*

mere—*adj.* unmixed, uninfluenced, unaffected, mundane, simple, pure, absolute, unadulterated. *(compound, biased, mixed, blended, impure.)*

merit—*n.* worth, desert, integrity, excellence, goodness, worthiness, virtue, ability. *(demerit, worthlessness, imperfection, defect, failing, dishonor, badness, unworthiness, weakness, error, fault.)*

meteoric—*adj.* phosphorescent, flashing, coruscant, brilliant, volcanic, momentary, displosive, pyrotechnic. *(beaming, steady, enduring, inconspicuous, permanent, burning, persistent.)*

method—*n.* system, way, mode, process, arrangement, technique, order, rule, manner, course, regularity, procedure. *(conjecture, empiricism, assumption, chaos, guess-work, disorder, quackery, experimentation.)*

methodical—*adj.* orderly, systematic, irregular, efficient, methodic, organized, disciplined. *(haphazard, irregular, disorderly, random, unsystematical.)*

meticulous—*adj.* scrupulous, fastidious, finicky, careful, perfectionist, exacting, nice, punctilious. *(careless, inexact, negligent, slovenly, perfunctory, sloppy.)*

middling—*adj.* average, well enough, mediocre, not bad, ordinary, moderate. *(first-rate, fine, good, glowing, splendid, excellent.)*

midst—*n.* center, throng, core, heart, middle, thick, nucleus, interior. *(confine, limit, purlieu, periphery, outskirt, edge, margin, extreme.)*

might—*n.* force, ability, potency, strength, power. *(infirmity, frailty, feebleness, weakness.)*

migrate—*v.* journey, emigrate, relocate, move, travel, resettle. *(bide, alight, settle, sojourn, remain, alight.)*

mild—*adj.* lenient, gentle, calm, tempered, meek, placid, genial, amiable, moderate, soft, tender. *(wild, savage, severe, harsh, balmy, bitter, violent, fierce, strong, merciless.)*

mind—*n.* spirit, memory, understanding, will, sentiment, belief, inclination, purpose, impetus, conception, remembrance, recollection, soul, liking, opinion, judgement, choice, desire, intellect. *(organization, proceeding, object, coolness, forgetfulness, body, action, conduct, resist, obviousness, indifference, aversion, ignore.)*

mindful—*adj.* attentive, careful, cautious, recollective, regardful, thoughtful. *(inattentive, oblivious, thoughtless, regardless, mindless.)*

mingle—*v.* compound, confound, intermingle, amalgamate, coalesce, mix, blend, confuse, associate. *(segregate, sort, discompound, classify, avoid, divide, separate, sift, analyze, eliminate, unravel.)*

minimize—*v.* little, diminutive, small, dwarf, microscopic, petite, tiny, minute, mini, wee. *(enlarge, expand, exaggerate, increase, maximize, stress, emphasize, magnify.)*

minister—*n.* officer, official, subordinate, clergyman, parson, preacher, shepherd, curate, religious, vicar, servant, delegate, ambassador, ecclesiastic, priest, divine, pastor, reverend. *(government, superior, head, fold, congregation, secular, monarch, master, principal, layman, flock.)*

minute—*adj.* microscopic, miniature, exact, specific, diminutive, tiny, searching, detailed, petite. *(enormous, tremendous, general, comprehensive, huge, monstrous, superficial, broad, momentous.)*

mischief—*n.* hurt, disservice, injury, damage, devilment, harm, damage, detriment, annoyance, ill-turn. *(good-turn, favor, advantage, gratification, benefit, compensation.)*

mischievous—*adj.* injurious, wanton, annoying, detrimental, spiteful. *(advantageous, conservative, protective, orderly, beneficial, reparatory, careful.)*

miscreant—*adj.* evil, corrupt, villainous, wicked, infamous, depraved, degenerate. *(moral, noble, ethical, virtuous, righteous, good.)*

miser—*n.* churl, curmudgeon, scrimp, cheapskate, hoarder, niggard, skinflint, screw. *(spendthrift, wastrel, rake, prodigal.)*

miserable—*adj.* forlorn, wretched, despicable, pathetic, disconsolate, abject, pitiable, worthless. *(happy, worthy, comfortable, joyous, respectable, contented.)*

misery—*n.* heartache, unhappiness, anguish, wretchedness, woe. *(glee, cheerfulness, joy, happiness.)*

misguided—*adj.* ill-advised, misled, mistaken, unwarranted, foolish, indiscreet, misdirected, unwise, erroneous. *(wise, sound, judicious, sagacious, prudent.)*

mitigate—*v.* alleviate, extenuate, relieve, temper, soothe, placate, mollify, allay, moderate, ameliorate. *(aggravate, intensify, increase, harden, magnify, augment, enhance.)*

mock—*v.* ridicule, mimic, ape, deceive, taunt, imitate, jeer, flout, insult, deride. *(welcome, admire, esteem, salute, respect, compliment, praise.)*

model—*n.* pattern, type, design, facsimile, standard, kind, example, mold. *(copy, execution, work, imitation, deformity, distortion.)*

moderate—*v.* soften, regulate, govern, abate, temper, control, allay, repress. *(disorganize, misconduct, aggravate, disturb, excite.)*

moderate—*adj.* temperate, sober, dispassionate, abstinent, steady, typical, ordinary, limited, calm, sparing. *(intemperate, excessive, extraordinary, drastic, extravagant, rigorous, violent.)*

modern—*adj.* existent, new-fangled, recent, novel, contemporary, later, present, new, new-fashioned, late. *(bygone, olden, old-fashioned, obsolete, archaic, past, former, ancient, antiquated.)*

modesty—*n.* diffidence, humility, simplicity, pure-mindedness, sobriety, bashfulness, reserve, shyness. *(conceit, self-admiration, coxcombry, shamelessness, pride, effrontery, vanity, self-sufficiency, foppery, wantonness.)*

moisture—*n.* dampness, wet, damp, humidity, dew, evaporation, vapor, mist, drizzle, perspiration. *(aridity, dryness, dehumidification, drought, barrenness, dehydration.)*

moment—*n.* second, twinkling, weight, gravity, avail, jiffy, instant, importance, trice, force, consequence. *(period, generation, insignificance, unimportance, unconcern, inefficacy, age, century, triviality, worthlessness.)*

monopoly—*n.* engrossment, trust, exclusiveness, impropriation, privilege, appropriation, cartel, preoccupancy. *(partnership, competition, accessory, free-trade, participation, community.)*

monotonous—*adj.* unvaried, humdrum, tedious, repetitious, uniform, dull, undiversified. *(changing, diversified, varying.)*

monstrous—*adj.* portentous, deformed, hideous, intolerable, grotesque, prodigious, marvelous, abnormal, preposterous. *(familiar, fair, shapely, natural, just, typical, ordinary, unnoticeable, comely, regular, reasonable.)*

moody—*adj.* sullen, temperamental, unstable, melancholy, erratic, morose, petulant, dismal, pessimistic, lugubrious, unhappy. *(cheerful, amiable, happy, stable, phlegmatic, stoic, calm, compatible.)*

moral—*adj.* ideal, spiritual, probable, presumptive, virtuous, scrupulous, mental, intellectual, ethical, inferential, analogous, well-conducted, honest. *(material, demonstrative, immoral, unethical, vicious, physical, practical, mathematical, unprincipled.)*

mortal—*adj.* ephemeral, short-lived, fatal, destructive, corporeal, human, sublunary, deadly, perishable. *(immortal, life-giving, eternal, divine, celestial, venial, imperishable.)*

motive—*n.* purpose, prompting, reason, incitement, motivation, inducement, design, stimulus, impulse. *(action, deed, project, deterent, maneuver, execution, dissuasive, effort, attempt, preventive.)*

move—*v.* go, stir, agitate, impel, advance, instigate, migrate, provoke, change, progress, affect, actuate, propose, propel. *(stop, rest, allay, prevent, withdraw, remain, stand, lie, stay, deter, arrest.)*

movement—*n.* move, change of place, progress, motion, action. *(rest, stillness, inertia, quietness, pause, stop.)*

much—*adj.* plenteous, abundantly, considerable, ample, abundant, greatly, far, substantial. *(scant, shortly, near, sparse, little, slightly, short.)*

muddle—*v.* waste, confuse, misarrange, entangle, fail, fritter away, derange. *(manage, classify, organize, clarify, economize, arrange, simplify.)*

muggy—*adj.* misty, damp, dim, cloudy, humid, foggy, dank, murky, vaporous. *(bright, vaporless, airy, pleasant, clear.)*

multitude—*n.* swarm, throng, number, mob, horde, rabble, crowd, accumulation, assemblage, host. *(scantiness, paucity, sprinkling, minority, nothing.)*

munificent—*adj.* princely, generous, lavish, liberal, bounteous, philanthropic. *(beggarly, stingy, niggardly, penurious.)*

murmur—*v.* whisper, grumble, mutter, complain, drone, repine, purr. *(vociferate, clamor, bawl.)*

muscular—*adj.* brawny, sinewy, stalwart, lusty, husky, sturdy, powerful, robust, strong, athletic. *(flabby, lanky, frail, debile, feeble, soft.)*

musical—*adj.* harmonious, concordant, tuneful, euphonious, mellifluous, melodious, dulcet, rythmical. *(inharmonious, discordant, unmelodious, harsh, dissonant.)*

musty—*adj.* rank, frowzy, sour, mildewed, decaying, fusty, moldy, stale, fetid. *(fresh, aromatic, refreshing, odorous, fragrant, balmy.)*

mutter—*v.* mumble, sputter, murmur, grunt, grumble. *(exclaim, vociferate, enunciate, pronounce, articulate.)*

mysterious—*adj.* obscure, unexplained, reserved, hidden, incomprehensible, inexplicable, cryptic, dim, veiled, unrevealed, unaccountable, secret, mystic. *(plain, explained, easy, simple, communicative, apparent, clear, obvious, understood, explainable, frank.)*

mystery—*n.* puzzle, secrecy, shrowd, quandry, arcanum, enigma, obscurity, veil. *(solution, truism, answer, publication, matter-of-fact, commonplace.)*

mystify—*v.* bamboozle, puzzle, mislead, perplex, confuse, hoodwink, confound, obfuscate, elude. *(enlighten, guide, interpret, illumine, inform, disclose.)*

mythical—*adj.* fictitious, unreal, fantastic, imaginary, legendary, fabricated, invented, fanciful, nonexistent. *(actual, true, factual, palpable, real.)*

N

nadir—*n.* foundation, floor, zero, base, root, rock bottom, nothing, minimum, bedrock. *(acme, summit, apex, zenith, peak, pinnacle.)*

naked—*adj.* bare, denuded, defenseless, unqualified, nude, unvarnished, simple, stripped, unclothed, undraped, destitute, uncolored, mere. *(robed, muffled, qualified, shrouded, varnished, embellished, dressed, draped, protected, veiled, colored.)*

name—*n.* cognomenation, title, reputation, appointment, fame, representation, nomenclature, designation, appelation, stead, authority. *(anonymousness, alias, pseudonym, ingloriousness, individuality, namelessness, misnomer, obscurity, disrepute, person.)*

name—*v.* designate, indicate, label, specify, call, nominate, title. *(miscall, misindicate, suggest, adumbrate, mention, misname, misdesignate, hint, shadow.)*

narrate—*v.* recite, tell, rehearse, describe, portray, relate, reveal, recapitulate, enumerate, paint. *(cover, withhold, veil, screen, smother, hide, conceal, shade.)*

narrow—*adj.* straightened, thin, contracted, cramped, scant, slender, scrutinizing, bigoted, tight, straight, confined, spare, near, limited, pinched, close, niggardly. *(broad, thick, easy, spacious, liberal, wide, ample, expanded.)*

nasty—*adj.* offensive, disagreeable, impure, unclean, loathsome, obscene, fowl, odious, indelicate, gross. *(pleasant, savory, agreeable, kind, pure, nice, sweet, admirable.)*

natural—*adj.* essential, normal, true, consistent, artless, inherent, original, intrinsic, regular, cosmical, probable, spontaneous. *(adventitious, monstrous, fictitious, affected, unsupposable, artful, ascetitious, incidental, abnormal, unnatural, improbable, forced.)*

nature—*n.* creation, structure, truth, kind, character, affection, attributes, naturalness, essence, constitution, disposition, sort, regularity, species. *(object, man, creature, unnaturalness, fiction, thing, invention, subject, being, art, monstrosity, romance, soul.)*

near—*adj.* close, neighboring, adjoining, nigh, adjacent. *(distant, remote, past, far.)*

neat—*adj.* immaculate, tidy, orderly, methodical, clean, shipshape, uncluttered, trim. *(disorderly, slovenly, unkempt, messy, disorganized.)*

necessary—*adj.* inevitable, certain, requisite, compulsory, expedient, unavoidable, indispensable, essential, needful. *(casual, free, discretional, unessential, optional, contingent, unnecessary, unrequired.)*

necessity—*n.* inevitableness, need, indigence, want, destiny, essential, indispensableness, requirement, fate. *(uncertainty, uselessness, affluence, contingency, choice, abundance, dispensableness, superfluity, competence, casualty, freedom.)*

nefarious—*adj.* atrocious, evil, despicable, odious, foul, vile, heinous, wicked, detestable, horrendous. *(honest, virtuous, noble, exalted, just, laudable, praiseworthy.)*

neglect—*v.* overlook, disregard, despise, omit, fail, slight, abandon, forget. *(respect, observe, esteem, attend, study, care for, consider, notice, regard, tend faster.)*

neglect—*n.* disregard, failure, slight, remissness, oversight, negligence, omission, default, carelessness. *(consideration, notice, esteem, care, attention, respect, regard.)*

nerve—*n.* firmness, boldness, resolution, endurance, strength. *(forceless, weak, impotent, cowardice, nerveless, feeble, enfeebled, palsied, bashfulness.)*

neutral—*adj.* impartial, remote, uninvolved, unbiased, indifferent, withdrawn, aloof, peaceful, pacifist. *(partisan, prejudiced, committed, biased, definite, active, belligerent.)*

new—*adj.* recent, modern, unused, current, novel, fresh, original. *(ancient, antiquated, passe, used, obsolete, old, antique.)*

nice—*adj.* scrupulous, neat, dainty, agreeable, fine, exact, particular, delightful, fastidious, accurate, discerning, pleasant, finished. *(unscrupulous, rude, undiscriminating, nauseous, miserable, coarse, disagreeable, inaccurate, rough, nasty.)*

niggardly—*adj.* penurious, miserly, cheap, parsimonious, small, mercenary, frugal, stingy, thrifty, avaricious. *(liberal, generous, munificent, lavish, charitable, bountiful, profuse, ample.)*

nobility—*n.* dignity, peerage, loftiness, rank, grandeur, aristocracy, distinction, lordship, generosity. *(meanness, serfdom, contemptibleness, simplicity,* *plebeianism, obscurity, commonalty, paltriness.)*

noble—*adj.* aristocratic, illustrious, worthy, dignified, lofty-minded, fine, patrician, grand, generous, exalted, excellent, magnanimous, honorable. *(plebeian, paltry, humble, mean, ignoble, despicable.)*

noisome—*adj.* harmful, odorous, pestilential, hurtful, nocuous. *(salutary, beneficial, curative, wholesome, salubrious.)*

noisy—*adj.* clamorous, loud, stunning, riotous, uproarious, hectic, deafening. *(soft, whispering, musical, harmonious, subdued, noiseless, peaceful, still, inaudible, soothing, melodious, tuneful, gentle.)*

nominal—*adj.* suppositious, professed, formal, trivial, trifling, ostensible, pretended. *(deep, important, substantial, intrinsic, essential, genuine, real, serious, grave, actual, veritable.)*

nondescript—*adj.* indefinite, colorless, commonplace, vague, unclassifiable, indistinct, characterless, stereotyped. *(unusual, distinctive, definite, vivid, unique, extraordinary.)*

nonsense—*n.* trash, pretense, balderdash, foolishness, absurdity, folly, jest. *(wisdom, fact, philosophy, reason, reality, sense, truth, gravity, science.)*

notice—*n.* cognizance, advice, consideration, mark, attention, note, observation, heed, news, visitation. *(disregard, mistidings, slight, ignorance, heedlessness, omission, misjudge, oversight, misinformation, neglect, amnesty, connivance, incognizance.)*

notion—*n.* idea, judgment, belief, sentiment, thought, apprehension, conception, opinion, expectation. *(falsification, misjudgment, misconception, misunderstanding, misapprenhension, misbelief, frustration.)*

notorious—*adj.* undisputed, allowed, scandalous, known, recognized. *(reputed, suspected, decent, reported.)*

nude—*adj.* bare, naked, stark, undressed, denuded, disrobed, unadorned, exposed. *(covered, clad, dressed, robed, appareled, clothed.)*

nuisance—*n.* annoyance, pest, vexation, trouble, offense, plague. *(delight,* *gratification, pleasure, benefit, blessing, joy.)*

nullify—*v.* veto, cancel, repeal, abolish, revoke, rescind, annul, invalidate, obliterate, abrogate. *(decree, ratify, establish, power, existence, viability.)*

O

oasis—*n.* retreat, shelter, haven, sanctum, refuge, sanctuary, asylum, island. *(desert, jungle, crossroads, thick, mainstream.)*

obedience—*n.* compliance, meekness, subservience, submission. *(rebellion, obstinate, transgression, disobedience, resistance, violation, antagonism.)*

obese—*adj.* corpulent, fleshy, fat, stout, heavy, rotund, portly, plump, gross, overweight. *(thin, emaciated, gaunt, lean, slender, angular, lanky, skinny.)*

obey—*v.* comply, concur, yield, submit. *(disobey, refuse, transgress, resist.)*

object—*n.* sight, end, motive, view, goal, target, appearance, design, aim, intent. *(notion, fancy, idea, proposal, effect, illusion, conception, subject, purpose.)*

object—*v.* contravene, demur to, gainsay, protest, oppose, obstruct, disapprove, complain. *(approve of, applaud, agree, justify.)*

oblige—*v.* coerce, force, favor, gratify, constrain, please, compel, necessitate, benefit, accommodate, bind. *(acquit, persuade, disoblige, inconvience, release, induce, annoy.)*

obliging—*adj.* considerate, kind, complaisant, accommodating, amiable, compliant. *(rude, perverse, disobliging, hostile, discourteous, inconsiderate, unaccommodating.)*

obliterate—*v.* eradicate, raze, destroy, ruin, pulverize, crush, extinguish, annihilate, level, abolish. *(create, reconstruct, rehabilitate, restore, preserve, build.)*

oblivious—*adj.* distracted, heedless, unconscious, careless, forgetful, unaware, inattentive, disregardful. *(aware, alert, careful, watchful, mindful, cognizant, concerned, worried.)*

obscene—*adj.* immodest, lewd, indelicate, disgusting, vulgar, foul-mouthed, impure, foul, indecent, filthy. *(modest, pure, decent, innocent, respectable.)*

obscure—*adj.* dim, indistinct, uncertain, unascertained, unintelligible, cloudy, dark, mean, lowering, enigmatical, doubtful, humble. *(luminous, lucid, plain spoken, unambiguous, eminent, resplendent, prominent, bright, distinct, plain, intelligible, ascertained.)*

observance—*n.* fulfilment, rule, celebration, ceremony, form, practice, adherence, attention, respect, performance, custom. *(inattention, disuse, disrespect, desuetude, omission, nonperformance, unceremoniousness, evasion, inobservance, breach, disregard, informality.)*

observant—*adj.* attentive, obedient, heedful, perceptive, regardful, mindful, watchful. *(neglectful, heedless, disobedient, indifferent, oblivious, disregardful, unmindful.)*

observation—*n.* study, attention, comment, watching, contemplation, remark, notice. *(oversight, inattention, ignorance, apathy, disregard, inadvertence, silence.)*

obsolete—*adj.* archaic, outmoded, old-fashioned, passé, ancient, antiquated, out-of-date, old, extinct. *(up-to-date, modern, current, prevalent, new, present-day.)*

obstacle—*n.* obstructive, objection, difficulty, hurdle, check, bar, impediment, hindrance. *(proceeding, course, advancement, support, career.)*

obstinate—*adj.* stubborn, self-willed, obdurate, intractable, determined, headstrong, refractory, pertinacious, perverse. *(complaisant, docile, characterless, wavering, flexible, amenable, yeilding, ductile, irresolute.)*

obvious—*adj.* self-evident, explicit, open, perceptible, patent, plain, manifest, apparent. *(obscure, involved, vague, latent, remote, farfetched.)*

occasion—*n.* opportunity, cause, event, necessity, ground, happening, conjuncture, occurrence, need, reason, opening. *(unseasonableness, frustration, untimeliness.)*

occult—*adj.* hidden, mysterious, dark, mystic, unknown, latent, unrevealed, secret, supernatural. *(plain, clear, exposed, aware, open, developed, patent, familiar.)*

occupation—*n.* avocation, usurpation, tenure, pursuit, business, career, holding, employment, possession, encroachment, calling, trade.

(vacancy, abandonment, resignation, loafing, idleness, leisure, vacation.)

odd—*adj.* sole, remaining, alone, fragmentary, singular, queer, fantastical, nondescript, unique, unmatched, over, uneven, peculiar, quaint, uncommon. *(consociate, balanced, integrant, common, regular, systematic, normal, aggregate, matched, squared, even, usual.)*

odious—*adj.* offensive, abominable, repugnant, hated, hateful, detestable. *(grateful, acceptable, agreeable, delectable, pleasant, delightful.)*

odorous—*adj.* redolent, scented, fragrant, odoriferous, aromatic, heady, perfumed, spicy, ambrosial. *(smelly, noesome, rancid, noxious, malodorous, fetid.)*

offense—*n.* sin, umbrage, misdeed, wrong, outrage, trespass, vice, misdemeanor, attack, crime, transgression, injury, affront, insult, indignity. *(innocence, virtue, guiltlessness, defense, honor.)*

offensive—*adj.* obnoxious, displeasing, fetid, repugnant, unsavory, aggressive, distasteful, foul. *(grateful, pleasant, amiable, savory, defensive.)*

offer—*v.* exhibit, present, extend, volunteer, donate, propose, proffer, tender, adduce. *(withdraw, retain, divert, deny, withhold, retract, alienate.)*

office—*n.* duty, function, station, post, incumbency, service, appointment, employment, business. *(vacancy, sinecure, loafing, resignation, leisure.)*

officious—*adj.* interfering, forward, intermeddling, snooping, meddling, pushing, intrusive. *(negligent, unofficious, modest, reticent, backward, remiss, retiring.)*

often—*adv.* repeatedly, habitually, frequently. *(seldom, infrequently, scarcely.)*

old—*adj.* pristine, ancient, antiquated, senile, sedate, antique, aged, long-standing, preceding, obsolete. *(young, fresh, immature, subsequent, current, youthful, recent, modern, new-fashioned.)*

ominous—*adj.* suggestive, foreboding, unpropitious, sinister, portentous, threatening, premonitory. *(propitious, encouraging, promising, auspicious.)*

oncoming—*adj.* impending, imminent, approaching, looming, immediate, arriving, growing, successive, developing. *(retiring, distant, subsiding, retreating, receding, remote.)*

ongoing—*adj.* progressing, growing, continuing, advancing, prosperous, successful, viable, evolving, proceeding, unfolding. *(declining, flagging, terminating, abortive, concluding, regressive, deteriorating.)*

onslaught—*n.* assult, foray, raid, invasion, charge, offense, encounter, coup, aggression. *(retreat, stampede, recession, flight, counterattack, defense.)*

opaque—*adj.* murky, dense, clouded, obscure, impervious, hazy, muddy, nontranslucent. *(transparent, shiny, clear, lucid, limpid, translucent, pellucid.)*

open—*v.* lay-open, expose, disclose, begin, unfasten, commence, unclose, lay bare, explain, initiate. *(shut up, inclose, misinterpret, cover, seal, close, conceal, mystify, conclude.)*

open—*adj.* free, unshut, public, unrestricted, unaffected, accessible, barefaced, above-board, available, unclosed, frank, unsettled, unbarred, undetermined, genuine, liberal, candid, ingenuous, unfolded, unreserved, undisguised. *(closed, unavailable, close, reserved, determined, blocked, inaccessible, barred, shut, secretive, settled.)*

opening—*n.* gap, space, chasm, initiation, inauguration, start, fissure, beginning, aperture, hole, opportunity, commencement, chink. *(obstruction, end, unreasonableness, inopportuneness, termination, conclusion, close, blockage, occlusion, stopgap, contretemps, enclosure.)*

operation—*n.* action, production, performance, manipulation, agency, exercise, influence, functioning *(inaction, cessation, inoperativeness, inefficiency, powerlessness, rest, inefficacy, misoperation, repose.)*

opinion—*n.* view, notion, idea, impression, theory, sentiment, conviction, judgment, estimation. *(actuality, fact, act, certainty, reality, happening, deed.)*

opportune—*adj.* auspicious, apt, favorable, timely, seasonable, convenient, fortunate, appropriate, suitable, proper. *(untimely, unfortunate, inopportune, unseasonable, inconvenient, unsuitable.)*

opposition—*n.* hostility, obstruction, antagonism, resistance, obstacle, rejection, aversion. *(cooperation, attraction, collaboration, combination, synergism, approval.)*

opposite—*adj.* adverse, opposed, inconsistent, contrary, counter, facing, repugnant, irreconcilable, antagonistic, contradictory. *(coincident, similar, identical, consentaneous, agreeing.)*

oppressive—*adj.* overpowering, galling, grinding, tyrannical, heavy, unjust, extortionate. *(just, lenient, compassionate, light.)*

oratorical—*adj.* eloquent, rhetorical, sermonizing, declamatory, orotund, elecutionary, bombastic. *(intimate, chatty, conversational, informal.)*

order—*n.* condition, direction, grade, decree, series, injunction, command, system, arrangement, sequence, rank, class, method, succession, precept. *(mess, jumble, chaos, disorder, anarchy.)*

order—*v.* dispose, adjust, command, ordain, appoint, mandate, manage, arrange, regulate, direct, classify, enjoin, prescribe. *(confusion, inversion, disorder, scramble, disarrangement, unsettlement, execution.)*

ordinary—*adj.* wonted, plain, commonplace, matter of fact, habitual, settled, conventional, inferior, humdrum. *(unusual, rare, superior, extraordinary, uncommon.)*

organization—*n.* form, method, construction, structure. *(disorder, disorganization, confusion.)*

origin—*n.* commencement, cause, rise, inception, beginning, source, spring, derivation. *(conclusion, extinction, finish, termination.)*

original—*adj.* initiatory, peculiar, ancient, first, fundamental, primary, primordial, pristine, former. *(terminal, later, ultimate, derivative, subsequent, modern.)*

ostentatious—*adj.* showy, flashy, pretentious, flamboyant, immodest, garish, grandiose, overdone, gaudy. *(modest, plain, inconspicuous, reserved, somber, sedate, unpretentious.)*

ostracize—*v.* avoid, banish, expel, isolate, boycott, blackball, reject, shun, exclude, blacklist. *(accept, invite, include, welcome, embrace, acknowledge.)*

oust—*v.*dispossess, evict, dislodge, banish, remove,

eject, deprive. *(reinstate, restore, induct, install, readmit.)*

outbreak—*n.* epidemic, invasion, eruption, outburst, explosion, display, demonstration. *(recession, decline, waning, decrease, subsidence, tranquillity, quiet.)*

outcast—*n.* reprobate, vagabond, fugitive, exile, castaway, vagrant. *(hero, saint, leader, philanthropist, gentleman, queen, angel.)*

outlandish—*adj.* queer, foreign, barbarous, bizarre, rude, strange, grotesque, rustic. *(modish, ordinary, native, fashionable, commonplace.)*

outline—*n.* sketch, draft, plan, diagram, delineation, contour. *(substance, object, field, bulk, core, space, form, figure, subject, ground.)*

outrage—*n.* offense, mischief, ebullition, indignity, insult, cruelty, outbreak, wantonness, abuse, violence, affront. *(self-control, soothe, subsidence, calmness, moderation, self-restraint, coolness.)*

outrageous—*adj.* unwarrantable, wanton, nefrarious, violent, diabolical, excessive, flagrant, unjustifiable, atrocious. *(reasonable, equitable, moderate, justifiable.)*

outset—*n.* start, exordium, opening, inauguration, inception, preface, commencement, beginning. *(termination, peroration, finale, close, conclusion.)*

outward—*adj.* apparent, sensible, ostensible, extrinsic, perceptible, extraneous, external, visible, superficial, forthcoming. *(intrinsic, inner, inapparent, interior, inward, internal, withdrawn.)*

overcome—*v.* conqùer, exhaust, overwhelm, vanquish, defeat, surmount. *(capitulate to, give up, admit defeat, surrender to, give in to.)*

overflow—*v.* exuberance, deluge, surge, inundation, redundancy, superabundance. *(subsidence, dearth, deficiency, exhaustion.)*

overlook—*v.* connive, oversee, inspect, review, pardon, neglect, slight, condone, disregard, supervise, survey, excuse, forgive. *(scrutinize, mark, remember, visit, investigate.)*

oversight—*n.* omission, neglect, inadvertence, superintendence, heedless, error, mistake, slip, inspection. *(correction, attention, notice,* *diligence, scruting, emendation, mark.)*

overthrow—*v.* subvert, overturn, demolish, rout, discomfit, overset, capsize, reverse, destroy, upset, ruin, defeat, overcome, invert. *(reinstate, regenerate, revive, conserve, re-edify, restore, construct, reintegrate.)*

overwhelm—*v.* quell, drawn, swamp, inundate, crush, extinguish, subdue. *(reinvigorate, reestablish, extricate, capitulate, raise, reinstate, rescue.)*

owing—*adj.* imputable, overdue, attributable, due, ascribable. *(perchance, by accident, settled, casualty, by chance, paid.)*

own—*v.* hold, acknowledge, admit, maintain, confess, possess, have, avow. *(forfeit, disclaim, disinherit, abjure, deprive, alienate, lose, disavow, abandon, disown.)*

P

pacify—*v.* conciliate, still, quiet, placate, tranquilize, appease, calm, soothe. *(agitate, irritate, provoke, aggravate, exasperate, excite, rouse.)*

pack—*v.* compact, cook, cram, stow, compress. *(unsettle, displace, dissipate, unload, neutralize, unpack, jumble, misarrange.)*

pack—*n.* bundle, lot, load, weight, burden, package, parcel.

pain—*n.* suffering, uneasiness, labor, anguish, agony, torment, penalty, distress, grief, effort, torture. *(remuneration, delight, gratification, pleasure, relief, enjoyment, gladness, reward, ease, joy, felicity, alleviation.)*

pain—*v.* grieve, torment, hurt, agonize, torture, annoy, harass, distress, afflict, rack, trouble, aggrieve. *(please, rejoice, relieve, refresh, comfort, gratify, delight, charm, ease.)*

painful—*adj.* distressful, grievous, hurting, agonizing, afflicting, grieving, excruciating. *(soothing, painless, comforting, pleasing, enjoyable, delightful.)*

painstaking—*adj.* attentive, laborious, meticulous, careful, diligent. *(negligent, careless, sloppy, haphazard.)*

palatable—*adj.* savory, delicious, delectable, toothsome, tasteful, appetizing. *(unsavory, bitter, nauseating, distasteful, repugnant.)*

palatial—*adj.* splendid, glorious, superb, grand, imposing, luxurious, majestic, stately, grandiose. *(humble, mean, unpretentious, ramshackle.)*

pale—*adj.* wan, dim, etiolated, cadaverous, ashen, pallid, faint, undefined, sallow. *(high-colored, deep, florid, ruddy, conspicuous.)*

palliate—*v.* extenuate, minimize, excuse, soften, apologize for, mitigate, varnish, alleviate. *(inflame, intensify, magnify, exaggerate, aggravate.)*

palmy—*adj.* glorious, victorious, enjoyable, flourishing, prosperous, distinguished. *(inglorious, gloomy, unflourishing, depressed, undistinguished.)*

paltry—*adj.* shabby, trifling, shifty, pitiable, worthless, trashy, niggardly, mean, vile, shuffling, prevaricating, contemptible, beggarly. *(honorable, conscientious, straightforward, admirable, magnificent, weighty, noble, candid, determined, estimable, worthy.)*

pamper—*v.* indulge, cater to, cosset, spoil, cherish, please, satisfy, flatter, fondle, humor. *(mistreat, domineer, oppress, abuse, maltreat, bully, intimidate, chastise.)*

pang—*n.* throe, convulsion, anguish, twinge, discomfort, paroxysm, agony, smart, pain. *(enjoyment, delight, fascination, solace, refreshment, pleasure, gratification, delectation.)*

panicky—*adj.* alarmed, shocked, panic-stricken, stunned, fearful, stupefied, aghast, immobilized, speechless. *(imperturbable, cool, unruffled, steady, composed.)*

paradox—*n.* enigma, absurdity, dilemma, ambiguity, contradiction, mystery. *(proposition, truism, proverb, postulate, precept, axiom.)*

parallel—*adj.* congruous, abreast, analogous, equidistant, correspondent, correlative, concurrent. *(opposed, irrelative, divergent, distinct, different, contrariant, incongruous, unanalogous.)*

paralyze—*v.* benumb, enervate, enfeeble, stupefy, deaden, prostrate, debilitate. *(strengthen, lift up, sustain, restore, give life, nerve.)*

paramount—*adj.* principal, main, leading, dominant, superior, greatest, supreme, cardinal, primary, utmost, essential. *(minimum, immaterial, least, minor, slightest, secondary, subordinate, inconsequential.)*

pardon—*v.* condone, acquit, excuse, discharge, overlook, forgive, absolve, remit. *(visit, accuse, condemn, punish, incriminate.)*

parsimonious—*adj.* close, frugal, illiberal, miserly, stingy, sparing, penurious, niggardly. *(unsparing, extravagant, lavish, liberal, profuse.)*

part—*n.* piece, fraction, member, element, share, concern, lot, participation, party, faction, duty, ingredient, portion, side, fragment, division, constituent, ingredient, interest, behalf, item. *(completeness, integrity, mass, body, transaction, unite, affair, whole, entirety, totality, bulk, compound.)*

partake—*v.* participate, derive, share, accept, sample, enjoy. *(relinquish, cede, afford, abstain, forfeit, forego, yield.)*

partial—*adj.* local, specific, inequitable, biased, peculiar, fragmentary, restricted, favoring, unfair, particular. *(total, general, equitable, fair, thorough, unbiased, unrestricted, universal, impartial, just.)*

particular—*adj.* specific, detail, special, minute, careful, exact, precise, nice, unique, local, subordinate, partial, fastidious, scrupulous, accurate, delicate, circumstantial. *(general, uncareful, comprehensive, inexact, coarse, undiscriminating, abundant, universal, unspecial, inaccurate, unscrupulous, rough, indiscriminate.)*

partisan—*n.* follower, henchman, supporter, promoter, disciple, adherent, party man, clansman. *(renegade, apostate, maverick, independent.)*

partition—*n.* division, compartment, separation, allotment, severance, screen, barrier, enclosure, demarcation, distribution. *(non-distinction, inclusion, combination, juncture, union, incorporation, generalization, collection, non-partition, non-separation, comprehension, coalition, amalgamation, concatenation.)*

partner—*n.* sharer, colleague, confederate, partaker, spouse, collaborator, associate, coadjutor, participator, accomplice, companion. *(opponent, alien, counter-agent, rival, enemy, competitor.)*

passable—*adj.* navigable, admissible, ordinary, mediocre, traversable, tolerable, penetrable. *(impervious, inadmissible, superior, excellent, impassable, impenetrable).*

passage—*n.* thoroughfare, course, route, clause, sentence, corridor, paragraph, journey, road, avenue, channel, phrase. *(book, chapter, part, clause.)*

passionate—*adj.* fiery, emotional, excitable, avid, impassioned, eager, enthusiastic, zestful, ardent. *(apathetic, unresponsive, phlegmatic, unconcerned, serene, placid.)*

passive—*adj.* inert, unresisting, negative, patient, apathetic, inactive, quiescent, unquestioning, enduring. *(alert, positive, malcontent, impatient, aggressive, active, resistant, insubmissive, vehement.)*

pastime—*n.* entertainment, diversion, sport, relaxation, recreation, amusement, play. *(study, task, work, profession, business, labor, occupation.)*

patent—*adj.* evident, plain, apparent, obvious, indisputable. *(questionable, cryptic, ambiguous, dubious.)*

pathetic—*adj.* moving, tender, poignant, meeting, affecting, emotional. *(unimpassioned, unaffecting, humorous, ludicrous, farcical.)*

patience—*n.* resignation, perseverance, sufferance, endurance, submission. *(insubmissiveness, rebellion, impatience, resistance, exasperation, repining, inconsistency.)*

pattern—*n.* sample, exemplar, shape, mold, prototype, model, archetype, specimen, precedent, design. *(caricature, mockery, misrepresentation, perversion, monstrosity.)*

pause—*n.* cessation, halt, rest, interlude, stop, suspension, intermission. *(advancement, perseverance, continuance, furtherance.)*

pause—*v.* suspend, forbear, wait, demur, desist, cease, delay, intermit, stay, hesitate, stop. *(proceed, persist, maintain, perserve, advance, continue.)*

peace—*n.* tranquility, repose, order, reconciliation, concord, amity, quiet, calm, pacification, calmness, harmony. *(disturbance, agitation, disorder, war, variance, conflict, strife, noise, tumult, hostility, embroilment, discord.)*

peaceable—*adj.* inoffensive, peaceful, mild, serene, orderly, placid, unwarlike, quiet, innocuous, unquarrelsome. *(warlike, fierce, quarrelsome, violent, restless, chaotic, pugnacious, litigious, savage, hostile, bellicose.)*

peculiar—*adj.* personal, special, exceptional, particular, singular, strange, odd, eccentric, private, characteristic, exclusive, specific, unusual, uncommon, rare. *(common, universal, ordinary, conventional, public, general, unspecial.)*

peculiarity—*n.* individuality, idiosyncrasy, uniqueness, speciality, distinctiveness. *(universality, uniformity, homogeneity, normalcy, generality, community, homology.)*

peevish—*adj.* testy, crabby, irritable, grouchy, touchy, petulant, querulous, sullen. *(amiable, genial, complaisant, jovial, good-natured, affable.)*

penetrating—*adj.* piercing, acid, sharp, severe, pungent, caustic, biting, shrill, harsh, deafening. *(dull, muted, bland, blunt, soft, mild, shallow, apathetic, dense.)*

pensive—*adj.* dreaming, sad, wistful, melancholy, somber, serious, solemn, thoughtful, reflective. *(happy, gay, jovial, carefree, frivolous, joyous, cheerful.)*

people—*n.* community, mob, herd, vulgar, mass, inhabitants, fellow-creatures, race, society, group, nation, populace, crowd, persons, commonalty, tribe. *(nobility, ruler, gentry, oligarchy, aristocracy, government, blue bloods.)*

perceive—*v.* distinguish, observe, touch, recognize, know, detect, discern, descry, feel, see, understand. *(misobserve, misunderstand, misperceive, miss, ignore, overlook, misconceive.)*

perception—*n.* apprehension, sight, understanding, vision, discernment, cognizance. *(ignorance, misapprehension, unawareness, incognizance, misunderstanding, imperception.)*

peremptory—*adj.* express, absolute, dictatorial, imperious, positive, categorical, decisive, authoritative, dogmatic, despotic. *(entreative, mild, postulatory, untenable, docile, flexible, suggestive.)*

perfect—*adj.* complete, indeficient, absolute, impeccable, unblemished, unexceptionable, ripe, flawless, pure, consummate, full, mature, immaculate, faultless, infallible, blameless. *(meagre, scant, deficient, imperfect, fallible, marred, defective, spoilt, incomplete, faulty, short, defective, blemished, inept.)*

perfectly—*adv.* wholly, completely, exactly, impeccably, fully, accurately, entirely, totally. *(incompletely, inaccurately, defectively, imperfectly, partially.)*

perform—*v.* do, transact, enact, execute, fulfil, complete, perpetrate, accomplish, act, achieve, discharge, effect, consumate. *(mar, misexecute, misenact, spoil, neglect, miss, misperform, botch, misconduct.)*

perhaps—*adv.* peradventure, maybe, probably, possibly, perchance. *(inevitably, certainly, positively.)*

perilous—*adj.* dangerous, risky, insecure, hazardous, tricky. *(secure, certain, guarded, safe.)*

period—*n.* date, era, duration, limit, end, determination, interval, time, epoch, age, continuance, bound, conclusion. *(datelessness, infinity, illimitability, indefiniteness, beginning, indeterminateness, eternity, immemoriality, perpetuity, endlessness.)*

periodic—*adj.* recurrent, stated, systematic, alternate, calculable, regular. *(eccentric, incalculable, fitful, incessant, indeterminate, irregular, spasmodic.)*

peripheral—*adj.* borderline, marginal, surrounding, outlying, tangential, incidental, exterior, outer, surface. *(primary, basic, intrinsic, proximal, central, inner, essential.)*

permanence—*n.* endurance, stability, survival, permanency, continuance, duration, perpetuity. *(mortality, brevity, transience, evanescence.)*

pernicious—*adj.* deadly, malignant, hurtful, damaging, lethal, destructive, ruinous, fatal, harmful. *(beneficial, tonic, healthful, salubrious, innocuous, invigorating.)*

perpetual—*adj.* unceasing, eternal, unfailing, continual, incessant, infinite, constant, uninterrupted, endless, everlasting, perennial, enduring. *(periodic, temporary, failing, occasional, casual, unstable, inconstant, recurrent, transient, exhaustible, momentary.)*

perplex—*v.* puzzle, involve, complicate, bewilder, harass, nonplus, entangle, embarrass, entangle, encumber, confuse, mystify. *(enlighten, disentangle, elucidate, explain, disencumber, clear, explicate, simplify.)*

perseverance—*n.* steadfastness, indefatigability, tenacity, endurance, persistence, constancy, resolution, stamina. *(unsteadfastness, caprice, vacillation, indecision, levity, hesitation, volatility, inconstancy, fit-*

fulness, irresoluteness, wavering, variableness.)

persuade—*v.* influence, convince, urge, incite, cajole, induce, incline, dispose, allure. *(disincline, compel, mispersuade, coerce, discourage, deter, indispose, misinduce.)*

pertinent—*adj.* applicable, material, apropos, suited, relevant, apt, germane, significant, fitting, appropriate. *(foreign, irrelevant, unrelated, alien, unsuitable, extraneous, impertinent.)*

perverse—*adj.* untoward, fractious, unmanageable, crochety, forward, eccentric, stubborn, wayward, intractable. *(ductile, governable, accommodating, obliging, normal, docile, amenable, complacent, pleasant.)*

pet—*adj.* favorite, darling, dear, cherished, precious, beloved, dearest. *(despised, unloved, detested, scorned, disliked.)*

petite—*adj.* dainty, little, diminutive, small, wee, undersized, slight. *(large, big, gross, ample.)*

petition—*n.* entreaty, application, salutation, request, invocation, instance, supplication, craving, appeal, prayer. *(expostulation, command, claim, requirement, dictation, censure, deprecation, protest, injunction, demand, exaction.)*

petty—*adj.* mean, ignoble, narrow, contemptible, insignificant, small, paltry, trifling, trivial. *(large, chivalrous, broad, magnificent, great, magnanimous, liberal, noble, generous.)*

philanthropy—*n.* generosity, charity, munificence, benevolence, humanity, charitableness, beneficence. *(stinginess, cynicism, misanthropy, ill will, selfishness, hostility.)*

philosopher—*n.* savant, master, thinker, schoolman, doctor, teacher. *(sciolist, tyro, foal, dunce, simpleton, ignoramus, freshman, greenhorn, apprentice.)*

philosophical—*adj.* sound, calm, scientific, enlightened, tranquil, unprejudiced, wise, conclusive, rational, accurate. *(crude, loose, popular, sciolistic, emotional, unphilosophical, unsound, vague, inaccurate, unscientific.)*

physical—*adj.* material, tangible, corporeal, concrete, natural, visible, substantial, objective, real. *(moral, immaterial, intangible, supernatural, psychic, mental,* *intellectual, hyperphysical, invisible, unsubstantial, spiritual.)*

picture—*n.* resemblance, painting, image, photograph, engraving, likeness, drawing, representation. *(mirror, original, pattern.)*

picturesque—*adj.* seemly, scenic, pictorial, photogenic, graphic, comely, graceful, artistic. *(uncouth, dead, unpicturesque, flat, monotonous, unseemly, banal, rude, ugly, tame.)*

piece—*n.* element, fragment, portion, section, share, unit, swatch, quantity, amount, bit, division. *(whole, sum, entirety, assemblage, set, total, zero, none.)*

pinion—*v.* restrain, manacle, shackle, fetter, fashion, bind, tether, fasten, strap. *(free, release, unloose, liberate, loosen, unshackle.)*

piquant—*adj.* sharp, racy, biting, smart, keen, tart, savory, pungent, lively, severe, cutting, stimulating, stinging. *(dull, characterless, bland, insipid, tame, flat.)*

pithy—*adj.* forceful, expressive, spongy, succinct, terse, laconic, concise. *(characterless, weak, pointless, vapid, redundant, diluted, flat.)*

pity—*n.* compassion, commiseration, sympathy, empathy, condolence, mercy, tenderness, ruth. *(hard-heartedness, scorn, pitilessness, apathy, rancor, ruthlessness, cruelty, rage, relentlessness.)*

place—*v.* assign, establish, attribute, put, situate, set, locate, fix, settle, deposit. *(remove, unsettle, disestablish, misattribute, uproot, extirpate, transport, detach, disturb, disarrange, misplace, misassign, transplant, eradicate.)*

plain—*adj.* even, smooth, clear, unobstructed, manifest, obvious, simple, natural, homely, open, unembellished, artless, lucid, level, feat, unencumbered, uninterrupted, evident, unmistakable, easy, unaffected, unvarnished, unsophisticated, unreserved. *(undulating, rough, abrupt, confused, obstructed, questionable, dubious, enigmatical, obtruse, fair, sophisticated, varnished, complicated, embellished, uneven, rugged, broken, encumbered, uncertain, interrupted, ambiguous, hard, affected, beautiful, artful.)*

plan—*n.* drawing, sketch, scheme, project, strategem,

system, design, draft, contrivance, device.

plan—*v.* devise, design, picture, contrive, sketch out, hatch, illustrate. *(confuse, twist, distort, falsify, obscure, perplex.)*

platonic—*adj.* intellectual, cold, mental, ecstatic, philosophical, unsensual. *(animal, sexual, passionate, intense, ardent, sensual.)*

plausible—*adj.* superficial, unctuous, pretentious, right, colorable, probable, credible, specious, passable, fair-spoken, ostensible, apparent, feasible. *(sterling, absurd, unlikely, profound, genuine, unmistakable.)*

playful—*adj.* sportive, frolicsome, vivacious, frisky, sprightly, lively, jocund, gay. *(dull, somber, sedate, earnest, grave.)*

plea—*n.* vindication, ground, apology, request, appeal, excuse, justification, defense, entreaty. *(accusation, action, charge, impeachment, indictment.)*

pleasant—*adj.* agreeable, pleasurable, gratifying, enlivening, delicious, jocular, exquisite, congenial, merry, grateful, acceptable, desirable, cheerful, sportive, delectable, satisfactory. *(ungrateful, obnoxious, offensive, lugubrious, ill-humored, distasteful, unpleasant, disagreeable, dull, unacceptable, unlively.)*

pleasure—*n.* gratification, choice, self-indulgence, will, purpose, favor, indulgence, entertainment, enjoyment, sensuality, voluptuousness, preference, inclination, determination, satisfaction. *(suffering, trouble, self-denial, disinclination, indisposition, refusal, elation, pain, affliction, asceticism, abstinence, aversion, denial.)*

plebian—*adj.* vulgar, low-bred, ignoble, crude, low, low-born, coarse. *(noble, refined, high-bred, elite, patrician, aristocratic, high-born.)*

pliable—*adj.* limber, plastic, supple, lithe, docile, flexible, pliant. *(stiff, firm, rigid, hard, stubborn.)*

plot—*n.* plan, combination, machination, scheme, intrigue, stratagem, conspiracy.

plot—*v.* concoct, contrive, hatch, scheme, devise, conspire, frame, plan.

plump—*adj.* bloated, distended, fat, chubby, massive, swollen, portly, rotund, corpulent. *(lean, emaciated, angular, slender, skinny, thin, bony, lank, weazen.)*

plunge—*v.* dive, duck, sink, immerse, thrust under, spurt, pitch headlong, dip, douse, submerge, precipitate, overwhelm. *(issue, raise, rescue, rise, emerge, soar, extricate.)*

plural—*adj.* many, manifold, multiple, several, numerous, multiplex. *(singular, unique, solitary, lone, single, sole.)*

poetic—*adj.* lyric, creative, imaginative, inspired, metrical, dreaming, rhythmic, lilting. *(prosaic, literal, stolid, unimaginative, routine, matter-of-fact.)*

poisonous—*adj.* infectant, toxic, corruptive, noxious, malignant, peccant, pestiferous, deleterious, venomous, vicious, vitiative, baneful, morbific, virulent, mephitic. *(genial, sanative, healthful, restorative, hygeian, salubrious, wholesome, beneficial, invigorative, innoxious, remedial.)*

polite—*adj.* refined, courteous, complaisant, courtly, genteel, gracious, accomplished, elegant, well-bred, obliging, civil, polished. *(rude, ill-bred, boorish, disobliging, insolent, awkward, uncouth, discourteous, clownish.)*

politic—*adj.* wise, provident, judicious, wary, discreet, tactful, prudent, sagacious, diplomatic, cunning, well, devised. *(unwise, undiplomatic, blundering, impolitic, imprudent, improvident.)*

pompous—*adj.* gorgeous, showy, ostentatious, lofty, bombastic, stiff, pretentious, assuming, arrogant, magnificent, splendid, sumptuous, stately, grand, turgid, inflated, coxcombical. *(unobtrusive, unassuming, humbleminded, retiring, unpretending, modest, plain-mannered.)*

ponderous—*adj.* bulky, heavy, massive, cumbersome, hefty, big, weighty, enormous, awkward. *(flimsy, airy, fragile, delicate, light, small, dainty.)*

poor—*adj.* moneyless, penniless, meager, deficient, unsatisfactory, thin, bold, destitute, indigent, impecunious, weak, insufficient, faulty, inconsiderable, scanty. *(wealthy, affluent, liberal, ample, sufficient, considerable, prosperous, rich, copious, abundant, large, moneyed, satisfactory.)*

popular—*adj.* current, public, received, beloved, approved, liked, prevalent, common, vulgar, general, favorite, prevailing, wide-spread. *(restricted, detested, esoteric,* *odious, disliked, exclusive, scientific, unpopular.)*

portentous—*adj.* menacing, fateful, impending, alarming, sinister, ominous, inauspicious, prophetic. *(auspicious, cheering, comforting, encouraging, propitious.)*

positive—*adj.* actual, absolute, real, unconditional, explicit, settled, indisputable, express, assured, direct, overbearing, decisive, dogmatical, substantial, fixed, independent, unequivocal, definitive, conclusive, enacted, confident, dogmatic. *(insubstantial, fictitious, relative, dependent, implied, questionable, uncertain, indirect, suspicious, doubtful, negative, unreal, imaginary, contingent, conditional, dubious, moral, fallacious, occasional.)*

possess—*v.* enjoy, hold, own, inherit, occupy, have, entertain. *(renounce, resign, surrender, forfeit, abandon, abjure, lose, submit.)*

possible—*adj.* teasible, potential, conceivable, practicable, likely. *(impossible, impracticable, absurd, unfeasible.)*

postpone—*v.* delay, procrastinate, suspend, defer, prorogue. *(accelerate, sustain, dispatch, expedite.)*

posterity—*n.* progeny, children, issue, heirs, descendents, offspring, scions. *(forbears, ancestors, progenitors, forefathers.)*

potent—*adj.* effective, stiff, strong, powerful, compelling, powerful, impressive, serious, cogent, vigorous, solid. *(feeble, weak, mild, impotent, ineffectual, dubious, frail, inefficient.)*

poverty—*n.* need, destitution, penury, want, indigence. *(wealth, affluence, prosperity.)*

power—*n.* capacity, potentiality, strength, might, susceptibility, dominion, command, agency, rule, effectiveness, strength, faculty, capability, ability, force, energy, influence, sway, government, authority, jurisdiction. *(incapability, inability, imbecility, insusceptibility, powerlessness, subservience, feebleness, incapacity, impotence, weakness, inertness, subjection, obedience, ineffectiveness.)*

powerful—*adj.* potent, energetic, masterful, mighty, strong, puissant. *(poor, weak, feeble, fragile.)*

practice—*n.* habit, experience, action, manner, routine, performance, usage, exercise, exercitation, custom.

(dishabituation, theory, nonperformance, disuse, inexperience, speculation, abolition.)

practice—*v.* exercise, carry on, perform, deal in.

praise—*v.* laud, honor, puff, compliment, applaud, flatter, panegyrize, eulogize, commend, glorify, celebrate, extol. *(censure, reprove, disparage, blame, discommend.)*

prayer—*n.* supplication, orison, suit, worship, request, petition, entreaty, benediction. *(expostulation, restriction, disrespect, irreverence, mockery.)*

precaution—*n.* provision, anticipation, care, prudence, providence, forethought, premonition, pre-arrangement. *(improvidence, thoughtlessness, carelessness, negligence.)*

precede—*v.* forego, lead, preface, introduce, herald, usher, anticipate, head, pave the way, forerun. *(follow, result, ensue, succeed, postdate.)*

precious—*adj.* valuable, cherished, beloved, of great value, dear, priceless, costly, treasured, estimable. *(valueless, unvalued, unappreciated, useless, vile, cheap, worthless, disesteemed.)*

precise—*adj.* exact, pointed, correct, formal, scrupulous, punctilious, formal, explicit, definite, nice, accurate, particular, specific, terse, ceremonious. *(vague, rough, loose, ambiguous, informal, casual, unceremonious, indefinite, inexact, inaccurate, circumlocutory, tortuous.)*

predict—*v.* foretell, prognosticate, foreshadow, anticipate, prophesy, forecast, forebode.)

prediction—*n.* prognostication, fore-announcement, foretelling, presage, foreshowing, augury, anticipation, prophecy, vaticination, premonstration, forebodement. *(relation, account, report, narration, history, description.)*

preface—*n.* proem, prologue, premiss, preliminary, introduction, prelude, preamble. *(sequel, epilogue, supplement, postscript, peroration, appendix.)*

prefer—*v.* elect, fancy, advance, favor, further, choose, select, promote. *(postpone, withhold, depress, exclude, reject, defer, degrade.)*

prejudice—*n.* prejudgment, bias, injury, impairment, partiality, damage, preconception, prepossession, predisposition, unfairness, harm, detriment, disadvantage. *(fairness, judgment, advantage, detachment, impartiality.)*

premature—*adj.* crude, untimely, precipitate, rash, inopportune, unseasonable, hasty, precocious, unauthenticated, too early. *(timely, opportune, mature, ripe, seasonable.)*

premium—*n.* guerdon, douceur, bribe, bonus, bounty, reward, remuneration, encouragement, enhancement, recompense, prize. *(fine, mulct, penalty, amercement, forfeit.)*

preparation—*n.* readiness, provision, development, apprenticeship. *(without, provision, unpreparedness, unawareness.)*

prepare—*v.* adapt, adjust, fit, arrange, lay, equip, ready, qualify, groom, provide, order, plan, furnish. *(misadapt, derange, demolish, disconcert, confuse, misfit, misprovide, disarrange, subvert.)*

prepossessing—*adj.* alluring, winning, engaging, personable, attractive, charming, taking. *(sinister, repulsive, unpleasant, unattractive.)*

preposterous—*adj.* exorbitant, absurd, foolish, fantastic, ridiculous, monstrous, unreasonable, irrational. *(due, sound, reasonable, right, orderly, sensible, just, fair, moderate, judicious.)*

presence—*n.* influence, closeness, attendance, nearness, intercourse. *(absence, distance, remoteness, separation, distraction.)*

preserve—*v.* guard, keep safe, protect, rescue, shield, spare, defend, save, uphold, maintain. *(destroy, damage, ruin, dilapidate.)*

president—*n.* moderator, chairman, superintendent, commander-in-chief, principal. *(subordinate, corporation, ward, component, institution, member, constituent, society.)*

press—*v.* crowd, force, squeeze, compress, constrain, instigate, impress, encroach, harass, palpate, urge, compel, crush, express, hurry, inculcate, throng. *(inhibit, entice, solicit, skim, free, ease, relieve, touch, relax, persuade, allure, graze, liberate, avoid, manipulate.)*

presume—*v.* anticipate, venture, conjecture, deem, surmise, assume, suppose, apprehend, take for granted, believe. *(deduce, argue, withdraw, distrust, conclude, infer, prove, retire, hesitate.)*

pretend—*v.* simulate, allege, propound, profess, imitate, feign, offer, exhibit, affect. *(unmask, test, refute, verify, detect, substantiate, corroborate.)*

pretense—*n.* pretext, simulation, mask, show, plea, make believe, pretension, mimicry, excuse, fabrication, cloak, color, garb, assumption, hoax. *(reality, simplicity, guilelessness, veritableness, fact, frankness, verity, truth, candor, openness, actuality.)*

pretty—*adj.* attractive, trim, pleasing, fine, delicate, comely, handsome, neat, tasteful, beautiful. *(grotesque, homely, ugly, ungainly, plain.)*

prevailing—*adj.* ruling, operative, prevalent, ascendant, most, common, current, controlling, influential, predominant, rife, most general. *(diminishing, powerless, uneffectual, mitigated, subordinate.)*

prevent—*v.* obstruct, neutralize, thwart, anticipate, frustrate, checkmate, preclude, hinder, bar, nullify, intercept, forefend, obviate. *(aid, expedite, instigate, advance, induce, produce, promote, facilitate, encourage, accelerate, cause.)*

price—*n.* figure, compensation, appraisement, expenditure, worth, cost, charge, expense, value. *(discount, remittance, reduction, abatement, donation, allowance.)*

pride—*n.* haughtiness, self-exaltation, conceit, vanity, loftiness, lordliness, arrogance, gratification. *(meekness, self-distrust, humility, lowliness, modesty.)*

priggish—*adj.* dandified, affected, conceited, pedantic, coxcombical, foppish, prim. *(sensible, simple-minded, casual, plain, unaffected, informal.)*

prim—*adj.* precise, starched, self-conscious, priggish, puritanical, formal, demure, stiff, unbending. *(easy, unaffected, free, libertine, naive, unformal, genial, natural.)*

primary—*adj.* original, elementary, chief, important, primitive, first, embryonic, pristine, earliest, main, principal, leading. *(subordinate, unimportant, subsequent, later, following, secondary, posterior, inferior.)*

primitive—*adj.* primeval, pristine, simple, archaic, aboriginal, old-fashioned, quaint, unsophisticated. *(new-fangled, modish, civilized, modern, sophisticated.)*

princely—*adj.* munificent, superb, regal, supreme, distinguished, imperial, august, magnificent, royal. *(mean, ig-*

noble, beggarly, niggardly, vulgar.)

principal—*adj.* first, leading, primary, pre-eminent, main, paramount, prominent, highest, chief, foremost. *(subordinate, minor, supplemental, auxiliary, peripheral, inferior, secondary subject.)*

principle—*n.* origin, cause, substance, power, truth, law, axiom, rule, postulate, ethics, source, motive, energy, element, faculty, tenet, doctrine, maxim. *(manifestation, action, development, exercise, formation, dishonesty, exhibition, application, issue, operation.)*

private—*adj.* peculiar, secret, retired, secluded, privy, special, individual, not public. *(public, unconcealed, general, open, available.)*

privilege—*n.* immunity, right, advantage, exemption, priority, prerogative, franchise, liberty, claim. *(disqualification, prohibition, subordination, inhibition, disfranchisement, exclusion.)*

prize—*n.* spoil, prey, trophy, guerdon, honors, palm, award, booty, plunder, forage, laurels, premium, ovation. *(forfeiture, penalty, sacrifice, failure, stigma, mulct, taint, loss, fine, amercement, disappointment, brand, infamy.)*

probability—*n.* presumption, chance, expectation, verisimilitude, appearance, likelihood. *(improbability, inconceivableness, unlikelihood, impossibility, doubtfulness.)*

probable—*adj.* presumable, reasonable, anticipated, likely, credible. *(incredible, unlikely, unreasonable, implausible.)*

problem—*n.* question, dilemma, puzzle, conundrum, query, riddle, difficulty, predicament, paradox, mystery. *(answer, solution, response, discovery, finding out, deciphering.)*

proceed—*v.* pass, progress, issue, flow, initiate, arise, move, advance, continue, emanate. *(deviate, stand, stop, stay, discontinue, retire, ebb, regress, recede, retreat, desist.)*

procession—*n.* march, file, train, cavalcade, parade, retinue, caravan, cortege. *(herd, rush, mob, rout, rabble, disorder, confusion, disarray.)*

prodigal—*adj.* profuse, reckless, squandering, profligate, improvident, lavish, extravagent, wasteful. *(saving, economical, miserly, close-*

fisted, cautious, frugal, hoarding, niggardly, close.)

prodigious—*adj.* portentous, vast, astounding, monstrous, huge, surprising, extraordinary, marvelous, wonderful, gigantic, enormous, amazing, remarkable. *(common-place, usual, moderate, picayune, ordinary, every-day, familiar.)*

produce—*n.* yield, profit, effect, consequence, amount, product, agricultural products, fruit, result.

produce—*v.* bear, afford, create, yield, prolong, render, cause, furbish, lengthen, exhibit, originate, extend. *(retain, withhold, destroy, curtail, contract, stifle, withdraw, neutralize, annihilate, shorten, reduce, subvert.)*

product—*n.* result, consequence, emanation, generate, work, fruit, issue, effect. *(principle, motive, operation, tendency, cause, law, power, energy, action, force.)*

production—*n.* evolution, genesis, manufacture, creation, growth, origination, formation, product. *(consumption, use.)*

profane—*v.* secular, unsanctified, irreligious, ungodly, godless, blasphemous, pervert, temporal, unconsecrated, unholy, irreverent, wicked, impious. *(consecrated, spiritual, reverent, godly, devout, glorify, holy, sacred, sanctified, religious, pious.)*

profess—*v.* avow, own, pretend, lay claim to, certify, declare, acknowledge, confess, proclaim. *(suppress, disavow, renounce, rebuff, abjure, conceal, disown, repudiate.)*

profit—*n.* emolument, avail, benefit, use, value, gain, advantage, acquisition, service, improvement. *(detriment, disadvantage, harm, waste, loss, damage.)*

profitable—*adj.* advantageous, beneficial, productive, gainful, lucrative, worthwhile, desirable, useful, remunerative. *(disadvantageous, detrimental, unprofitable, vain, unproductive, damaging, useless, unremunerative, unprofitable, undesirable, unbeneficial, fruitless.)*

program—*n.* notice, catalogue, performance, calendar, plan, advertisement, schedule. *(rehearsal, resume,* précis, recital, review, analysis, repetition.)

progress—*n.* advance, proceeding, journey, speed, progression, growth, advancement, movement, way, proficiency. *(stoppage, stay, delay, failure, relapse, retardation, retreat, retrogression.)*

project—*n.* purpose, scheme, device, undertaking, venture, plan, design, contrivance. *(chance, hazard, peril.)*

prominent—*adj.* protuberant, embossed, manifest, eminent, main, leading, distinctive, jutting, protrusive, relieved, extended, conspicuous, distinguished, important, characteristic. *(concave, indented, engraved, withdrawn, minor, unimportant, undistinguishable, secondary, subordinate, receding, rebated, hallowed, entailed, average, inconspicuous, indistinctive.)*

promiscuous—*adj.* confused, unselected, undistributed, common, casual, unordered, heterogeneous, mingled, undistinguished, unarranged, unassorted, unreserved, disorderly. *(select, arranged, reserved, exclusive, homogeneous, nice, sorted, orderly, distributed, assorted.)*

promise—*v.* engage, covenant, stipulate, guarantee, pledge, assure, warrant.

promise—*n.* assurance, pledge, covenant, stipulation, engagement, word, oath.

promote—*v.* further, excite, raise, prefer, encourage, aid, advance, exalt, elevate. *(repress, check, depress, dishonor, disable, discourage, hinder, allay, degrade.)*

prompt—*v.* alert, active, brisk, unhesitating, incite, ready, responsive, quick, apt. *(sluggish, inactive, deter, unready, irresponsive.)*

pronounce—*v.* utter, propound, express, assert, enunciate, proclaim, articulate, declare, affirm, deliver. *(mispropound, suppress, silence, swallow, mumble, subdue, mispronounce, misaffirm, stifle, choke, gabble.)*

proof—*n.* trial, criterion, test, establishment, demonstration, testimony, verification, essay, examination, comprobation, evidence, scrutiny, authentication. *(failure, short-coming, undemonstrativeness, error, reprobation, disproof, invalidity, fallacy.)*

proper—*adj.* appertinent, own, special, adapted, suitable, just, equitable, decent, fit, applicable, peculiar, personal, constitutional, befitting, suited, appropriate, fair, right, becoming. *(inappertinent, universal, unbefitting, unsuited, indecent, inappropriate, improper, common, in-*

congruous, alien, nonspecial, unadopted, unsuitable, wrong, unbecoming, unorthodox.)

property—*n.* attribute, nature, possessions, wealth, gear, ownership, acquisitions, quality, peculiarity, characteristic, goods, estate, resources.

proportion—*n.* relation, distribution, symmetry, uniformity, harmony, correlation, adaptation, rate, adjustment, interrelationship. *(misadjustment, disparity, disorder, disproportion, irregularity, misproportion, incongruity, disharmony, irrelation.)*

propose—*v.* tender, bring forward, intend, propound, design, move, suggest, offer, proffer, purpose, mean. *(denounce, deprecate, dispute, discount, deny, protest, contradict.)*

prosaic—*adj.* matter-of-fact, prolix, unimaginative, dull, tedious. *(animated, lively, eloquent, provocative, graphic, poetic, interesting, fervid.)*

prospect—*n.* vision, landscape, anticipation, assurance, view, field, hope, probability, promise. *(dimness, darkness, veiling, hopelessness, shadow, improbability, viewlessness, obscurity, cloud, occultation.)*

prospectus—*n.* plan, announcement, scheme, brochure, synopsis, program, catalogue, bill, compendium. *(proceeding, subject, transaction, enactment.)*

prosperity—*n.* weal, good fortune, good luck, affluence, success, welfare, well-being. *(woe, failure, depression, reverse, unsuccess, adversity.)*

protect—*v.* fortify, shield, cover, save, screen, vindicate, defend, guard, preserve, secure. *(endanger, abandon, forsake, expose, betray, imperil.)*

prototype—*n.* original, first, norm, example, precedent, sample, absolute, pattern, model. *(imitation, rerun, facsimile, reproduction, copy.)*

protracted—*adj.* prolonged, lengthy, extensive, extended, diffuse, rambling, interminable. *(short, concise, brief, abbreviated, limited.)*

proud—*adj.* haughty, supercilious, boastful, vain, elated, lofty, magnificent, appreciative, self-conscious, arrogant, imperious, presumptuous, prideful, imposing, ostentatious, self-satisfied. *(humble, unpresuming, lowly, unimposing, humiliated,* *deferential, affable, meek, mean, ashamed.)*

prove—*n.* assay, establish, ascertain, show, examine, validate, attest to, verify, try, test, demonstrate, argue, confirm, substantiate. *(pretermit, misindicate, disprove, disestablish, invalidate, pass, misdemonstrate, refute, contradict, neutralize.)*

proverbial—*adj.* current, customary, unquestioned, notorious, acknowledged. *(unfounded, suspected, unfamiliar, dubious, questionable, suspicious.)*

provide—*v.* arrange, afford, cater, contribute, get, produce, stipulate, donate, prepare, procure, supply, yield, furnish, agree, collect. *(neglect, withhold, appropriate, deny, divert, retain, mismanage, disallow, overlook, misprovide, refuse, alienate, misemploy.)*

province—*n.* region, section, domain, precinct, territory, tract, department, sphere. *(capital, metropolis, center, center of government.)*

provision, provisions—*n.* arrangement, supply, food, victuals, eatables, rations, preparations, produce, anticipation, supplies, edibles. *(pittance, misprovision, thoughtlessness, destitution, dearth, dole, neglect, scantiness, forgetfulness, want, oversight, starvation.)*

provoke—*v.* summon, irritate, challenge, impel, exasperate, tantalize, infuriate, educe, rouse, excite, vex, offend, anger. *(relegate, soothe, propitiate, conciliate, allay, pacify.)*

proxy—*n.* substitution, agent, representative, commissioner, delegate, deputy, agency, representation, substitute, surrogate, lieutenant. *(personality, person, deputer, principalship, principal, authority, superior.)*

prudent—*adj.* wary, circumspect, careful, vigilant, judicious, wise, cautious, discreet. *(unwary, indiscreet, uncircumspect, imprudent, reckless, foolish, incautious, rash, audacious, silly, liberal.)*

prudish—*adj.* over-modest, squeamish, demure, puritanical, coy, over-nice, reserved. *(promiscuous, free, uninhibited.)*

public—*adj.* notorious, social, open, exoteric, generally known, universal, common, national, general. *(secret, domestic, close, solitary, individual, parochial, private, secluded, personal.)*

pull—*v.* drag, extract, haul, tug, magnetize, pluck, draw, adduce. *(eject, propel, thrust, push, extrude.)*

punch—*v.* pierce, pommel, bore, strike, perforate, poke, puncture. *(plug, bung, stop, seal, snap.)*

punish—*v.* castigate, correct, discipline, scourge, penalize, chastise, chasten, whip. *(recompense, indemnify, exonerate, reward, remunerate.)*

pupil—*n.* learner, tyro, ward, disciple, scholar, student, novice. *(master, adept, tutor, guardian, teacher, proficient.)*

puppy—*n.* fop, prig, coxcomb, youth, dude. *(clown, lout, boor, bumpkin.)*

pure—*adj.* unmixed, genuine, mere, quietless, unadulterated, unsullied, chaste, clean, immaculate, unspotted, sheer, innocent, unpolluted, clear, simple, absolute, uncorrupted, unblemished, real, spotless, undefiled, guileless. *(turbid, adulterated, corrupt, stained, defiled, guilty, faulty, foul, impure, mixed.)*

purpose—*n.* design, meaning, object, end, point, objective, resolve, intention, mind, view, aim, scope. *(fortune, accident, lot, lottery, incident, hit, chance, fate, hazard, casualty.)*

purpose—*v.* determine, resolve, propose, persist, intend, design, mean. *(risk, revoke, venture, jeopardize, stake, chance, hazard, miscalculate.)*

push—*v.* drive, shove, press against, butt, urge, accelerate, jostle, reduce, press, impel, propel, thrust, expedite. *(draw, adduce, pull, drag, haul.)*

put—*v.* lay, propose, situate, place, set. *(raise, transfer, dislodge, withdraw, remove, displace.)*

putrid—*adj.* rancid, decaying, spoiled, moldering, moldy, rotten, contaminated, decomposed, bad. *(pure, fresh, wholesome, healthy, untainted.)*

puzzle—*n.* bewilderment, confusion, intricacy, enigma, embarrassment, doubt, conundrum, labyrinth, quandary. *(solution, extrication, lucidity, clue, disentanglement, explanation.)*

puzzle—*v.* perplex, bewilder, mystify, complicate, confuse, pose, embarrass, confound. *(instruct, clarify, illumine, enlighten.)*

Q

quack—*n.* mountebank, impostor, humbug, fraud, empiric, charlatan, pretender. *(gull, victim, dupe, prey.)*

quaint—*adj.* recondite, elegant, odd, affected, archaic, singular, charming, old-fashioned, curious, abstruse, nice, whimsical, antique, fanciful. *(ordinary, coarse, modern, fashionable, current, dowdy, commonplace, usual, common, modish.)*

qualified—*adj.* adapted, suitable, eligible, fitted, competent. *(unable, deficient, impotent, inept.)*

quality—*n.* character, attribute, disposition, sort, description, power, nature, stature, tendency, condition, property, peculiarity, temper, kind, capacity, virtue. *(heterogeneousness, incapacity, indistinctiveness, disqualification, disability, mediocrity, anomalousness, nondescript, weakness, triviality, ineffectiveness, negation.)*

qualm—*n.* scruple, uneasiness, regret, pang, twinge, fear, compunction, apprehension, uncertainty. *(security, comfort, firmness, confidence, invulnerability, easiness.)*

quandry—*n.* dilemma, perplexity, entanglement, impasse, crisis, plight, predicament, fix, doubt. *(relief, assurance, ease, certainty, plain sailing.)*

quantity—*n.* amount, size, measure, portion, magnitude, share, volume, division, bulk, sum, aggregate, part. *(deficiency, want, scantiness, loss, diminution, wear, dearth, margin, waste, deduction, inadequacy, leakage, insufficiency, deterioration.)*

quarrel—*n.* altercation, squabble, tumult, wrangle, disagreement, hostility, embroilment, broil, controversy, brawl, affray, feud, dispute, variance, misunderstanding, quarreling, bickering. *(conversation, pleasantry, friendliness, amity, agreement, goodwill, confabulation, chat, conciliation, peace.)*

quarrelsome—*adj.* irascible, litigious, brawling, hot-tempered, choleric, irritable, argumentative, petulant, pugnacious, fiery, contentious. *(amenable, mild, unquarrelsome, conciliatory, bland, meek, suave, accommodating, peaceable, genial, inoffensive.)*

quarter—*n.* district, territory, forbearance, source, pity, region, locality, mercy.

(mercilessness, cruelty, pitilessness, extermination, ruthlessness, unsparingness.)

queasy—*adj.* sick, nauseated, edgy, squeamish, restless, upset, giddy. *(relaxed, content, comfortable, easy, untroubled.)*

queer—*adj.* whimsical, cross, crochety, eccentric, weird, odd, quaint, strange, singular. *(common, familiar, orthodox, customary, ordinary, usual.)*

quell—*v.* quiet, subdue, reduce, disperse, scatter, vanquish, pacify, tranquillize, curb. *(excite, stimulate, kindle, incite, spur, irritate, enrage.)*

question—*v.* inquire, doubt, ask, dubitate, dispute, catechize, interrogate, investigate, controvert. *(state, pronounce, concede, affirm, allow, answer, dictate, assert, enunciate, grant, endorse.)*

question—*n.* interrogation, inquiry, scrutiny, topic, investigation, doubt, debate. *(response, answer, admission, retort, concession, reply, solution, explanation.)*

questionable—*adj.* dubious, suspicious, disputable, uncertain, hypothetical, doubtful, problematical, debatable. *(evident, obvious, unequivocal, indisputable, certain, self-evident.)*

quick—*adj.* rapid, expeditious, hasty, ready, sharp, adroit, keen, active, nimble, agile, sprightly, fast, intelligent, precipitous, irasible, speedy, swift, prompt, clever, shrewd, fleet, brisk, lively, alert, transient. *(tardy, inert, dull, gradual, insensitive, slow, sluggish, inactive.)*

quiet—*n.* repose, calm, rest, pacification, peace, stillness, tranquillity, appeasement, silence. *(motion, agitation, disturbance, tumult, uproar, unrest, noise, excitement, turmoil.)*

quiet—*v.* appease, pacify, lull, soothe, silence, calm, allay, still, hush, tranquilize. *(excite, agitate, urge, blare, goad, rouse, disturb, stir.)*

quit—*v.* resign, relinquish, cease, release, give up, forsake, leave, abandon, discharge, surrender, depart from. *(occupy, bind, haunt, continue, enter, seek, invade, enforce.)*

quite—*adv.* entirely, wholly, altogether, fully, totally, perfectly, completely, truly. *(imperfectly, scarcely, insufficiently, partially, hardly, barely.)*

quixotic—*adj.* impractical, idealistic, romantic, lofty, fantastic, chivalrous, visionary. *(practical, prosaic, pragmatic, realistic, hardheaded.)*

quote—*v.* name, plead, note, cite, repeat, paraphrase, adduce, allege. *(refute, oppose, traverse, misadduce, deny, rebut, disprove, retort, contradict, misquote.)*

R

rabid—*adj.* zealous, dedicated, fanatical, bigoted, unreasonable, deranged, frantic, maniacal, frenzied. *(reasonable, normal, moderate, sound, sober, lucid, rational, sane, steady.)*

racy—*adj.* fresh, piquant, spicy, smart, vivacious, animated, rich, fine-flavored, pungent, spirited, lively. *(stupid, flavorless, languid, dull, morose.)*

radiant—*adj.* luminous, bright, lustrous, sparkling, shining, brilliant, ecstatic, beaming, elated, merry. *(dull, murky, dim, gloomy, downcast, somber, sad, blurred.)*

radical—*adj.* fundamental, natural, unsparing, entire, immanent, underived, profound, deep-seated, original, thorough-going, extreme, innate, essential, ingrained. *(ascititious, partial, superficial, conservative, derived, traditional, acquired, adventitious, extraneous, moderate.)*

rage—*n.* rabidity, indignation, fury, anger, dudgeon, passion, ferocity, wrath, choler, frenzy, ire, mania, madness. *(moderation, temperateness, quiescence, assuagement, mildness, serenity, softness, reason, gentleness, calmness, mitigation.)*

rage—*v.* storm, be furious, rave, seethe, be violent, fume. *(be peaceful, be calm, mollify, be composed, lull.)*

raise—*v.* heave, exalt, promote, lift, enhance, rouse, call forth, rear, collect, erect, propagate, intensify, elevate, advance, heighten, awaken, excite, cultivate, produce, summon, originate. *(cast, degrade, dishonor, depreciate, compose, calm, destroy, disband, hush, neutralize, curtail, confute, lay, depress, retard, lull, lower, quiet, blight, disperse, stifle, silence.)*

rampant—*adj.* wild, flagrant, excessive, unrestrained, prevalent, menacing, boisterous, ungovernable, comprehensive, universal. *(bland, mild, calm, decorous, local, moderate, contained, dispassionate.)*

range—*n.* dispose, place, collocate, concatenate, stroll, scope, rove, rank, class, order, file, ramble. *(disconnection, derangement, disturbance.)*

rank—*n.* line, order, grade, series, dignity, row, tier, degree. *(disorder, incontinuity, intermission, plebianism, commonalty, breach, hiatus, disconnection, solution, meanness.)*

rank—*adj.* exuberant, excessive, proliferating, luxuriant, rampant, extreme. *(sparse, fragrant, scanty, pure, wholesome.)*

rankle—*v.* smoulder, irritate, disquiet, embitter, fester, burn, gall. *(cool, calm, compose, improve, heal, close, quiet.)*

rapid—*adj.* swift, accelerated, instantaneous, flying, quick, speedy. *(tardy, cumbrous, deliberate, slow, lazy, retarded.)*

rapture—*n.* delight, exultation, joy, ecstasy, felicity, bliss, passion, rejoicing, transport. *(misery, revulsion, disgust, distress, discontent, affliction.)*

rare—*adj.* choice, excellent, volatile, exceptional, unusual, uncommon, extraordinary, dispersed, precious, sporadic, scarce, infrequent, few, sparse, singular, incomparable, unique, valuable, thin. *(frequent, numerous, ordinary, regular, dense, common, worthless, valueless, mediocre, abundant, mean, usual, crowded, vulgar, cheap.)*

rash—*adj.* audacious, precipitate, foolhardy, adventurous, indiscreet, overventuresome, unwary, impulsive, headstrong, hasty, reckless, careless, thoughtless, venturesome, heedless, incautious. *(cautious, discreet, dubitating, reluctant, prudent, timid, wary, calculating, unventuresome, hesitating.)*

rate—*n.* impost, duty, allowance, quota, price, status, tax, assessment, standard, ratio, worth, value. *(rebate, discount, allowance, percentage.)*

rate—*v.* calculate, value, abuse, evaluate, appraise, compute, estimate, scold. *(repose, be quiescent, loaf.)*

rational—*adj.* sound, reasoning, judicious, sensible, equitable, fair, logical, sane, intelligent, reasonable, sober, probable, moderate. *(unsound, silly, absurd, fanciful, preposterous, unreasonable, exorbitant, emotional, insane, weak, unintelligent,* *injudicious, extravagant, unreasoning, irrational.)*

ravel—*v.* undo, unwind, fray, disentangle, separate, untwist. *(complicate, confuse, mend, entangle, conglomerate.)*

ravish—*v.* transport, enrapture, violate, debauch, captivate, entrance, enchant, charm, outrage. *(disgust, pique, rile, displease, provoke, harass.)*

raw—*adj.* unprepared, unripe, unseasoned, fresh, unpracticed, bare, exposed, chill, piercing, crude, uncooked, unfinished, bleak, inexperienced, green, untried, bald, galled, unrefined. *(dressed, finished, cooked, mature, seasoned, expert, healed, habituated, practiced, tried, genial, processed, prepared, ripe, mellow, experienced, adept, familiar, trained, covered, balmy.)*

reach—*v.* thrust, obtain, attain, grasp, strain, lengthen, aim, extend, stretch, arrive at, gain, penetrate. *(stop, revert, miss, drop, recoil, fail, cease, rebate.)*

read—*v.* interpret, unravel, recognize, comprehend, learn, persue, decipher, discover. *(misinterpret, misobserve, misunderstand, overlook.)*

ready—*adj.* responsive, alert, speedy, dexterous, skillful, expert, easy, fitted, disposed, free, compliant, quick, accessible, prompt, expeditious, unhesitating, apt, handy, facile, opportune, prepared, willing, cheerful. *(tardy, hesitating, dubitating, unhandy, remote, unavailable, unsuited, unwilling, unprepared, grudging, incompliant, difficult, unready, slow, reluctant, awkward, clumsy, inaccessible, inopportune, unfitted, indisposed, constrained, unaccommodating, irresponsive, doubtful.)*

real—*adj.* veritable, authentic, true, developed, tangible, actual, existent, legitimate, genuine. *(imaginary, non-existent, false, adulterated, pretended, possible, counterfeit, fictitious, unreal, untrue, artificial, assumed, potential.)*

really—*adv.* truly, unquestionably, indubitably, veritably, indeed. *(possibly, falsely, fictitiously, doubtfully, questionably, perhaps, untruly.)*

reason—*n.* account, explanation, proof, understanding, rationality, propriety, order, sake, target, purpose, ground, cause, motive, apology, reasoning, right, justice, object. *(pretense, falsifica-*

tion, disproof, absurdity, irrationality, unreason, unfairness, aimlessness, nonsense, unaccountableness, pretext, misinterpretation, misconception, unreasonableness, fallacy, wrong, impropriety, folly.)

reason—*v.* discuss, infer, deduce, conclude, cogitate, debate, argue. *(back up, comply, abet, encourage, agree.)*

reassure—*v.* restore, inspirit, countenance, bolster, rally, encourage, animate. *(cow, intimidate, unnerve, discountenance, discourage, brow-beat.)*

rebuff—*v.* repel, check, oppose, reject, rebuke, repulse, snub. *(encourage, welcome, abet, accept, support.)*

rebuff—*n.* discouragement, check, refusal, rebuke, repulsion. *(encouragement, spur, acceptance, welcome.)*

rebuke—*v.* chide, reprimand, berate, censure, reprove, rebuff. *(encourage, applaud, extol, incite, approve, eulogize.)*

receipt—*n.* reception, acknowledgement, acquisition, voucher, custody. *(rejection, exclusion, emission, expulsion.)*

receive—*v.* accept, hold, assent to, acquire, take, admit, entertain. *(impart, reject, emit, expend, give, afford, discharge.)*

reception—*n.* admittance, acceptation, salutation, entertainment, admission, acceptance. *(protest, rejection, dismissal, renunciation, abjuration, denial, repudiation, non-acceptance, discardment, adjournment.)*

recess—*n.* nook, retirement, seclusion, vacation, depression, holiday, cavity, withdrawal, retreat, privacy. *(protrusion, publicity, promontory, work time, projection, discharge.)*

reckless—*adj.* heedless, foolhardy, rash, regardless, improvident, venturesome, careless, incautious, thoughtless, precipitate, inconsiderate. *(heedful, timid, thoughtful, provident, wary, prudent, circumspect, careful, cautious, chary, calculating, considerate.)*

reckon—*v.* calculate, regard, value, consider, infer, enumerate, judge, compute, count, estimate, account, argue. *(miscalculate, misreckon, miscompute, misestimate, miscount.)*

reclusive—*adj.* solitary, recluse, secluded, isolated, cloistered, ascetic, withdrawn, eremitic. *(sociable,* *gregarious, convivial, companionable, wordly, accessible.)*

recognize—*v.* acknowledge, know, avow, allow, discern, identify, concede, own, recollect. *(overlook, repudiate, disown, scrutinize, disallow, ignore, misobserve, disavow.)*

recollect—*v.* recall, bethink, reminisce, think of, recreate, recover, remember, bring to mind. *(lose, forget, obliterate, overlook.)*

recommend—*v.* confide, applaud, advise, sanction, commend, praise, approve. *(disapprove, warn, dissuade, disparage, condemn, deter.)*

recompense—*v.* remunerate, indemnify, repay, compensate, repair, requite, reward, satisfy, reimburse. *(injure, spoil, dissatisfy, damnify, mar, misrequite.)*

recompense—*n.* indemnification, remuneration, requital, reward, amends, satisfaction.

reconcile—*v.* conciliate, pacify, adjust, suit, appease, reunite, unite, propitiate, harmonize, adapt. *(sever, estrange, derange, antagonize, separate, incite, disharmonize, alienate, conflict.)*

record—*n.* entry, list, inventory, catalogue, schedule, scroll, roll, instrument, remembrance, memorandum, chronicle, register, enrollment, index, registry, archive, enumerative, memento. *(oblivion, desuetude, immemorality, amnesty, disremembrance, obliteration, nonregistration, obsolescence.)*

recover—*v.* repossess, retrieve, save, heal, revive, reanimate, recapture, regain, resume, recruit, cure, restore. *(forfeit, sacrifice, impair, decline, succumb, relapse, lose, miss, deteriorate, decay.)*

recovery—*n.* regaining, vindication, restitution, retrieval, replacement, reanimation, revival, improvement, redemption, repossession, reinstatement, renovation, re-establishment, rectification, reanimation. *(forfeiture, deprival, loss, abandonment, retrogression, ruin, declension, defection, privation, sacrifice, relapse, decay, incurableness.)*

recreation—*n.* cheer, amusement, revival, sport, relaxation, regeneration, refreshment, holiday, reanimation, diversion, pastime. *(toil, labor, work, employ-*

ment, drudgery, weariness, lassitude, fatigue, assiduity.)

redeem—*v.* regain, make amends for, ransom, rescue, satisfy, liberate, discharge, reconvert, repurchase, retrieve, recompense, recover, fulfill. *(lose, abandon, surrender, rescind, sacrifice, pledge, forfeit, betray.)*

reduce—*v.* diminish, attenuate, narrow, weaken, subdue, bring, subject, curtail, convert, lessen, abridge, impoverish, contract, impair, subjugate, refer, classify. *(magnify, augment, exalt, extend, broaden, renovate, expand, restore, liberate, except, transform, enlarge, increase, produce, amplify, invigorate, repair, free, dissociate.)*

redundant—*adj.* expendable, extra, superfluous, marginal, wasteful, additional, dispensable, repetitious, unnecessary. *(essential, central, necessary, concise, brief, indispensable.)*

refer—*v.* associate, advert, relate, belong, apply, relegate, attribute, assign, connect, point, allude, appeal. *(dissociate, misappertain, misbeseem, disunite, disresemble, disconnect, misapply, alienate.)*

refinement—*n.* purification, sublimation, elegance, civilization, finesse, polish, clarification, filtration, delicacy, cultivation, subtility, sophistry, discernment. *(grossness, turbidity, coarseness, unrefinement, foulness, inelegance, broadness, vulgarity, bluntness, impurity, rudeness, boorishness, unsophisticatedness.)*

reflect—*v.* image, mirror, consider, cogitate, contemplate, muse, heed, animadvert, reverberate, return, exhibit, think, meditate, ponder, ruminate, advert. *(dissipate, dream, rove, wool-gather, disregard, absorb, overlook, divert, idle, wander, star-gaze, connive.)*

reform—*v.* ameliorate, rectify, reclaim, remodel, reorganize, regenerate, improve, amend, correct, better, rehabilitate, reconstitute. *(vitate, deteriorate, stabilitate, impair, stereotype, degenerate, corrupt, worsen, perpetuate, confirm, deform.)*

refresh—*v.* refrigerate, revive, renovate, renew, cheer, brace, revitalize, cool, invigorate, reanimate, recreate, restore, freshen. *(oppose, burden, annoy, fatigue, debilitate, relax, depress,* *heat, weary, afflict, tire, exhaust, enervate.)*

refuse—*v.* withhold, decline, veto, repudiate, deny, reject. *(afford, concede, permit, acquiesce, grant, yield.)*

refuse—*n.* scum, sediment, sweepings, offscourings, remains, waste, dross, offal, dregs, recrement, trash, debris. *(pickings, flower, prime, merchandise, cream, first-fruits, chattels.)*

regard—*v.* view, esteem, deem, respect, revere, conceive, notice, behold, mind, contemplate, consider, affect, reverence, value, heed, scrutinize. *(overlook, despise, miss, contemn, loathe, misconceive, misjudge, reject, disregard, dislike, hate, misconsider, misestimate.)*

regardless—*adj.* inconsiderate, unmindful, unobservant, indifferent, imprudent, heedless, despising, careless, inattentive, disregarding. *(considerate, alert, attentive, cautious, scrupulous, careful, mindful, regardful, prudent, circumspect.)*

regenerate—*v.* rehabilitate, improve, remedy, edify, reform, uplift, redeem, rejuvenate, reanimate, redo, recreate, convert, better, civilize. *(debase, lower, corrupt, degenerate, defile, demolish, crush, deprove.)*

regret—*v.* lament, miss, deplore, brood, grieve, repent, desiderate. *(hail, abandon, forget, overlook, disregard, welcome, approve, abjure.)*

regret—*n.* grief, remorse, concern, repentance, sorrow, lamentation, anguish. *(contentment, tranquillity, peace of mind, comfort, solace.)*

regular—*adj.* normal, orderly, stable, recurrent, systematic, established, formal, certain, customary, ordinary, stated, periodical, methodic, recognized, symmetrical. *(exceptional, capricious, irregular, fitful, variable, erratic, abnormal, uncertain, unusual, habitual, rare, disordered, unsymmetrical, eccentric.)*

regulation—*n.* law, disposal, rule, government, control, organization, arrangement, adjustment, method, order, statute. *(disorder, misgovernment, disarrangement, caprice, insubjection, license, uncontrol, misrule, anarchy, maladministration, nonregulation, chaos.)*

reject—*v.* renounce, cast away, repel, decline, refuse, ignore, exclude, throw out, repudiate, discard. *(welcome, appropriate, hail, select, endorse, admit, accept, choose.)*

rejoice—*v.* glory, joy, gladden, revel, cheer, enliven, jubilate, gratify, delight, exult, triumph, be glad, please. *(grieve, weep, repent, afflict, weary, disappoint, darken, pain, vex, mope, annoy, mourn, lament, sorrow, trouble, oppress, depress, burden, distress, sadden.)*

relation—*v.* aspect, narration, fitness, bearing, homogeneity, relevancy, ratio, agreement, kindred, reference, correlation, appurtenancy, connection, proportion, affinity, association, pertinency, harmony, relative, kinsman. *(disconnection, irrelevancy, disproportion, unfitness, heterogeneity, disagreement, isolation, alien, irrelation, dissociation, disharmony, impertinency, misproportion, independence, unsuitableness.)*

release—*v.* loose, discharge, acquit, extricate, indemnify, exempt, free, liberate, quit, parole, disengage. *(constrain, shackle, fetter, enslave, yoke, bind, confine.)*

relevant—*adj.* apt, contingent, pertinent, apropos, related, germane, suitable, appropriate, connected, applicable, on target. *(inappropriate, alien, unrelated, irrelevant, foreign, immaterial.)*

relief—*n.* support, extrication, respite, mitigation, help, remedy, exemption, refreshment, succor, comfort, release, alleviation, aid, assistance, redress, deliverance. *(aggravation, burdensomeness, exhaustion, discomfort, hamper, oppression, intensification, trouble, weariness.)*

religion—*n.* creed, belief, piety, godliness, denomination, holiness, faith, theology, profession, sanctity. *(irreligion, atheism, unbelief, sacrilege, blasphemy, profanity, sanctimoniousness, formalism, irreverence, reprobation, scoffing, skepticism, hypocrisy, pharisaism, godlessness, impiety.)*

religious—*adj.* godly, devotional, holy, reverent, sacred, pious, devout, divine. *(ungodly, sacrilegious, skeptical, agnostic, impious, profane, undevout, blasphemous.)*

relish—*n.* recommendation, flavor, gusto, appetite, sapidity, allure, zest, enhancement, savor, taste, piquancy. *(disflavor, nauseousness, insipidity, antipathy, unsavoriness, drawback, disrecommendation, disrelish.)*

remain—*v.* continue, stop, halt, rest, abide, endure, loiter, accrue, stay, wait, tarry, sojourn, dwell, last. *(vanish,* *depart, hasten, flit, pass, transfer, fly, remove, speed, press, disappear.)*

remarkable—*adj.* noticeable, unusual, striking, notable, famous, rare, prominent, eminent, singular, observable, extraordinary, noteworthy, distinguished, peculiar. *(unnoticeable, mean, every-day, inconspicuous, undistinguished, unremarkable, ordinary, commonplace.)*

remedy—*v.* restorative, reparation, relief, specific, rectify, cure, counteraction, redress, help. *(disease, infection, ill, deterioration, provocation, undermine, evil, hurt, plague, impairment, aggravation.)*

remember—*v.* recall, bear in mind, review, mind, recollect, retain. *(obliviate, overlook, forget, disregard, ignore.)*

remembrance—*n.* memory, token, memento, nostalgia, reminiscence, recollection, memorial, souvenir. *(oblivion, forgetfulness, obscurity.)*

remiss—*adj.* careless, inattentive, slow, idle, dilatory, remissful, delinquent, slack, negligent, wanting, slothful, lax, tardy. *(careful, active, alert, diligent, meticulous, strict, energetic, attentive, assiduous, painstaking.)*

remit—*v.* pardon, forego, surrender, resign, condone, relax, absolve, discontinue, forgive. *(intensity, exact, deteriorate, increase, enforce.)*

remorse—*n.* anguish, penitence, qualm, contrition, compunction, self-condemnation, regret. *(self-approval, pride, self-congratulation, complacency, satisfaction.)*

remote—*adj.* indirect, unrelated, alien, separate, inaccessible, contingent, distant, unconnected, foreign, heterogeneous. *(close, connected, actual, homogeneous, proximate, present, urgent, current, near, direct, related, immediate, essential, pressing.)*

remove—*v.* separate, transport, transfer, oust, suppress, depart, uproot, displace, abstract, carry, eject, dislodge, migrate, obliterate. *(conserve, perpetuate, reinstate, install, fasten, fix, stand, remain, abide, sustain, restore, stabilitate, establish, reinstall, dwell, stay.)*

render—*v.* present, restore, give, apportion, surrender, requite, submit, deliver, return, give up, assign, pay. *(retain, appropriate, misapportion, misrequite, refuse, keep,* *withhold, alienate, misappropriate.)*

renegade—*adj.* heretical, insurgent, rebellious, traitorous, dissident, mutinous, maverick, apostate, disloyal. *(faithful, obedient, loyal, steadfast, unswerving.)*

renew—*v.* restore, renovate, furbish, repeat, reissue, reform, modernize, transform, recreate, refresh, rejuvenate, recommence, reiterate, regenerate. *(wear, vitiate, discontinue, weaken, deprove, cancel, impair, deteriorate, exhaust, corrupt, defile.)*

renounce—*v.* abjure, disown, disavow, quit, abandon, resign, relinquish, reject, repudiate, disclaim, forego, deny, resign, recant. *(recognize, maintain, propound, vindicate, profess, retain, accept, defend, acknowledge, claim, assert, own, avow, hold.)*

renowned—*adj.* celebrated, famous, illustrious, prominent, wonderful. *(obscure, unknown, anonymous, unrecognized.)*

repay—*v.* reimburse, reward, requite, indemnify, refund, remunerate, recompense, retaliate. *(misappropriate, waste, extort, exact, circumvent, defraud, embezzle, alienate, confiscate.)*

repeal—*n.* rescission, annulment, termination, abrogation, recall, revocation. *(establishment, perpetuation, endurance, continuance.)*

repeal—*v.* revoke, cancel, recall, reverse, invalidate, abolish, rescind, annul, abrogate, discontinue, delete. *(establish, institute, enact, confirm, secure, continue, pass, sanction, perpetuate.)*

repeat—*v.* iterate, cite, relate, quote, recapitulate, reaffirm, reproduce, reiterate, renew, rehearse. *(drop, abandon, suppress, misquote, misrepresent, misconvey, discontinue, discard, ignore, misrepeat, misrecite, neglect, misinterpret.)*

repeatedly—*adv.* frequently, often, again and again, many times. *(rarely, seldom, occasionally.)*

repentance—*n.* contrition, regret, sorrow, self-condemnation, remorse, contrition, penitence, compunction, self-reproach. *(obduracy, hardness, self-approval, smugness, impenitence, recusancy, reprobation.)*

repetition—*n.* reiteration, iteration, diffuseness, relation, verbosity, recapitulation, dwelling upon. *(precedence, newness, freshness, singularity, uniqueness.)*

replace—*v.* supply, reinstate, re-establish, supersede, restore, substitute, rearrange. *(abstract, remove, move, deprive, deviate, withdraw, damage.)*

reply—*v.* answer, rejoin, rebut, replicate, respond. *(drop, pass, question, disregard, ignore, pretermit.)*

reply—*n.* rejoinder, replication, retaliation, answer, response. *(ignoring, pass by, stimulus.)*

report—*v.* relate, circulate, narrate, describe, communicate, divulge, declare, announce, tell, notify, recite, detail. *(hush, misreport, misrelate, expunge, falsify, silence, suppress, misrepresent.)*

report—*n.* announcement, narration, description, declaration, rumor, repute, reverberation, disclosure, tidings, relation, recital, news, communication, fame, noise. *(suppression, silence, fabrication, reticence, noiselessness, misannouncement.)*

represent—*v.* delineate, exhibit, state, indicate, enact, denote, dramatize, symbolize, resemble, portray, play, reproduce, personate, describe, embody, illustrate. *(misdelineate, falsify, misrepresent, misportray, distort, caricature, minimize.)*

representative—*n.* commissioner, agent, deputy, embodiment, delegate, proxy, vicigerent, soverign, emissary, constituency, substitute, personation, vicar, principal. *(dictator, autocrat, despot.)*

repress—*v.* control, inhibit, block, restrain, hinder, stifle, squelch, swallow, curb, quell, subdue. *(liberate, encourage, allow, permit, free, sanction, authorize.)*

reproach—*n.* censure, rebuke, blame, reprobate, lecture, taunt, reprove, upbraid. *(praise, approval, laud, glory, esteem.)*

reprobate—*n.* villain, miscreant, scalawag, degenerate, castaway, ruffian, rascal. *(pattern, model, paragon, example, mirror, saint.)*

repudiate—*v.* disown, abjure, disclaim, revoke, disavow, discard, divorce, renounce, contradict. *(own, assert, vaunt, profess, acknowledge, concede, accept, avow, vindicate, retain, claim, recognize.)*

repulsive—*adj.* deterrent, odious, unattractive, revolting, repugnant, forbidding, ungenial, ugly, disagreeable.

(agreeable, winning, fascinating, seductive, enchanting, pleasant, charming, attractive, captivating, alluring.)

reputable—*adj.* creditable, reliable, estimable, dependable, honorable, respectable. *(discreditable, disgraceful, unrespectable, dishonorable, disreputable, notorious.)*

rescue—*v.* recover, liberate, save, preserve, salvage, retake, recapture, extricate, deliver. *(imperil, surrender, expose, endanger, betray, abandon, impede.)*

resemblance—*n.* similarity, affinity, semblance, portrait, likeness, reflection, image, similitude, representation. *(dissimilarity, difference, contrast, contrariety, unlikeness, disresemblance.)*

resent—*v.* resist, recalcitrate, be indignant at, repel, rebel, take exception to. *(submit, pardon, approve, overlook, acquiesce, condone.)*

reserve—*n.* retention, accumulation, shyness, modesty, reservation, limitation, coldness, coyness, evasiveness. *(rashness, immodesty, spontaneity, boldness, recklessness.)*

residence—*n.* stay, home, domicile, dwelling, mansion, sojourn, abode, habitation.

resist—*v.* oppose, check, baffle, disappoint, frustrate, withstand, hinder, thwart. *(yield, surrender, comply, weaken, capitulate.)*

resolute—*adj.* decided, constant, steadfast, bold, unshaken, decisive, determined, fixed, steady, persevering, firm. *(infirm, cowardly, faltering, inconstant, weak, shy.)*

resource—*n.* means, expedients, riches, assets, material, supplies, wealth. *(exhaustion, drain, poverty, want, destitution, lack, nonplus.)*

respect—*v.* esteem, revere, appreciate, regard, honor, venerate. *(disrespect, deride, dishonor, scorn.)*

respond—*v.* rejoin, answer, reply, acknowledge, notice. *(disregard, neglect, ignore, overlook.)*

rest—*n.* relaxation, indolence, lassitude, idleness, leisure, retirement, siesta, repose, tranquillity, calm. *(work, activity, exertion, sweat, toil, turmoil, agitation.)*

restless—*adj.* uneasy, disquieted, agitated, unsettled, wandering, turbulent, unquiet, disturbed, sleepless, anxious, roving. *(settled, steady, calm, quiet, peaceful.)*

restrain—*v.* hinder, withhold, curb, coerce, abridge, confine, tether, check, stop, repress, suppress, restrict, limit. *(let go, free, liberty, give full rein to, release, flow.)*

result—*n.* consequence, inference, event, effect, conclusion, issue, aftermath. *(origin, beginning, cause, seed.)*

retain—*v.* restrain, keep, hold, withhold. *(give up, yield, abandon.)*

retire—*v.* leave, secede, abdicate, withdraw, deport, recede. *(continue, advance, proceed.)*

retort—*v.* answer, repartee, retaliate.

retreat—*n.* departure, seclusion, privacy, shelter, evacuation, refuge, retirement, withdrawment, solitude, asylum. *(forward march, progress, advance.)*

return—*v.* requite, recompense, remit, restore, repay, render, report, remember. *(question, assert, claim, displace, remove.)*

reveal—*v.* disclose, unveil, open, impart, announce, show, communicate, divulge, uncover, discover. *(withhold, conceal, disguise, hide, keep secret, cover.)*

revengeful—*adj.* resentful, spiteful, malicious, vindictive, merciless. *(ingenuous, hearty, kind, charitable, cordial, open, frank, generous.)*

revenue—*n.* returns, proceeds, result, wealth, dividends, receipts, income. *(outgo, expense, disbursements.)*

reverence—*n.* honor, adoration, esteem, veneration, awe. *(disdain, contempt, scorn, arrogance.)*

review—*n.* resurvey, survey, revise, revision, evaluation, re-examination, retrospect, reconsideration.

reward—*n.* compensation, pay, retribution, accolade, recompense, remuneration, requital. *(fine, punishment, penalty, damages.)*

rhetorical—*adj.* eloquent, articulate, fluent, pompous, expressive, pretentious. *(inarticulate, ill-spoken, tongue-tied, fumbling.)*

rich—*adj.* affluent, ample, abundant, costly, precious, luscious, lavish, wealthy, opulent, copious, fruitful, sumptuous, generous. *(weak, cheap, sordid, destitute, poor, straitened, scanty.)*

ridicule—*n.* wit, raillery, irony, mockery, satire, gibe, sneer, sarcasm, derision, banter, burlesque, travesty, jeer.

(praise, respect, honor, homage, deference.)

ripe—*adj.* mellow, finished, developed, mature, complete. *(young, unfinished, tender, green, incomplete.)*

rise—*v.* ascend, mount, climb, arise, scale, emanate. *(sink, decline, fall, slump.)*

risk—*n.* hazard, jeopardy, peril, vulnerability, exposure, danger. *(security, safeness, safety, protection.)*

rival—*n.* emulator, competitor, antagonist, opponent. *(colleague, associate, collaborator, ally, partner.)*

road—*n.* highway, lane, route, course, way, street, pathway, passage, thoroughfare.

robbery—*n.* depredation, despoliation, pillage, piracy, theft, steal, plunder, caper, looting.

romance—*n.* novel, tale, mystery, fable, fiction.

romantic—*adj.* fanciful, glamorous, extravagant, chimerical, wild, sentimental, fictitious. *(familiar, timorous, aloof, unromantic, frigid, cold.)*

room—*n.* compass, latitude, space, apartment, scope, chamber.

rotund—*adj.* rounded, spherical, circular, globular, plump, fat, corpulent, chubby, stout. *(slim, lean, trim, svelte, thin, slender.)*

round—*adj.* spherical, globose, orbed, full, rotund, curved, circular, globular, orbicular, cylindrical, plump. *(oblong, lean, slender, thin, square, angular.)*

rout—*v.* smite, conquer, defeat, vanquish. *(recede, retire, withdraw.)*

route—*n.* path, track, roadway, passage. *(drift, digression, twist, meander.)*

royal—*adj.* regal, imperial, noble, princely, majestic, splendid, magnanimous, aristocratic, kingly, monarchical, kinglike, august, superb, illustrious. *(low, humble, plebian, coarse, vulgar, tawdry, common.)*

ruin—*n.* downfall, fall, defeat, subversion, bane, mischief, destruction, perdition, overthrow, pest, collapse. *(construction, creation, improve, enhance, build.)*

rule—*n.* law, maxim, canon, method, control, sway, authority, empire, regulation, precept, guide, order, direction, government. *(misrule, violence, revolt, misgovernment, confusion, riot, rebellion, conflict.)*

rustic—*adj.* rude, inelegant, honest, awkward, coarse, unadorned, artless, uncouth, rural, plain, unpolished, untaught, rough, simple. *(stylish, elegant, sophisticated, blasé,* chic.)

ruthless—*adj.* pitiless, heartless, unfeeling, hardened, cold, cruel, brutal, relentless, merciless. *(tenderhearted, gentle, indulgent, compassionate, sympathetic.)*

S

sabotage—*v.* disable, sap, wreck, subvert, vandalize, hamper, damage, obstruct, incapacitate. *(enhance, strengthen, abet, assist, cooperate, reinforce.)*

sacred—*adj.* divine, consecrated, devoted, venerable, blessed, holy, hallowed, dedicated, religious, reverend, sanctified. *(secular, sinful, profane, violable, impious, temporal, unconsecrated.)*

sacrifice—*n.* slaughter, offering victim, martyr, scapegoat, oblation, homage, holocaust, corban, hecatomb. *(gain, seizure, usurpation, confiscation, appropriation, profit.)*

sad—*adj.* mournful, dejected, cheerless, sedate, grave, afflictive, sorrowful, despondent, calamitous, gloomy, depressed, downcast, serious, grievous. *(lively, spirited, jolly, seductive, cheerful, gay, happy, sprightly, fortunate.)*

safe—*adj.* unendangered, sure, protected, secure, unscathed. *(hazardous, dangerous, risky, exposed, in danger.)*

sagacious—*adj.* acute, keen, judicious, intelligent, shrewd, cunning, wise, rational, prudent, sensible, tactful. *(irrational, stupid, foolish, obtuse, silly, ignorance, fatuous.)*

salient—*adj.* outstanding, noticeable, striking, signal, conspicuous, prominent, obvious, palpable, manifest. *(depressed, minor, trifling, insignificant, trivial, unimportant.)*

salutary—*adj.* healthful, remedial, beneficial, advantageous, useful, wholesome, profitable, salubrious. *(tainted, unhealthy, detrimental, infectious.)*

sample—*n.* illustration, specimen, instance, example.

sanction—*v.* endorse, support, approve, ratify. *(disapprove, forbid, hinder, censure.)*

sarcasm—*n.* irony, ridicule, sneering, scorn, contempt, jeer, taunting, vitrial, bitterness. *(compliment, praise, flattery, admiration, eulogy, commendation, enthusiasm.)*

satire—*n.* sarcasm, ridicule, burlesque, humor, pasquinade, lampoon, irony, mockery, wit.

satisfaction—*n.* content, pleasure, compensation, remuneration, atonement, felicity, contentment, gratifiation, recompense, amends, indemnification. *(discomfort, want, displeasure, discontent, resentment, shame, unhappiness.)*

satisfy—*v.* content, gratify, fulfill, compensate, indemnify, satiate, please, recompense, remunerate. *(renege, fail, trouble, sadden, deplete, drain, vex.)*

saucy—*adj.* insolent, impudent, disrespectful, impertinent, rude. *(well-bred, demure, respectful, mannerly, amiable.)*

savage—*adj.* wild, untaught, feral, unpolished, brutish, heathenish, cruel, fierce, merciless, murderous, ferocious, uncultivated, rude, uncivilized, brutal, barbarous, inhuman, pitiless, unmerciful. *(refined, gentle, humane, domesticated, tame, cultured, kind, merciful, human.)*

save—*v.* rescue, protect, reserve, redeem, prevent, preserve, deliver, spare. *(expose, throw away, sacrifice, abandon, give up.)*

saying—*n.* speech, maxim, by-word, apothegm, proverb, utterance, declaration, adage, aphorism, saw.

scandal—*n.* detraction, calumny, reproach, disgrace, outrage, defamation, slander, opprobrium, shame. *(glory, respect, honor, esteem, praise.)*

scanty—*adj.* gaunt, scarce, deficient, meager, inadequate. *(plenty, full, ample, copious.)*

scarce—*adj.* infrequent, uncommon, rare, unique, deficient. *(general, frequent, common, usual, abundant.)*

scatter—*v.* dissipate, strew, diffuse, sprinkle, disperse, spread. *(keep together, preserve, assemble, gather, collect, unite.)*

scheme—*n.* project, contrivance, device, strategy, plot, plan, design, purpose.)

scholar—*n.* intellectual, sage, pupil, disciple, professor, academician. *(ignoramus, illiterate, simpleton, dunce, dolt.)*

science—*n.* art, knowledge, literature, expertness, skill. *(illiteracy, ignorance, sciolism.)*

scoff—*v.* mock, jeer, ridicule, belittle, sneer, deride, taunt, revile. *(exalt, extol, value, praise, appreciate.)*

scorn—*n.* disdain, contumely, slight, contempt, disregard, derision, despite, dishonor. *(respect, admiration, approval, flattery, love, honor.)*

scrimp—*v.* save, stint, economize, hoard, grudge, scrape, withhold, be parsimonious. *(spend, pour, lavish, squander, waste.)*

scrupulous—*adj.* careful, hesitating, meticulous, cautious, ethical, conscientious. *(careless, daring, reckless, dishonest, negligent, unscrupulous, scatterbrained.)*

scurrilous—*adj.* abusive, low, insulting, offensive, vile, mean, foul-mouthed, scurrile, obscene, opprobrious, reproachful, insolent, gross, vulgar, foul, indecent. *(proper, delicate, polite, decent, refined, well-bred.)*

seasoned—*adj.* mature, knowing, ripe, weathered, experienced, veteran, practiced, hardened. *(immature, green, innocent, starry-eyed, untried.)*

secret—*adj.* concealed, unseen, private, recondite, covert, privy, confidential, hidden, secluded, unknown, obscure, latent, clandestine. *(free, public, revealed, known, open.)*

sectarian—*adj.* partisan, heretic, schismatic, fanatic, clannish. *(nonpartisan, broadminded, nonsectarian.)*

section—*n.* division, portion, segment, part, component. *(entirety, all, whole, totality.)*

security—*n.* defense, shelter, certainty, assurance, confidence, pledge, invulnerability, protection, guard, safety, ease, carelessness, surety. *(exposure, uncertainty, hazard, danger, doubt.)*

sedate—*adj.* demure, calm, quiet, settled, passive, unruffled, sober, serious, grave, serene. *(frolicsome, ruffled, disturbed, excitable, flighty, indiscreet, agitated.)*

seem—*v.* look, appear, manifest.

seemly—*adj.* fit, proper, congruous, decent, conventional, becomingly, suitable, appropriate, meet, decorous, polite. *(immodest, gross, outrageous, rude, improper, unconventional.)*

segregate—*v.* disconnect, seclude, isolate, sequester, exclude, quarantine, ghettoize, divorce, disunite. *(blend, integrate, unify, desegregate, mix.)*

seize—*v.* grasp, snatch, arrest, capture, embrace, catch, clutch, append, take. *(relinquish, liberate, free, let go, loose, let pass.)*

selective—*adj.* choosy, critical, discriminating, finicky, fastidious, percipient, exacting, cautious, careful. *(random, inclusive, promiscuous, careless, unselective, undemanding.)*

self-control—*n.* self-discipline, independence, self-restraint, equilibrium, stability, balance, fortitude, willpower. *(instability, weakness, hotheadedness, excitability.)*

selfish—*adj.* egotistic, self-centered, greedy, mean, tight, egotistical, self-interested, mercenary, rapacious, stingy. *(selfless, generous, altruistic, giving, magnanimous, charitable.)*

sense—*n.* reason, sensation, meaning, signification, opinion, reaction, judgment, understanding, perception, feeling, import, notion. *(anesthesia, atrophy, paralysis, numbness.)*

sensible—*adj.* wise, satisfied, astute, persuaded, intelligent, cognizant, logical. *(foolish, dense, obtuse, scatterbrained, impractical.)*

sentiment—*n.* opinion, sensibility, emotion, feeling, thought, notion.

sepulchral—*adj.* funereal, dismal, somber, dreary, morbid, ghastly, melancholy, cheerless, lugubrious. *(bright, vivacious, lively, inviting, cheerful.)*

serene—*adj.* fair, balmy, cool, peaceful, tranquil, placid, relaxed, dignified, nonchalant. *(agitated, anxious, excitable, stormy, turbulent, hectic.)*

serious—*adj.* solemn, weighty, pensive, grave, important, thoughtful. *(lively, light, happy, frivolous, gay, unimportant.)*

serve—*v.* minister to, promote, obey, help, benefit, officiate, succor, subserve, aid, assist, support. *(obstruct, dissatisfy, thwart, hinder, betray, deceive.)*

set—*v.* settle, decline, consolidate, establish, harden, sink, subside, compose. *(ascend, mount, agitate, run, melt, fuse, dislodge, flow, rise, soar, stir, loosen, soften, mollify.)*

set—*adj.* established, determined, formal, conventional, fixed, firm, regular. *(unorthodox, eccentric, unusual, unconventional.)*

settle—*v.* establish, arrange, adjust, decide, quiet, still, fall, lower, acquiesce, agree, stabilize, fix, regulate, compose, determine, allay, adjudicate, sink, subside, calm, abate. *(disestablish, derrange, aggravate, disturb, misdetermine, misplace, rise, move, increase, scramble, remove, misregulate, discompose, disorder, confuse, heighten, misarrange, unsettle, ascend, disagree.)*

settlement—*n.* dregs, precipitation, location, stabilization, colony, subsidence, residuum, colonization, arrangement. *(perturbation, fluctuation, disorder, turbidity, excitement.)*

several—*adj.* distinct, sundry, various, numerous, different, separate, diverse, divers. *(same, indistinguishable, united, integral, communal, one, identical, inseparable, total.)*

severe—*adj.* austere, grave, harsh, rigorous, afflictive, violent, exact, censorious, sarcastic, keen, cruel, serious, stern, strict, rigid, sharp, distressing, extreme, critical, caustic, cutting, better, demanding. *(smiling, relaxed, mild, jocund, indulgent, trivial, loose, inconsiderable, lenient, moderate, considerate, tender, compassionate, gentle, gay, genial, cheerful, jocose, joyous, light, trifling, inexact, uncritical, inextreme, kind, feeling.)*

shabby—*adj.* threadbare, beggarly, impoverished, ragged, contemptible, paltry, mangy. *(dapper, debonair, admirable, new, spendthrift.)*

shadowy—*adj.* cloudy, dark, gloomy, somber, mysterious, dim, obscure, murky. *(brilliant, sunny, bright, clear, sharp, dazzling.)*

shallow—*adj.* slight, trifling, superficial, trivial, unprofound, shoal, flimsy, simple. *(profound, deep, serious, meaningful.)*

sham—*n.* ghost, illusion, delusion, shadow, counterfeit, deception, phantom, mockery, pretense, unreality, affectation. *(reality, substantiality, authenticity, sincerity, verity, truth, substance.)*

shame—*n.* humiliation, decorum, shamefacedness, dishonor, contempt, discredit, remorse, dispraise, abashment, modesty, decency, reproach, ignominy, degradation. *(barefacedness, impudence, indecorum, honor, exaltation, credit, shamelessness, glory, immodesty, indecency, impropriety, renown, pride.)*

shameful—*adj.* degrading, outrageous, indecent, despicable, unbecoming, disgraceful, scandalous, dishonorable. *(respectable, estimable, honorable, reputable.)*

shape—*v.* mould, adapt, adjust, create, make, fashion, form, figure, delineate, contrive, execute. *(distort, misdelineate, discompose, misproduce, destroy, pervert, misadapt, derange, miscontrive, caricature, ruin.)*

shape—*n.* form, mould, pattern, model, silhouette, figure, outline, fashion, cost. *(disorder, disarray, confusion.)*

share—*n.* apportionment, division, allowance, contingent, segment, portion, lot, participation, quota, allotment, dividend. *(mass, entirety, aggregate, whole, total.)*

sharp—*adj.* fine, shrewd, clever, acute, aculeated, pungent, shrill, afflictive, harsh, cutting, active, sore, animated, perceptive, spirited, thin, keen, discerning, sarcastic, pointed, penetrating, acid, piercing, distressing, severe, eager, ardent, hard. *(indifferent, blunt, obtuse, light, rounded, mellow, hollow, trivial, gentle, tender, sluggish, indifferent, spiritless, ambiguous, tame, thick, dull, knobbed, bluff, bass, deep, trifling, mild, soft, lenient, inactive.)*

shatter—*v.* dissipate, derange, rend, shiver, disintegrate, burst, split, disrupt, break in pieces, demolish, dismember. *(organize, fabricate, rear, strengthen, constitute, construct, collocate, compose.)*

sheer—*adj.* mere, unqualified, absolute, unadulterated, gauzy, pure, unmixed, unmitigated, simple. *(qualified, modified, partial, limited, adulterated.)*

shelve—*v.* discard, stifle, postpone, dismiss, swamp, shift. *(prosecute, revive, expedite, agitate, start, pursue.)*

shift—*v.* alter, shelve, remove, rearrange, change, transfer, displace. *(fasten, insert, plant, restrain, place, fix, locate, pitch.)*

shift—*n.* expedient, pretext, change, device, resource, deviation, transference, contrivance, artifice, substitute, motive, evasion. *(fixity, retention, gripe, per-*

manence, miscontrivance, steadiness, location.)

shocking—*adj.* horrible, hateful, abominable, foul, astounding, sad, disgraceful, revolting, loathsome. *(honorable, delightful, edifying, attractive, enticing, comforting, pleasing, charming, creditable, exemplary, alluring.)*

short—*adj.* limited, inadequate, near, condensed, lacking, defective, weak, incomplete, inextensive, abrupt, brief, concise, abridged, scanty, insufficient, less, deficient, imperfect, soon, narrow, incomprehensive, blunt. *(protracted, unlimited, ample, adequate, exuberant, long, large, complete, deferred, strong, extensive, bland, inabrupt, diffuse, elongated, extended, plentiful, abundant, sufficient, liberal, copious, distant, wide, comprehensive, exceeding, courteous, expanded.)*

shortsighted—*adj.* imprudent, myopic, unthinking, unwise, reckless, impulsive, indiscreet, thoughtless, foolish. *(prudent, circumspect, cautious, thoughtful, sagacious.)*

show—*v.* present, unfold, teach, conduct, evince, prove, verify, explain, exhibit, demonstrate, reveal, inform, manifest. *(suppress, withhold, mystify, misdemonstrate, contradict, deny, misinterpret, misexplain, screen, conceal, hide, obscure, wrap, misdeclare, refute, disprove, falsify.)*

show—*n.* exhibition, parade, illusion, semblance, pretext, pretense, pageantry, appearance, pomp, demonstration, likeness, profession. *(disappearance, suppression, disguise, unlikeness, reality, substance, deception, nonappearance, concealment, secrecy, sincerity, dissimilarity, ungenuineness.)*

showy—*adj.* gaudy, gorgeous, tinsel, garish, gay, high-colored, flashy. *(unnoticeable, quiet, subdued, dingy, inconspicuous.)*

shrewd—*adj.* penetrating, discriminating, discerning, perceptive, sagacious, astute, intelligent, acute, keen. *(undiscerning, dull, stupid, ignorant, stolid, unsagacious.)*

shrink—*v.* shrivel, retire, revolt, deflate, contract, withdraw, recoil. *(expand, venture, dare, dilate, amplify, stretch.)*

shrivel—*v.* dry up, wrinkle, decrease, degenerate, contract, wither, corrugate. *(flatten, unfold, dilate, rejuvenate, expand, develop, spread.)*

shuffle—*v.* interchange, intershift, derange, wade, equivocate, cavil, mystify, dissemble, jumble, confuse, shift, intermix, agitate, prevaricate, quibble, sophisticate, palter. *(distribute, arrange, reveal, confuse, declare, elucidate, deal, apportion, order, compose, propound, explain.)*

shy—*adj.* reserved, bashful, chary, shrinking, sheepish, timid, modest, suspicious. *(brazen-faced, audacious, aggressive, reckless, bold, impudent.)*

sick—*adj.* ill, distempered, weak, disgusted, feeble, nauseated, corrupt, valetudinarian, queasy, disordered, indisposed, ailing, morbid, impaired, diseased. *(well, sound, strong, salubrious, vigorous, whole, healthy, robust, well-conditioned.)*

sickly—*adj.* diseased, ailing, pining, morbid, vitiated, tainted, languishing, valetudinary, weak, disordered, feeble, drooping, unhealthy, delicate. *(healthy, flourishing, sound, rugged, robust, strong, vigorous, salubrious.)*

side—*n.* edge, border, face, plane, interest, policy, boundary, behalf, margin, verge, laterality, aspect, party, cause. *(body, interior, neutrality, severance, opposition, detachment, center, core, essence, disconnection, secession.)*

sight—*n.* perception, vision, spectacle, inspection, representation, image, appearance, seeing, view, visibility, show, examination. *(invisibility, obscuration, oversight, undiscernment, blunder, non-perception, blindness, disappearance, non-appearance.)*

sign—*n.* indication, memorial, symbol, prefiguration, type, symptom, mark, presage, gesture, token, proof, expression, emblem, badge, premonition, prognostic, signal, wonder. *(misrepresentation, misleader, misindication, falsification.)*

signal—*adj.* conspicuous, extraordinary, memorable, important, distinguished, prominent, eminent, remarkable, notable, illustrious, salient. *(common, mediocre, unimportant, obscure, ordinary, unnoticeable, unmemorable.)*

signify—*v.* purport, mean, indicate, denote, declare, forebode, imply, presage, portend, prognosticate, represent, communicate, betaken, utter. *(suppress, misdenote, refute, preclude, obviate, conceal, misindicate, nullify, neutralize.)*

silence—*n.* stillness, peace, quiet, muteness, oblivion, tactiturnity, calm, hush, secrecy, lull. *(loquacity, chatter, brawl, clatter, babel, agitation, storm, roar, reverberation, fame, commotion, proclamation, celebrity, remembrance, effusiveness, garrulity, talkativeness, noise, clamor, din, tumult, restlessness, unrest, bruit, resonance, cackling, publicity, rumor, repute.)*

silly—*adj.* foolish, shallow, weak, unwise, imprudent, fatuous, absurd, simple, witless, indiscreet. *(intelligent, wise, discreet, sound, mature, rational, deep, sagacious, astute, prudent.)*

similar—*adj.* resembling, common, concordant, congruous, kindred, correspondent, alike, homogeneous, harmonious. *(unlike, alien, discordant, contrary, incongruous, different, dissimilar, heterogeneous.)*

simple—*adj.* incomplex, unblended, pure, mere, plain, unartificial, sincere, single-minded, silly, homely, unsophisticated, elementary, primal, transparent, rudimentary, single, uncompounded, isolated, unmixed, absolute, unadorned, artless, undesigning, unaffected, weak, humble, lowly, ultimate. *(complex, blended, fused, multigenerous, compound, eminent, subdivided, connected, complicated, artificial, designing, double-minded, self-conscious, sophisticated, complete, perfect, embellished, double, compounded, mixed, multi-form, various, articulated, organized, modified, elaborate, artful, insincere, affected, sagacious, great, illustrous, developed.)*

simultaneous—*adj.* concomitant, synchronous, contemporary, con-current, synchronic. *(separate, intermittent, diachronic, periodic, inconcurrent, apart.)*

sin—*n.* iniquity, ungodliness, evil, crime, immorality, wrongdoing, transgression, unrighteousness, wickedness, impurity. *(obedience, righteousness, godliness, virtue, goodness, sinlessness, holiness, purity.)*

sincere—*adj.* unmixed, unadulterated, honest, unvarnished, cordial, unfeigned, genuine, true, pure, heartfelt, hearty, unaffected, candid, frank. *(adulterated, insincere, feigned, false, duplicity, impure, dishonest, hypocritical, pretended.)*

single—*adj.* one, alone, individual, solitary, sole, uncombined, separate, unmarried, private, isolated, unaccompanied. *(many, united, frequent, conglomerate, plural, collective, numerous, married, blended.)*

singular—*adj.* individual, eminent, conspicuous, unusual, odd, quaint, unexampled, solitary, eccentric, exceptional, remarkable, queer, unparalleled, single, unique, extraordinary, consummate, uncommon, peculiar, whimsical, unprecedented, sole, fantastic, particular, curious. *(frequent, ordinary, unnoticeable, customary, regular, nondescript, common, numerous, usual, every-day, general.)*

sinister—*adj.* evil, pernicious, malevolent, noxious, ominous, corrupt, malign, disastrous, menacing. *(good, auspicious, benign, fortunate, promising.)*

situation—*n.* position, state, post, condition, aspect, office, plight, standing, dilemma, locality, birth, topography, seat, place, residence, footing, predicament. *(non-location, non-assignment, displacement, non-appearance, dislodgement, non-situation, absence, unfixedness.)*

skeptical—*adj.* suspicious, cynical, doubtful, agnostic, dubious, questioning, quizzical, incredulous, unbelieving, unconvinced. *(credulous, certain, gullible, confident, believing, sure.)*

skillful—*adj.* skilled, polished, expert, proficient, adroit, deft, capable, clever, competent, versed. *(clumsy, awkward, inept, unskilled, bungling, unqualified.)*

slander—*v.* injure, malign, discredit, asperse, smear, defame, libel, vilify, denigrate. *(commend, defend, praise, eulogize, laud, extol.)*

slender—*adj.* narrow, slim, trivial, inadequate, feeble, meagre, superficial, spindly, thin, slight, small, spare, fragile, flimsy, inconsiderable. *(thick, robust, considerable, deep, pudgy, stout, broad, massive, ample.)*

sloppy—*adj.* messy, dirty, careless, tacky, slovenly, untidy, slipshod, substandard, frowzy. *(careful, trim, clear, immaculate, meticulous, tidy.)*

slow—*adj.* inactive, lazy, tardy, gradual, dull, lingering, inert, deliberate, sluggish, unready, slack, late, tedious, dilatory. *(quick, rapid, ready, early, immediate, punctual, active, fast, alert, prompt, sudden.)*

slur—*n.* smear, affront, insult, innuendo, detraction, disparagement, insinuation, reproach. *(commendation, honor, eulogy, compliment, praise, homage.)*

sly—*adj.* subtle, artful, underhanded, stealthy, covert, cunning, crafty, wily, astute. *(frank, undesigning, candid, open, artless.)*

small—*adj.* diminutive, minute, trivial, paltry, mean, slender, inferior, modest, little, slight, feeble, insignificant, narrow, weak, fine. *(large, considerable, extensive, spacious, strong, liberal, broad, weighty, great, big, bulky, ample, stout, important.)*

smart—*adj.* pungent, quick, sharp, active, brilliant, witty, spruce, fresh, showy, intelligent, keen, piercing, vigorous, severe, clever, vivacious, ready, brisk, dressy. *(heavy, slow, stupid, unready, unwitty, shabby, bland, clownish, dull, aching, inactive, sluggish, slow- minded, dowdy.)*

smooth—*adj.* plain, flat, glossy, soft, unobstructed, oily, silken, suave, even, level, polished, sleek, unruffled, bland. *(rough, abrupt, unpolished, blunt, abrasive, uneven, rugged, precipitous, harsh.)*

smother—*v.* stifle, gag, suppress, strangle, swallow, asphyxiate, suffocate, repress, conceal, choke, allay. *(ventilate, cherish, vent, publish, divulge, excite, fan, foster, nurture, promulgate, spread, purify.)*

smug—*adj.* complacent, cocky, serene, placid, self-satisfied, triumphant, conceited. *(apologetic, hesitant, sheepish, modest, diffident.)*

snappy—*adj.* energetic, curt, keen, animated, crisp, quick, fashionable, stylish, smart. *(slow, threadbare, dowdy, languid, lazy, shabby, seedy.)*

sneer—*n.* gibe, taunt, contempt, superciliousness, grimace, disdain, scoff, jeer, disparagement, scorn. *(eulogy, deference, laudation, complement, commendation.)*

snub—*n.* check, reprimand, insult, rebuke.

snug—*adj.* housed, compact, sheltered, cozy, close, compressed, comfortable. *(loose, uncompact, bare, uncovered, shivering, exposed, disordered, uncomfortable.)*

sober—*adj.* unintoxicated, calm, dispassionate, sound, serious, sedate, abstemious, rational, moderate, temperate, cool, reasonable, self-possessed, unexcited, grave, steady, deliberate, circumspect, lucid, staid, dignified, prim, severe, serious, somber. *(drunk, heated, extreme, impassioned, agitated, passionate, immoderate, erratic, befuddled, eccentric, intemperate, intoxicated, excited, unreasonable, furious, extravagant, exorbitant, flighty, besotted, crazed, gay, carefree, wanton, muddled.)*

society—*n.* polity, collection, fellowship, participation, sociality, intercourse, culture, sodality, community, company, association, companionship, connection, communion. *(personality, separation, unsociality, dissociation, privacy, individuality, segregation, solitariness, disconnection, seclusion.)*

soft—*adj.* pressible, smooth, fine, glossy, gentle, kind, flexible, sleek, luxurious, tender, undecided, mild, supple, yielding, impressible, delicate, balmy, feeling, effeminate, unmanly, irresolute. *(tough, unyielding, rigid, unimpressible, coarse, abrupt, rigorous, severe, unfeeling, austere, inflexible, self-denying, hard, determined, strident, stubborn, rough, harsh, ungentle, cutting, unkind, sharp, stern, ascetic, resolute.)*

soften—*v.* palliate, mitigate, dulcify, yield, humanize, compose, moderate, enervate, mollify, assuage, lenify, macerate, abate. *(indurate, excite, harden, infuriate, toughen, aggravate, consolidate, intensify.)*

solace—*v.* alleviate, calm, soothe, comfort, cheer, bolster, mitigate, console, reassure, ameliorate. *(depress, aggravate, irritate, undermine.)*

solemn—*adj.* formal, reverential, ceremonial, religious, serious, awesome, sacred, devotional, ritual, impressive, grave. *(undevotional, light, trivial, informal, frivolous, profane, secular, gay, unceremonial, unsolemn, flippant.)*

solicitous—*adj.* regardful, nervous, apprehensive, fearful, vigilant, anxious, troubled, caring, avid, yearning. *(relaxed, carefree, nonchalant, cool, apathetic, indifferent, unenthusiastic.)*

solid—*adj.* firm, resistant, strong, substantial, just, impenetrable, cubic, solidified, hard, compact, dense, weighty, valid, sound, stable. *(hollow, frail, flimsy, resilient, impressible, liquid, soft, light,* *weak, unsound, weakly, flexible, yielding, brittle, elastic, malleable, fluid, frivolous, trifling, invalid, fallacious.)*

solitude—*n.* remoteness, retirement, wildness, barrenness, privacy, withdrawal, loneliness, seclusion, isolation, desertion, wilderness. *(combination, continuity, conjunction, complication, union, mystification, integration, gregariousness, amalgamation, connection, entanglement, confusion, obscurity.)*

somber—*adj.* funereal, grim, dark, melancholy, sepulchral, dreary, sad, doleful, gloomy. *(festive, cheerful, gay, bright, joyous.)*

sophisticated—*adj.* experienced, knowledgeable, aware, worldy, cosmopolitan, blase, intellectual, cultured. *(simple, naive, primitive, provincial, unseasoned, ingenuous, sophomoric.)*

sore—*adj.* irritated, excoriated, scarified, grievous, heavy, raw, abscessed, painful, susceptible, ulcerous, afflictive, burdensome, chafed. *(sound, healthful, grateful, unbroken, light, unburdensome, untroublesome, delighted, painless, whole, healed, unsacrified, trivial, pleasant.)*

sorry—*adj.* pained, afflicted, hurt, doleful, mortified, dejected, mean, shabby, apologetic, worthless, grieved, woe-be-gone, down-hearted, vexed, poor, vile. *(rejoiced, pleased, fine, handsome, agreeable, glad, delighted, gratified, choice.)*

sort—*n.* species, class, character, manner, condition, designation, category, genus, kind, nature, order, rank, quality, description. *(solitariness, non-classification, heterogeneity, non-description, uniqueness, variegation.)*

sound—*adj.* unbroken, perfect, well-grounded, unimpaired, firm, vigorous, solid, irrefutable, valid, correct, logical, substantial, entire, whole, unhurt, uninjured, healthy, strong, weighty, irrefragable, thorough, wholesome. *(broken, impaired, frail, unsound, light, unfounded, weak, fallacious, unwholesome, risky, unsubstantial, partial, injured, unhealthy, fragile, trivial, hollow, imperfect, incorrect, invalid, feeble.)*

sour—*adj.* rancid, turned, crusty, crabbed, morose, churlish, tart, acetous, peevish, fermented, coagulated, harsh, austere, pungent, acid, bitter, acrimonious. *(wholesome, mellow,* *kindly, affable, sweet, genial, untainted.)*

sovereign—*adj.* enthroned, imperial, sanctioned, ruling, authoritative, almighty, free, dominant, paramount. *(dethroned, powerless, unauthorized, minor, subservient, secondary, petty.)*

spacious—*adj.* extensive, vast, large, roomy, voluminous, broad, expansive, ample, capacious, wide. *(restricted, narrow, cramped, inextensive, limited, uncomfortable, confined.)*

spare—*v.* afford, reserve, husband, retain, grudge, omit, withhold, abstain, liberate, save, grant, do without, economize, store, discard, forbear, refrain. *(squander, lavish, vent, expend, indulge, dissipate, spend, waste, scatter, pour.)*

spare—*adj.* unplentiful, meagre, chary, frugal, restricted, niggardly, thin, superfluous, available, additional, minimal, scanty, inabundant, economical, stinted, parsimonious, disposable, lean. *(plentiful, profuse, unrestricted, bountiful, ornate, unstinted, available, elaborate, ample, abundant, liberal, generous, unsparing, unbounded.)*

spasmodic—*adj.* irregular, fitful, erratic, occasional, transient, sudden, convulsive, changeable, transitory. *(continuous, lasting, regular, uninterrupted.)*

special—*adj.* specific, appropriate, distinctive, especial, unique, exceptional, particular, peculiar, proper, extraordinary. *(universal, generic, typical, general, common.)*

speculation—*n.* consideration, view, weighing, theory, hypothesis, assumption, conjecture, contemplation, thought, scheme. *(proof, verification, certainty, substantiation, fact, realization.)*

speed—*v.* expedite, urge, hasten, press, plunge, dispatch, accelerate, hurry. *(delay, obstruct, loiter, linger, stay, dawdle, retard, postpone, drag, creep, lag.)*

speed—*n.* swiftness, haste, promptness, nimbleness, rush, rapidity, agility, quickness. *(sluggishness, inertia, laziness, slowness, delay.)*

spend—*v.* waste, squander, lay out, disburse, dissipate, lavish, bestow, exhaust, expend, consume. *(save, accumulate, economize, conserve, retain, hoard, husband.)*

spirit—*n.* breath, soul, essential, ego, quality, immateriality, disembodiment, apparition, energy, enthusiasm, earnestness, zeal, temper, motive, courage, distillation, air, life, vital force, essence, intelligence, spectre, ghost, ardor, activity, courage, disposition, principle. *(body, materiality, deadness, organization, embodiment, dejection, listlessness, lifelessness, flesh, torpor, sluggishness, timidity, substance, corporeity, frame, spiritlessness, soullessness, dejection, slowness.)*

spirited—*adj.* lively, ardent, sprightly, enterprising, courageous, animated, vivacious, buoyant. *(dispirited, cowardly, inert, dull, depressed.)*

spiritual—*adj.* religious, ghostly, immaterial, intellectual, psychic, divine, holy, ethical, incorporeal. *(fleshly, gross, sensuous, secular, carnal, unspiritual, material.)*

spite—*n.* malevolence, pique, ill-will, rancor, bitterness, malice, spleen, grudge, hatred, vindictiveness. *(kindliness, benevolence, charity, good-will.)*

splendid—*adj.* showy, sumptuous, glorious, imposing, superb, heroic, signal, incredible, brilliant, magnificent, gorgeous, pompous, illustrious, famous, grand. *(obscure, somber, beggarly, ordinary, inglorious, dreadful, dull, tame, poor, unimposing, ineffective.)*

split—*v.* separate, cleave, rive, splinter, rend, disagree, divide, disunite, fragment, crack, burst, sunder, secede. *(unite, coalesce, agree, consolidate, integrate, cohere, amalgamate, conform, splice.)*

spoil—*v.* strip, devastate, denude, vitiate, deteriorate, damage, mar, plunder, rob, pillage, corrupt. *(enrich, replenish, improve, ameliorate, preserve, repair, invest, endow, renovate, better, rectify.)*

spontaneous—*adj.* self-generated, self-evolved, unbidden, extemporaneous, gratuitous, voluntary, self-originated, willing. *(imposed, unwilling, premeditated, involuntary, compulsionary, necessitated, calculated.)*

sporadic—*adj.* occasional, rare, spasmodic, unexpected, irregular, unscheduled, isolated, infrequent. *(regular, continuous, epidemic, extensive, frequent, general, unlimited.)*

sport—*n.* frolic, joke, fun, merriment, recreation, pastime, entertainment, play, wantonness, diversion, gaiety, amusement, game. *(seriousness, earnestness, work, toil, business.)*

spread—*v.* stretch, open, divulge, publish, diffuse, distribute, circulate, ramify, inflate, extend, expand, unfurl, propagate, disperse, overlay, scatter, disseminate. *(furl, fold, shut, suppress, restrict, hush, recall, stagnate, localize, close, condense, contract, gather, secrete, confine, repress, conceal, collect, concentrate.)*

spring—*v.* bound, start, issue, originate, emanate, burst, hurdle, flow, leap, jump, emerge, proceed, rise, germinate. *(alight, drop, issue, end, debouch, wither, disembogue, settle, land, arrive, eventuate, terminate.)*

squalid—*adj.* wretched, unkempt, dilapidated, shabby, dingy, filthy, untidy, poor, grimy, vulgar, disheveled, decayed. *(tidy, decent, neat, presentable, noble, well-kept, clean, respectable.)*

staid—*adj.* demure, sober, subdued, sedate, grave, steady, prudent, conservative. *(flighty, wanton, erratic, agitated, ruffled, capricious, unsteady, indiscreet, insedate, eccentric, discomposed.)*

stammer—*v.* hesitate, falter, mumble, stutter. *(speak unhesitantly, speak clearly.)*

stamp—*n.* kind, make, impression, print, cast, character, signature, type, genus, description, mark, imprint, brand, mould. *(non-description, heterogeneity, formlessness, unevenness.)*

stand—*v.* remain, be, suffer, rest, depend, consist, continue, pause, tolerate, halt, stop, exist, insist, await, hold, endure. *(move, advance, fail, succumb, lie, fade, depart, oppose, progress, proceed, fall, yield, drop, vanish, run.)*

standard—*n.* gauge, test, exemplar, flag, model, plummet, pennant, measure, criterion, rule, banner, type, scale, emblem. *(misrule, non-criterion, miscomparison, misfit, confusion, incommensurateness, inconformity, mismeasurement, misadjustment.)*

state—*n.* condition, circumstance, predicament, province, position, situation, plight, case, emotion.

state—*v.* declare, aver, narrate, particularize, recite, utter, say, propound, set forth, specify, avow. *(repress, imply,* *retract, contradict, repudiate, suppress, suppose, deny.)*

stately—*adj.* imposing, elevated, proud, pompous, grand, lofty, awesome, dignified, lordly, majestic, magnificent. *(unimposing, mean, commonplace, squalid, undignified, unstately.)*

staunch—*adj.* resolute, firm, faithful, trustworthy, loyal, devoted, stalwart, reliable, true. *(questionable, unreliable, faithless, vacillating, ambivalent.)*

stay—*v.* stop, withhold, hinder, obstruct, rest, remain, dwell, halt, wait, confide, lean, hold, restrain, arrest, delay, support, repose, continue, await, abide, tarry, trust, linger. *(liberate, expedite, free, hasten, depress, fail, proceed, depart, mistrust, facilitate, loose, send, speed, accelerate, oppress, burden, fall, move, overthrow.)*

steady—*adj.* fixed, uniform, equable, undeviating, permanent, well-regulated, firm, constant, consistent, regular. *(variable, inconstant, wavering, sporadic, ill-regulated, infirm, unsteady, changeable.)*

step—*n.* pace, grade, degree, walk, progression, trace, proceeding, measure, stride, advance, space, gradation, track, vestige, gait, action. *(recession, station, nongraduation, stand-still, tracklessness, non-impression, desistance, withdrawal, inaction, retreat, stop, halting, standing, non-progression, untraceableness, desinence.)*

stern—*adj.* austere, harsh, rigorous, unyielding, stringent, forbidding, severe, rigid, strict, unrelenting. *(genial, easy, lenient, encouraging, compassionate, kindly, flexible.)*

stiff—*adj.* inflexible, unyielding, strong, obstinate, constrained, starched, ceremonious, firm, difficult, unbending, rigid, forceful, stubborn, pertinacious, affected, formal. *(flexible, yielding, easy, unaffected, affable, pliable, unceremonious, pliant, flaccid, genial.)*

still—*adj.* calm, hushed, pacific, motionless, peaceful, tranquil, inert, stationary, quiet, noiseless, silent, serene, stagnant, quiescent. *(disturbed, moved, resonant, moving, dynamic, transitional, unquiet, agitated, noisy, turbulent.)*

stingy—*adj.* avaricious, niggardly, hide-bound, sparing, penurious, miserly, close, mean, frugal, parsimonious, sordid. *(generous, handsome,* *bountiful, munificent, unsparing, liberal, large, lavish.)*

stop—*v.* obstruct, cork, seal, suspend, rest, hinder, delay, terminate, end, thwart, close, plug, bar, arrest, halt, suppress, cease. *(expedite, broach, promote, farther, proceed, hasten, initiate, open, clear, unseal, advance, continue, speed.)*

stout—*adj.* lusty, robust, brawny, resolute, valiant, pudgy, durable, strong, vigorous, sturdy, corpulent, brave. *(debile, thin, lean, feeble, timid, fragile, weak, frail, attenuated, slender, irresolute, cowardly.)*

straight—*adj.* rectilinear, linear, unswerving, nearest, direct, undeviating, right, horizontal. *(winding, tortuous, serpentine, waving, devious, crooked, indirect, incurved, sinuous, circuitous.)*

strange—*adj.* alien, unfamiliar, odd, abnormal, surprising, marvelous, uncommon, anomalous, peculiar, foreign, exotic, unusual, irregular, exceptional, wonderful, astonishing. *(domestic, usual, common, customary, unsurprising, general, indigenous, familiar, ordinary, regular, commonplace, universal.)*

strength—*n.* vigor, security, sinew, vehemence, hardness, nerve, vitality, force, power, validity, intensity, soundness, fibre. *(imbecility, insolidity, invalidity, delicacy, flimsiness, vulnerability, hollowness, weakness, feebleness, insecurity, frailty, softness.)*

strenuous—*adj.* resolute, earnest, ardent, energetic, arduous, strong, determined, vigorous, bold, vehement. *(irresolute, feeble, unearnest, effortless, emasculate, weak, undetermined, debile.)*

strict—*adj.* exact, rigorous, close, stringent, precise, meticulous, accurate, severe, nice. *(inexact, lenient, lax, indulgent, negligent, loose, inaccurate, mild.)*

striking—*adj.* affecting, wonderful, notable, surprising, impressive, admirable. *(indifferent, minor, mediocre, ineffectual, commonplace.)*

stringent—*adj.* exacting, hard, severe, stern, rigorous, relentless, firm, compelling, obedient, harsh. *(relaxed, equivocal, flexible, moderate, lenient, easy.)*

strong—*adj.* vigorous, secure, forcible, hale, brawny, sound, cogent, dynamic, zealous, pungent, hardy, tenacious, powerful, solid, fortified, hearty, impetuous, sinewy, robust, patent, influential, muscular, staunch. *(weak, insecure, feeble, calm, delicate, inefficacious, frail, unconvincing, vapid, unavailing, debile, nerveless, moderate, powerless, defenseless, mild, gentle, sickly, unsatisfactory, unimpressive, impotent, lukewarm, flaccid, tender, indifferent, fragile.)*

stubborn—*adj.* unbending, hard, intractable, stiff, inflexible, harsh, refractory, contumacious, dogmatic, tough, unyielding, obstinate, heady, obdurate, pig-headed, headstrong. *(tractable, pliant, malleable, indecisive, flexible, docile, manageable pliable.)*

studious—*adj.* diligent, attentive, thoughtful, reflective, erudite, literary, desirous, careful, assiduous. *(illiterate, indulgent, regardless, thoughtless, idle, uneducated, unliterary, careless, inattentive, indifferent, negligent.)*

stupid—*adj.* senseless, doltish, dull, insensate, prosy, dull-witted, vacuous, stolid, besotted, obtuse, asinine. *(sharp, sensible, quick, penetrating, brilliant, bright, clever, sagacious.)*

subdue—*v.* reduce, break, quell, overwhelm, subjugate, conquer, overpower, tame, vanquish, master, suppress. *(exalt, strengthen, liberate, capitulate, enfranchise, aggrandize, fortify, empower.)*

subject—*adj.* subservient, liable, disposed, amenable, dependent, subordinate, exposed, prone, obnoxious. *(independent, dominant, indisposed, unamenable, exempt, superior, unliable.)*

submissive—*adj.* compliant, docile, obsequious, passive, subservient, humble, obedient, yielding, modest, acquiescent. *(incompliant, recusant, inobsequious, refractory, resistant, domineering, disobedient, unyielding, recalcitrant, proud, renitent.)*

substantial—*adj.* real, true, stout, material, bulky, durable, solid, existing, corporeal, strong, massive, tangible, stable. *(unreal, fictitious, incorporeal, visionary, weak, airy, spiritual, fragile, ghostly, frail, imaginary, insubstantial, chimerical, suppositious, immaterial, disembodied.)*

subtle—*adj.* artful, insinuating, astute, discriminating, fine, sophistical, elusive, jesuitical, sly, cunning, wily, nice, crafty, shrewd. *(frank,* *artless, open, rough, undiscerning, simple, obtuse, honest, undiscriminating, blunt, unsophisticated.)*

success—*n.* luck, prosperity, good-fortune, attainment, victory, achievement, consummation. *(defeat, ruin, disgrace, failure, disaster.)*

succession—*n.* supervention, progression, sequence, series, continuity, suite, following, order, rotation, supply. *(anticipation, antecedence, disorder, solution, intermission, gap, inconsecutiveness, interim, precedence, prevention, irregularity, non-sequence, failure, break.)*

succinct—*adj.* short, concise, crisp, laconic, condensed, compressed, compact, pithy, curt, clipped, abbreviated, terse. *(verbose, rambling, circuitous, wordy, loquacious, garrulous.)*

suffer—*v.* endure, undergo, grieve, permit, admit, experience, let, support, bear, sustain, allow, tolerate. *(repel, reject, repudiate, ignore, eliminate, resist, expel, disallow, forbid.)*

sufficient—*adj.* equal, satisfactory, qualified, suited, ample, fit, abundant, adequate, competent, adapted, enough. *(unequal, meagre, unqualified, insufficient, scanty, deficient, incomplete, inadequate, incompetent, short, unadapted, unsuited, bare.)*

suit—*v.* adapt, adjust, apportion, beseem, correspond, comport, serve, become, reconcile, accord, fit, match, harmonize, befit, tally, answer, please, agree. *(misadapt, misapportion, vary, disagree, dissatisfy, differ, miscomport, misfit, mismatch, unbeseem.)*

summary—*n.* tabulation, resume, digest, abstract, recapitulation, analysis, abridgment, compendium, epitome. *(dilution, expansion, dilatation, amplification.)*

superb—*adj.* magnificent, princely, showy, august, gorgeous, grand, exquisite, elegant, splendid, proud, stately. *(common, unimposing, inferior, shabby, mean, worthless.)*

supercilious—*adj.* contemptuous, arrogant, patronizing, insolent, haughty, disdainful. *(courteous, modest, humble, bashful, affable, respectful.)*

superficial—*adj.* slight, showy, flimsy, shallow, skin-deep, peripheral, light, imperfect, external, surface, smattering. *(profound, deep,* *recondite, exact, complex, abstruse, accurate, internal.)*

superior—*adj.* upper, preferable, loftier, remarkable, conspicuous, distinguished, higher, better, surpassing, excellent, eminent. *(lower, subordinate, common, average, mediocre, inferior, imperfect, worse, ordinary, mean, unremarkable.)*

supple—*adj.* bending, flexible, servile, cringing, sycophantic, limber, resilient, compliant, pliant, yielding, elastic, fawning, adulatory, lithe. *(unbending, stiff, inflexible, independent, rigid, supercilious, firm, unyielding, stubborn, inelastic, self-assertive.)*

supply—*v.* afford, accoutre, give, minister, contribute, replenish, furnish, provide, yield. *(use, waste, absorb, withhold, retain, deplete, expend, consume, exhaust, demand, withdraw.)*

support—*n.* stay, buttress, aid, influence, living, subsistence, food, prop, foundation, advocate, help, assistance, maintenance, patronage, livelihood.

support—*v.* uphold, underlie, help, assist, promote, suffer, foster, nourish, endorse, continue, stay, patronize, prop, sustain, bear, befriend, second, buttress, further, defend, nurture, cherish, maintain, countenance, subsidize, back, favor. *(betray, abandon, oppose, weaken, thwart, drop, disfavor, suppress, squelch, surrender, discontinue, discourage, exhaust, subvert.)*

suppose—*v.* presume, deem, fancy, regard, imagine, deduce, presuppose, guess, judge, consider, assume, believe, think, conceive, imply, conjecture, conclude. *(demonstrate, realize, conclude, deny, prove, substantiate, disbelieve.)*

sure—*adj.* secure, assured, stable, knowing, confident, unquestioning, unfailing, permanent, enduring, indisputable, absolute, fast, safe, certain, unmistakable, firm, strong, believing, trusting, positive, abiding, infallible. *(ignorant, doubtful, dubious, distrustful, vacillating, untrustworthy, insecure, transient, fallible, weak, loose, vulnerable, uncertain, hesitating, questioning, precarious, impermanent, evanescent, disputable.)*

surreptitious—*adj.* clandestine, covert, veiled, furtive, secret, stealthy, undercover, sneaky, concealed. *(exposed, candid, overt, public, open, straightforward.)*

susceptible—*adj.* impressible, sensitive, vulnerable, capable, tender. *(unimpressible, insusceptible, resistent, impassible, incapable, insensitive.)*

suspense—*n.* uncertainty, pause, solicitude, intermission, indecision, abeyance, indetermination, doubt, apprehension, protraction, cessation, waiting, discontinuance, stoppage. *(settlement, revival, continuance, finality, resolution, determination, execution, decision, uninterruption.)*

sway—*n.* influence, authority, supremacy, superiority, dominion, preponderance, ascendancy, force, jurisdiction, power, wield, rule, government, bias, control, domination, mastery, weight. *(inferiority, irresistance, subservience, weakness, debility, subjection, subordination, obedience.)*

sway—*v.* govern, bias, swing, teeter, wield, influence, rule, wave.

sweet—*adj.* luscious, dulcet, pure, harmonious, beautiful, wholesome, winning, fresh, amiable, genial, saccharine, fragrant, melodious, musical, lovely, pleasing, mild, agreeable, gentle. *(bitter, fetid, nauseous, stinking, inharmonious, unlovely, unwholesome, tainted, unamiable, repulsive, sour, unsweet, offensive, olid, nasty, discordant, repulsive, putrid, ungentle.)*

swell—*v.* extend, heighten, enhance, expand, augment, aggravate, dilate, distend, multiply, enlarge, heave, rise, increase, protuberate, amplify. *(curtail, diminish, shrivel, retrench, collapse, narrow, contract, concentrate, decrease, lessen, fold, reduce, condense.)*

sympathy—*n.* compassion, understanding, pity, tenderness, kindness, humanity, unselfishness. *(antagonism, animosity, pitilessness, compassionlessness, harshness, unkindliness, antipathy, incongeniality, mercilessness, unkindness.)*

system—*n.* scheme, regularity, arrangement, plan, organization, method, order, classification, rule. *(derangement, fortuity, medley, incongruity, non-classification, chaos, disorder, confusion, chance, haphazard, complication.)*

T

tact—*n.* delicacy, savoir faire, diplomacy, sensitivity, politeness, prudence, polish, subtlety, finesse. *(bluntness, grossness, crudeness, indiscretion, gaucherie, insensitivity, tactlessness.)*

take—*v.* grasp, capture, use, seize, pursue, follow, procure, catch, charm, engage, select, accept, admit, conduct, receive, apprehend, transfer, seige, obtain, employ, assume, captivate, interest, choose. *(reject, surrender, miss, release, repel, drop, abandon, lose.)*

tall—*adj.* lofty, elevated, high, towering, elongated. *(short, low, abbreviated.)*

tame—*adj.* reclaimed, subjugated, gentle, docile, spiritless, dull, subdued, domesticated, tamed, flat, broken, mild, meek, tedious. *(unreclaimed, wild, unbroken, spirited, ferine, exciting, lively, disobedient, savage, undomesticated, untamed, fierce, animated, interesting, stirring.)*

tangible—*adj.* real, solid, actual, concrete, palpable, manifest, veritable, specific, factual, substantial. *(imaginary, flimsy, elusive, vague, ethereal.)*

task—*n.* function, job, business, drudgery, lesson, assignment, work, labor, operation, undertaking, toil. *(leisure, hobby, rest, relaxation, amusement.)*

taste—*n.* savor, sapidity, choice, perception, discernment, critique, predilection, elegancy, aroma, refinement, gustation, flavor, relish, judgment, nicety, sensibility, zest, delicacy. *(ill-savor, disrelish, indiscrimination, indelicacy, inelegancy, abhorrence, nongustation, insipidity, nonperception, indiscernment, coarseness.)*

tasteful—*adj.* relishing, agreeable, toothsome, elegant, artistic, refined, sapid, savory, tasty, palatable. *(unrelishing, unpalatable, inelegant, vapid, unrefined, vulgar, insipid, unsavory, nauseous, tasteless.)*

teach—*v.* tell, instruct, counsel, educate, enlighten, indoctrinate, edify, train, impart, direct, inform, admonish, inculcate, advise. *(misteach, misinstruct, misguide, learn, mislead, withhold, misdirect, misinform.)*

teacher—*n.* school-master, tutor, pedagogue, educator, school-mistress, scholar, instructor, preceptor, professor, educationist. *(scholar, learner, student, pupil, disciple.)*

tedious—*adj.* tiresome, dilatory, sluggish, dull, prolix, prosaic, monotonous, wearisome, dreary, irksome. *(exciting, charming, delightful, challenging, stirring, amusing, interesting, fascinating.)*

tell—*v.* number, count, utter, state, disclose, betray, explain, promulgate, teach, report, discern, discriminate, decide, narrate, describe, mention, enumerate, recount, recite, verbalize, publish, divulge, acquaint, inform, communicate, rehearse, judge, ascertain. *(suppress, misnarrate, misdeclare, misjudge, conceal, misdescribe, repress, misrecount, miscommunicate, misrecite.)*

temporary—*adj.* immediate, limited, impermanent, momentary, present, partial, transient. *(lasting, complete, perfect, entire, settled, perpetual, confirmed, final, permanent.)*

tenacious—*adj.* firm, cohesive, obstinate, resolute, persistent, iron, mulish, perseverant, willful, obdurate, adamant, stalwart. *(flexible, loose, yielding, wavering, irresolute, lax, tractable.)*

tendency—*n.* proneness, gravitation, scope, disposition, proclivity, bias, inclination, conduciveness, penchant, course, vergency, drift, aim, predisposition, leaning, attraction. *(aversion, contravention, divergency, divarication, renitency, prevention, termination, hesitancy, disinclination, repulsive, deviation, tangency, opposition, reluctance, neutralization.)*

tender—*v.* proffer, bid, present, submit. *(withdraw, appropriate, withhold, retain, retract.)*

tender—*adj.* frail, susceptible, soft, weak, compassionate, careful, gentle, meek, merciful, sympathetic, pathetic, delicate, impressible, yielding, effeminate, feeble, jealous, affectionate, mild, pitiful. *(sturdy, robust, iron, unmerciful, hard-hearted, liberal, unchary, rough, coarse, unmoving, unimpressive, unimpressed, strong, insensitive, hardy, tough, pitiless, cruel, careless, lavish, ungentle, rude, unsentimental, unfeeling, unimpassioned.)*

tension—*n.* stretch, extension, rigidity, strain, tautness, worry, traction, anxiety, apprehension, stress. *(sag, calm, flexibility, serenity, tranquillity, looseness.)*

terminate—*v.* finish, stop, end, culminate, conclude, complete, expire, lapse, discontinue, cease. *(commence, initiate, pursue, begin, inaugurate, open, start.)*

terrible—*adj.* fearful, formidable, frightful, horrible, intimidating, shocking, awful, dreadful, terrific, tremendous. *(unastounding, unexcruciating, informidable, unstartling, unsevere.)*

terror—*n.* dread, fright, horror, panic, dismay, fear, alarm, consternation. *(fearlessness, confidence, reassurance, security, boldness.)*

test—*n.* trial, proof, standard, touchstone, ordeal, probe, cupel, examination, criterion, experiment, experience. *(misproof, misindication, misjudgment, miscomputation.)*

testimony—*n.* evidence, affirmation, confirmation, affidavit, proof, witness, attestation, corroboration. *(contradiction, confutation, invalidation, denial, refutation, disproof, contravention.)*

theatrical—*adj.* scenic, showy, gesticulatory, meretricious, thespian, dramatic, melodramatic, ceremonious, pompous. *(genuine, unaffected, subdued, plain, retiring, chaste, simple, quiet, mannerless.)*

thick—*adj.* close, turbid, coagulated, dull, foggy, crowded, solid, deep, inarticulate, voluminous, dense, massive, compact, luteous, muddy, misty, vaporous, numerous, bulky, confused. *(fine, sparse, pure, limpid, scanty, slight, laminated, articulate, narrow, distinct, race, thin, strained, percolated, clear, crystalline, incompact, shallow.)*

thicken—*v.* befoul, bemire, increase, amalgamate, intermix, multiply, expand, broaden, intensify, solidify, obscure, becloud, coagulate, commingle, crowd, enlarge, extend, deepen, confuse, obstruct. *(dissipate, attenuate, purify, percolate, defecate, free, brighten, open, diminish, reduce, contract, unravel, loosen, dilute, rarify, refine, clear, strain, clarify, depurate, lighten, filtrate, separate, narrow, liberate, extricate, disentangle.)*

thin—*adj.* slender, attenuated, watery, unsubstantial, translucent, lean, slim, flimsy, diluted, meagre. *(opaque, corpulent, thick, obese, solid, wide, dense.)*

think—*v.* meditate, reflect, conceive, hold, believe, judge, opine, cogitate, reckon, ponder, consider, contemplate, imagine, fancy, regard, deem. *(act rashly, forget, be thoughtless, act unreasonably.)*

thought—*n.* reasoning, supposition, sentiment, conception, opinion, view, conceit, design, intention, care, calculation, provision, reflection, cogitation, meditation, idea, fancy, judgment, purpose, deliberation. *(incogitation, dream, aberration, incogitancy, vacuity, improvidence, inattention, thoughtlessness, hallucination, misconception, carelessness, unreflectiveness, distraction.)*

threatening—*adj.* intimidating, foreboding, imminent, ominous, impending, menacing, unpromising. *(promising, enticing, overpast, auspicious, withdrawn, encouraging, reassuring, passed.)*

thwart—*v.* balk, frustrate, baffle, prevent, circumvent, prevent, outwit, defeat, fail, obstruct, hinder. *(support, abet, help, facilitate, cooperate, aid, magnify, encourage, assist.)*

tide—*n.* course, rush, influx, movement, avalanche, flow, flood, current, inundation, stream. *(arrestation, cessation, subsidence, discontinuance, stagnation, stoppage, motionlessness.)*

tight—*adj.* compact, close, neat, natty, secure, firm, fast, tidy, smart, tense. *(incompact, flowing, large, lax, flexible, loose, open, loose-fitting, untidy, relaxed, insecure.)*

time—*n.* duration, interval, era, opportunity, term, span, cycle, spell, period, season, date, age, occasion, space. *(eternity, indetermination, neverness, indeterminableness, perpetuity, non- duration.)*

timid—*adj.* pusillanimous, shy, diffident, timorous, cowardly, inadventurous, apprehensive, coy, fearful, afraid, faint-hearted. *(confident, courageous, rash, spirited, bold, venturesome, overventuresome, audacious, aggressive.)*

tinsel—*adj.* tawdry, garish, cheap, superficial, trashy, gaudy, meretricious, glittering. *(genuine, conservative, previous, understated, low-key, tasteful.)*

tint—*n.* hue, dye, shade, color, complexion, tinge, stain, tincture. *(decoloration, achromatism, pallor, etiolation, sallowness, cadaverousness, paleness, exsanguineousness, ashenness, bleaching, colorlessness, wanness.)*

tiresome—*adj.* wearisome, dull, monotonous, tedious, fatiguing, arduous, difficult, troublesome, exhausting, laborious. *(stimulating, restful, restorative, refreshing, exciting, delightful, fascinating.)*

title—*n.* heading, style, name, appellation, address, caption, inscription, denomination, designation, distinction, epithet. *(indistinction, namelessness, non-designation, nondescript, indenomination.)*

together—*adv.* conjointly, concertedly, coincidently, concurrently, unitedly, unanimously, contemporaneously, simultaneously, concomitantly. *(disconnectedly, variously, individually, separately, independently, incoincidently.)*

tolerable—*adj.* bearable, sufferable, permissible, passable, defensible, endurable, supportable, allowable, sufficient. (unbearable, insufferable, impermissible, intolerable, admissible, unendurable, insupportable, unallowable, insufficient.)

tolerate—*v.* permit, warrant, admit, indulge, authorize, sanction, concede, license, sustain, accord. *(forbid, ban, veto, prohibit, disapprove, repel, protest, refuse.)*

tongue—*n.* speech, dialect, articulation, idiom, discourse, language.

tool—*n.* implement, instrument, cat's-paw, appliance, hireling, utensil, machine, dupe.

topic—*n.* theme, subject-matter, thesis, question, subject.

torrid—*adj.* hot, fiery, suffocating, parched, scorching, tropical, fervent, amorous, erotic. *(cool, frigid, temperate, cold, arctic, indifferent.)*

tough—*adj.* stubborn, fibrous, refractory, unmanageable, firm, cohesive, strong, resistant, difficult, hard, tenacious. *(tender, soft, crumby, friable, yielding, fragile.)*

traditional—*adj.* usual, familiar, conventional, ritual, routine, prescriptive, normal, customary. *(unusual, rare, uncommon, unconventional, unfamiliar.)*

tragedy—*n.* calamity, adversity, grief, catastrophe, disaster, affliction, misfortune. *(delight, prosperity, fortune, joy, boon, comedy, merriment.)*

train—*n.* procession, cortege, series, appendage, suite, retinue, course.

train—*v.* rear, habituate, drill, practice, instruct, educate, familiarize with, lead, inure, accustom, exercise, discipline, bend. *(break, disaccustom, miseducate, misguide, disqualify, force, trail, dishabituate.)*

transfer—*v.* transport, sell, transplant, alienate, transmit, exchange, dispatch, convey, remove, assign, make over, give, translate, forward. *(withhold, retain, appropriate, keep, fix, retain.)*

transient—*adj.* fugitive, temporary, evanescent, momentary, brief, migratory, fleeting, transitory, passing, ephemeral. *(permanent, persistent, enduring, resident, abiding, perpetual, lasting.)*

transparent—*adj.* crystalline, limpid, obvious, indisputable, porous, self-evident, pellucid, translucent, diaphanous, clear. *(turbid, filmy, intransparent, dubious, thick, opaque, mysterious, questionable, complex.)*

travel—*n.* commuting, journey, progress, transportation, passage, expedition, cruising, tour, voyage. *(halt, cessation, pause, stay, rest.)*

treatise—*n.* essay, pamphlet, brochure, tractate, article, thesis, tract, paper, dissertation, monograph. *(notes, memoranda, ephemera, shedding, jottings, adversaria, effusion.)*

treaty—*n.* agreement, covenant, entente, negotiation, contract, convention, league, alliance. *(non-interference, non-agreement, indecision, non-convention, neutrality, non-alliance.)*

tremble—*v.* quake, tatter, shake, shudder, jar, pulsate, quiver, shiver, vibrate. *(steady, still, stand, compose, calm, settle.)*

tremendous—*adj.* dreadful, fearful, enormous, appalling, terrible, awful. *(unappalling, small, inconsiderable, little, unimposing.)*

tremulous—*adj.* quivery, spasmodic, throbbing, hesitant, palpitating, trembling, fearful, uncertain, flinching. *(motionless, brave, fixed, immobile, heroic, still, phlegmatic.)*

trial—*n.* gauge, temptation, proof, affliction, burden, attempt, criterion, tribulation, scrutiny, verification, test, experiment, trouble, grief, suffering, endeavor, essay, ordeal. *(non-probation, miscalculation, trifle, alleviation, disburdenment, comfort, oversight, delight, non-trial,* *mismeasurement, misestimate, triviality, relief, refreshment, attempt.)*

trick—*n.* contrivance, guile, wile, cheat, antic, finesse, deception, delusion, subterfuge, legerdemain, artifice, machination, stratagem, fraud, juggle, vagary, slight, imposition. *(exposure, mishap, botch, fumbling, maladroitness, blunder, openhandedness, betrayal, artlessness, bungling, inexpertness, genuineness.)*

tribulation—*n.* ordeal, oppression, adversity, depression, suffering, curse, misery, affliction, pain. *(pleasure, joy, happiness, ease, blessing.)*

trifle—*n.* bagatelle, straw, triviality, joke, bubble, toy, kickshaw, plaything, bauble, trinket, nothing, levity, cipher, gewgaw. *(portent, crisis, weight, importance, seriousness, muddle, treasure, phenomenon, conjuncture, urgency, necessity.)*

triumph—*n.* success, achievement, exultation, conquest, trophy, victory, ovation, coup. *(discomfiture, unsuccess, baffling, fiasco, disappointment, defeat, failure, abortion.)*

trivial—*adj.* trite, unimportant, nugatory, inconsiderable, paltry, frivolous, trifling, common, useless. *(weighty, original, trifle, novel, important, critical.)*

trouble—*n.* disturbance, perplexity, vexation, calamity, uneasiness, disaster, misfortune, anxiety, sorrow, grief, difficulty, toil, agony, effort, affliction, annoyance, molestation, inconvenience, distress, tribulation, torment, adversity, embarrassment, misery, depression, labor. *(composure, appeasement, assuagement, gratification, blessing, joy, ease, luck, amusement, indifference, inertia, treat, pleasure, indiligence, alleviation, delight, happiness, boon, exultation, gladness, facility, recreation, carelessness, indolence.)*

trouble—*v.* vex, confuse, distress, harass, molest, mortify, irritate, oppress, disturb, agitate, perplex, annoy, tease, grieve. *(calm, appease, soothe, gratify, entertain, refresh, elate, compose, allay, please, delight, recreate, relieve.)*

troublesome—*adj.* irksome, tedious, laborious, importunate, agitated, vexatious, tiresome, difficult, arduous, grievous. *(pleasant, facile, unlaborious, agree-*

able, untroublesome, easy, amusing, light.)

true—*adj.* veracious, precise, faithful, loyal, pure, literal, real, veritable, exact, accurate, actual, genuine. *(unreliable, untrustworthy, false, unfaithful, fickle, erroneous, perfidious, adulterated, inaccurate, fictitious, unhistorical, inveracious, faithless, treacherous, spurious, counterfeit.)*

trust—*n.* confidence, belief, faith, expectation, duty, charge, reliance, dependency, hope, credit, commission. *(suspicion, doubt, distrust, uncertainty.)*

trust—*v.* rely, believe, deposit, repose, depend, hope, confide, credit, charge, entrust. *(suspect, doubt, resume, despair, be wary of, distrust, discredit, disbelieve, withdraw.)*

try—*v.* endeavor, aim, test, gauge, fathom, venture, attempt, strive, examine, sound, probe. *(abandon, ignore, misexamine, neglect, misinvestigate, reject, discard.)*

turbid—*adj.* opaque, thick, dark, foul, smudgy, murky, vague, disoriented, incoherent, rattled, disturbed. *(clear, fresh, crystal, lucid, coherent, placid, limpid.)*

turn—*n.* winding, deflection, deed, alternation, occasion, act, purpose, convenience, gift, character, crisis, cast, manner, fashion, rotation, change, bend, vicissitude, curve, opportunity, time, office, treatment, requirement, talent, tendency, exigence, form, shape, mold, cut, pirouette, revolution, recurrence, alteration. *(fixity, stationariness, uniformity, indeflection, oversight, untimeliness, non-requirement, shapelessness, sameness, stability, immobility, unchangeableness, rectilinearity, continuity, incognizance, independence, malformation.)*

turn—*v.* shape, adapt, reverse, alter, convert, revolve, hinge, deviate, mold, diverge, change, swivel, round, spin, deflect, transform, rotate, metamorphose, depend, incline, decline. *(misadapt, stabilitate, fix, continue, maintain, proceed, misshape, perpetuate, stereotype, arrest.)*

turncoat—*n.* deserter, renegade, trimmer, defector, apostate.

tutor—*n.* governor, teacher, professor, savant, coach, guardian, instructor, preceptor, master. *(pupil, stu-*

dent, learner, ward, tyro, scholar, disciple, neophyte.)

twine—*v.* wind, entwine, wreath, unite, bend, coil, meander, twist, embrace. *(unwind, disunite, separate, unwreath, disentwine, straighten, untangle, untwist, detach, unravel, continue.)*

twist—*v.* convolve, pervert, wrest, wind, form, unite, braid, contort, complicate, distort, wreath, encircle, weave, insinuate, interpenetrate. *(untwist, verify, reflect, preserve, substantiate, unwind, disengage, disunite, disincorporate, attest, unravel, straighten, rectify, represent, render, express, unwreath, detach, separate, disentangle.)*

type—*n.* stamp, kind, sign, form, pattern, idea, likeness, cast, mark, fashion, species, emblem, model, character, symbol, archetype, image, expression, mold. *(nonclassification, misrepresentation, falsification, deviation, monstrosity, aberration, nondescription, inexpression, misindication, abnormity, caricature.)*

tyranny—*n.* autocracy, czarism, despotism, severity, sterness, coercion, terrorism, savagery, authoritarianism, oppression. *(relaxation, understanding, ease, mercy, humanity, benevolence, democracy.)*

tyro—*n.* amateur, neophyte, beginner, student, novice, appretice, freshman, novitiate, greenhorn. *(master, pro, veteran, professional, expert.)*

U

ugly—*adj.* hideous, frightful, ill-favored, ill—looking, hateful, homely, repulsive, loathsome, uncouth, unsightly, plain, ungainly, deformed, monstrous. *(fair, shapely, handsome, comely, attractive, seemly, beautiful.)*

ultimate—*adj.* final, conclusive, farthest, maximum, last, extreme, remotest. *(intermediate, preliminary, prior, proximate, initial.)*

umbrage—*n.* displeasure, antipathy, indignation, offense, pique, resentment, animosity, rancor, anger. *(good will, sympathy, amity, cordiality, harmony.)*

unanimous—*adj.* unified, solid, of one mind, agreeing, undivided, harmonious. *(disagreeing, split, discordant, differing.)*

unappetizing—*adj.* uninviting, stale, unpalatable, vapid, insipid, unpleasant, unappealing, unsavory. *(agreeable, pleasant, attractive, interesting, appealing.)*

unbelievable—*adj.* inconceivable, improbable, preposterous, incredible, untenable, irrational, suspicious, absurd. *(credible, persuasive, convincing, believable, obvious.)*

uncertain—*adj.* dubious, fitful, ambiguous, variable, problematic, fluctuating, doubtful, questionable, equivocal, indistinct. *(fixed, decided, definite, steady, reliable.)*

unconscious—*adj.* comatose, senseless, lethargic, asleep, numb, unaware, incognizant, narcotized, insensible. *(awake, aware, sensible, conscious, alert, cognizant, knowing.)*

undeniable—*adj.* indisputable, incontrovertible, irrefutable, incontestable, unquestionable. *(doubtful, debatable, deniable, untenable, controversial.)*

undergo—*v.* suffer, sustain, bear, tolerate, experience, endure. *(avoid, reject, miss, forego, refuse.)*

underhand—*adj.* furtive, unfair, surreptitious, deceitful, clandestine, dishonest, fraudulent. *(straightforward, honest, candid, undisguised, openhanded, fair.)*

understand—*v.* comprehend, perceive, conceive, recognize, imply, appreciate, apprehend, know, discern, learn, interpret. *(miscomprehend, misinterpret, state, express, misapprehend, ignore, declare, enunciate, neglect.)*

understanding—*n.* discernment, construction, intellect, mind, conception, brains, cognizance, knowledge, interpretation, agreement, intelligence, sense, reason. *(misapprehension, misinterpretation, mindlessness, ignorance, misunderstanding, misconstruction, irrationality, antipathy.)*

unethical—*adj.* dishonorable, shady, improper, corrupt, unscrupulous, immoral, conniving, unfair, unworthy, suspect. *(moral, ethical, upright, scrupulous, worthy, honorable.)*

unfit—*adj.* unsuitable, untimely, ineffective, incompetent, improper, inconsistent. *(suitable, competent, eligible, adequate, equipped, hale, sound.)*

unfortunate—*adj.* ill-fated, wretched, miserable, catastrophic, calamitous, unlucky, unhappy. *(lucky, successful, fortunate, affluent, happy, auspicious.)*

uniform—*adj.* invariable, regular, homogeneous, equal, alike, equable, undiversified, unvarying, even, conformable, consistent, unvaried, symmetrical. *(variable, irregular, incongruous, heterogeneous, diverse, multifarious, polymorphic, varying, eccentric, different, inconformable, inconsistent, unsymmetrical, erratic, multigenous, bizarre.)*

union—*n.* coalition, agreement, conjunction, league, alliance, concord, consolidation, fusion, junction, combination, harmony, concert, connection, confederacy, confederation. *(separation, divorce, discord, secession, multiplication, division, rupture, disjunction, severance, disagreement, disharmony, disruption, diversification.)*

unit—*n.* item, individual, part, piece, ace. *(aggregate, sum, total, mass, collection, composite.)*

unite—*v.* combine, attach, associate, embody, fuse, connect, add, cohere, integrate, converge, join, link, amalgamate, coalesce, merge, conjoin, couple, incorporate with, concatenate, reconcile. *(sever, separate, resolve, disintegrate, disrupt, multiply, sunder, segregate, diverge, disjoin, dissociate, disamalgamate, disunite, disconnect, divide, part.)*

unity—*n.* singleness, concord, agreement, indivisibility, identity, oneness, individuality, conjunction, uniformity. *(multitude, multiplicity, disjunction, severance, heterogeneity, incongruity, disharmony, divisibility, plurality, complexity, discord, separation, variety, diversity.)*

universal—*adj.* unlimited, total, entire, ecumenical, prevalent, pandemic, worldwide, common, comprehensive. *(unique, rare, limited, particular, exclusive.)*

universal—*adj.* embracing, all, unlimited, comprehensive, general, exhaustive, ecumenical, complete, total, boundless, entire, whole. *(local, incomplete, particular, unique, exceptional, partial, limited, exclusive, inexhaustive.)*

unlawful—*adj.* illegal, unlicensed, illicit, unconstitutional, forbidden, lawless. *(licit, authorized, permitted, legal, legitimate.)*

unreasonable—*adj.* silly, exorbitant, preposterous, ridiculous, foolish, extravagant, absurd, immoderate. *(sane, rational, sensible, logical, wise, equitable.)*

upright—*adj.* erect, honest, pure, conscientious, fair, ethical, just, equitable, vertical, perpendicular, honorable, principled. *(inclined, dishonest, dishonorable, unprincipled, unethical, unconscientious, inverted, corrupt.)*

urge—*v.* push, impel, force, press, solicit, incite, stimulate, good, expedite, dispatch, drive, propel, importune, animate, instigate, hasten, accelerate. *(hold, inhibit, restrain, hinder, discourage, obstruct, caution, repress, retain, coerce, cohibit, retard, damp.)*

urgent—*adj.* imperative, grave, importunate, strenuous, serious, indeferrible, pressing, immediate, forcible, momentous, demanding. *(insignificant, trivial, frivolous, deferrible, unimportant, trifling.)*

use—*n.* custom, practice, habit, utility, exercise, advantage, service.

use—*v.* exercise, practice, utilize, habituate, employ, inure, treat, accustom. *(suspend, avoid, dishabituate, save, disinure, discard, ignore, disaccustom.)*

useful—*adj.* profitable, serviceable, available, suited, utilitarian, conducive, advantageous, helpful, beneficial, adapted. *(unprofitable, obstructive, retardative, antagonistic, ineffectual, combersome, unbeneficial, hostile, inconducive, fruitless, applicable, disadvantageous, preventative, useless, burdensome, unavailable.)*

usual—*adj.* customary, normal, habitual, accustomed, prevalent, common, ordinary, regular, wonted, general, frequent. *(rare, uncustomary, abnormal, unusual, sparse, uncommon, exceptional, extraordinary, irregular.)*

utmost—*adj.* maximum, greatest, sovereign, remotest, terminal, uppermost, maximal, extreme, major, cardinal, foremost. *(minimal, adjacent, nearest, smallest, minimum, next, neighboring.)*

utter—*v.* issue, express, speak, pronounce, emit, circulate, promulgate, articulate. *(suppress, hush, check, conceal, swallow, recall, repress, stifle.)*

utter—*adj.* perfect, unqualified, thorough, entire, pure, sheer, unmitigated, extreme, complete, absolute, consummate. *(impure, limited, incomplete, imperfect, reasonable.)*

utterly—*adv.* completely, quite, entirely, extremely, totally, wholly, altogether. *(somewhat, rather, tolerably, partly, moderately, passably.)*

V

vacancy—*n.* void, hollowness, gap, blankness, vacuousness, hole, emptiness, depletion. *(plenitude, profusion, fullness, occupancy, completeness.)*

vacant—*adj.* leisure, unencumbered, void, mindless, depleted, empty, exhausted, unemployed, unoccupied, unfilled. *(replenished, employed, occupied, thoughtful, intelligent, full, business, engaged, filled.)*

vague—*adj.* lax, undetermined, intangible, unsettled, pointless, casual, general, indefinite, popular, equivocal, uncertain, ill-defined. *(definite, limited, pointed, specified, strict, specific, determined, scientific, mysterious.)*

vain—*adj.* worthless, unsatisfying, idle, egotistic, unreal, arrogant, conceited, complacent, empty, fruitless, unavailing, ineffectual, showy. *(substantial, worthy, effectual, potent, modest, humble, real, solid, sound, efficient, cogent, unconceited.)*

valid—*adj.* powerful, weighty, substantial, efficient, operative, logical, conclusive, strong, cogent, sound, available, sufficient. *(invalid, unsound, unavailable, insufficient, obsolete, superseded, vague, illogical, weak, powerless, unsubstantial, inefficient, inoperative, effete.)*

value—*v.* compute, estimate, treasure, prize, evaluate, appreciate, rate, esteem, appraise. *(misestimate, disregard, underrate, underestimate, scorn, despise, condemn, vilify, miscompute, disesteem, vilipend, undervalue, cheapen.)*

vanity—*n.* unsubstantiality, conceit, falsity, self-sufficiency, pride, triviality, narcissism, emptiness, unreality, ostentation, worthlessness. *(solidity, reality, modesty, simplicity, humility, diffidence, substance, substantiality, truth, self-distrust, unostentatiousness.)*

vaporize—*v.* mist, fume, spray, atomize, humidify,

steam, evaporate, volatilize. *(dry, dehydrate, dehumidify, desiccate.)*

variable—*adj.* mutable, capricious, unsteady, shifting, elastic, changeable, fickle, wavering, inconstant. *(unchangeable, constant, true, staunch, steady, invariable, predictable, firm, unchanging, immutable, fast, unwavering, unalterable.)*

variation—*n.* alteration, diversity, change, exception, transformation, discrepancy, deviation, mutation, departure, abnormity. *(fixity, exemplification, rule, harmony, regularity, law, agreement, continuance, indivergency, uniformity.)*

variety—*n.* diversity, miscellany, multiformity, heterogeneity, abnormity, difference, medley, multiplicity. *(species, specimen, sameness, uniformity, type.)*

various—*adj.* diverse, sundry, multitudinous, manifold, miscellaneous, diversified, different, multiform, several, uncertain. *(same, uniform, similar, equivalent, one, few, identical.)*

vast—*adj.* wild, extensive, huge, spacious, gigantic, boundless, enormous, colossal, far-reaching, substantial, desolate, widespread, wide, measureless, mighty, immense, prodigious. *(close, frequented, cultivated, tilled, bounded, moderate, paltry, narrow, confined, populated, tended, limited, circumscribed.)*

vassal—*n.* serf, underling, slave, hireling, subordinate, puppet, dependent, minion, yes-man. *(overlord, master, boss, ruler.)*

vegetate—*v.* deteriorate, stagnate, languish, waste away, idle, loaf, laze. *(develop, bloom, grow, participate, react, accomplish, bustle, respond.)*

vehement—*adj.* impetuous, urgent, burning, raging, passionate, eager, zealous, violent, ardent, fervent, furious, fervid, forcible. *(feeble, subdued, unimpassioned, cold, gentle, mitigated, timid, mild, inanimate, controlled, passionless, stoical, weak.)*

vengeance—*n.* retaliation, revenge, vindictiveness, retribution, fury. *(pardon, amnesty, remission, oblivion, reprieve, tolerance, forgiveness, condonation, grace, absolution, indulgence.)*

venom—*n.* spite, hate, rancor, malice, hostility, rage, truculence, animosity, resentment, enmity. *(charity, pity, mercy, benevolence, humanitarianism, kindness.)*

venture—*n.* risk, hazard, undertaking, experiment, wager, speculation, chance, stake, luck, gamble. *(caution, calculation, law, surveillance, method, non-speculation, reservation, certainty.)*

veracity—*n.* truthfulness, truth, exactness, integrity, accuracy, credibility. *(dishonesty, lying, mendacity, deceitfulness, guile, error.)*

verdict—*n.* judgment, opinion, sentence, evaluation, finding, answer, decision. *(indecision, bias, misconception, indetermination, nondeclaration.)*

verge—*v.* bend, incline, tend, approximate, bear, gravitate, slope, approach. *(deviate, depart, return, retrocede, deflect, decline, revert, recede, back.)*

verify—*v.* confirm, authenticate, identify, test, demonstrate, corroborate, establish, fulfill, substantiate, realize, warrant. *(subvert, falsify, fail, misrepresent, disappoint, refute, disestablish, mistake, misstate, invalidate.)*

versed—*adj.* practiced, acquainted, indoctrinated, familiar, proficient, qualified, skilled, conversant, initiated, clever, accomplished. *(Ill-versed, untaught, inconversant, uninitiated, awkward, unversed, incompetent, unskilled, unpracticed, unfamiliar, ignorant, strange.)*

vested—*adj.* absolute, independent, statutory, guaranteed, inalienable, established, sanctioned, fixed. *(contingent, occasional, provisional, variable.)*

vex—*v.* irritate, plague, worry, tantalize, trouble, afflict, annoy, tease, provoke, torment, bother, pester, disquiet, harass. *(appease, quiet, mollify, please, soothe, gratify.)*

vibrant—*adj.* pulsing, resonant, ringing, vibrating, throbbing, sonorous, energetic, animated, forceful. *(sluggish, weak, inactive, thin, feeble, dull, phlegmatic.)*

vice—*n.* fault, evil, immorality, badness, imperfection, defect, corruption, crime, sin. *(faultlessness, virtue, goodness, attainment, soundness, purity, perfection, immaculateness.)*

vicious—*adj.* faulty, bad, morbid, peccant, profligate, impure, immoral, depraved, corrupt, defective, debased, unruly. *(sound, virtuous, friendly, healthy, pure, perfect.)*

victory—*n.* triumph, success, domination, conquest, ovation. *(defeat, disappointment, miscarriage, downfall, non-success, failure, frustration, abortion.)*

view—*v.* examine, explore, consider, reconnoitre, regard, judge, glimpse, behold, inspect, survey, contemplate, observe, estimate. *(overlook, misconsider, misobserve, misjudge, ignore, disregard, misinspect, misestimate.)*

view—*n.* vision, examination, light, judgment, scene, apprehension, aim, conception, object, intention, sight, design, scrutiny, survey, estimate, inspection, representation, sentiment, opinion, purpose, end. *(occultation, darkness, deception, delusion, misrepresentation, aimlessness, error, non-intention, blindness, obscuration, misexamination, misjudgment, misconception.)*

vile—*adj.* worthless, low, mean, hateful, impure, abandoned, cheap, sinful, ignoble, villainous, base, wretched, profligate, valueless, despicable, bad, vicious, abject, sordid, wicked, degraded. *(rare, valuable, exalted, honorable, venerable, virtuous, costly, precious, high, noble, lofty.)*

villain—*n.* wretch, scoundrel, reprobate, ruffian. *(prince, idol, hero.)*

villainous—*adj.* knavish, infamous, detestable, base, depraved. *(heroic, moral, humane, virtuous, saintly, righteous.)*

vindicate—*v.* maintain, clear, defend, substantiate, establish, exonerate, assert, uphold, support, claim, justify. *(abandon, forego, disestablish, nullify, subvert, vitiate, pardon, waive, surrender, disprove, neutralize, destroy, annul.)*

violate—*v.* injure, disturb, rape, debauch, infringe, transgress, desecrate, disobey, ravish, abuse, hurt, outrage, break, profane. *(foster, regard, cherish, obey, esteem, respect, observe, preserve, protect.)*

violence—*n.* impetuosity, rape, rage, injustice, infringement, oppression, truculence, force, destructiveness, outrage, profanation, fury, fierceness. *(mildness, feebleness, respect, self-control, obedience, conservation, humaneness, lenity, protection, self-restraint,* *gentleness, forbearance, observance, preservation.)*

virtue—*n.* capacity, force, excellence, morality, uprightness, chastity, rectitude, power, strength, efficacy, value, goodness, purity, salubrity, honor. *(incapacity, inefficacy, corruption, immorality, dishonor, unchastity, malignancy, weakness, inability, badness, vice, impurity, virulence.)*

visible—*adj.* apparent, plain, conspicuous, discernible, clear, manifest, evident, detectable, perceptible, obvious, observable, palpable, distinguishable. *(non-apparent, hidden, impalpable, invisible, concealed, withdrawn, indistinguishable, imperceptible, inconspicuous, microscopic, unobservable, eclipsed, indiscernible.)*

visionary—*adj.* dreamy, baseless, imaginary, fabulous, idealized, romantic, fanciful, chimerical, shadowy, unreal. *(real, sound, veritable, palpable, sober, actual, truthful, substantial, unromantic.)*

vital—*adj.* palpable, animate, viable, functioning, essential, crucial, critical, decisive, fundamental, mortal. *(dead, weak, inanimate, irrelevant, phlegmatic, superficial.)*

vivid—*adj.* brilliant, resplendent, radiant, clear, animated, lively, striking, sunny, scintillant, dynamic, bright, luminous, lustrous, graphic, stirring, glowing. *(opaque, obscure, dim, lurid, non-reflecting, dusky, nebulous, wan, colorless, dull, non-luminous, rayless, somber, cloudy, pale, nondescript.)*

volume—*n.* body, dimensions, work, capacity, compass, magnitude, quantity, aggregate, size, bulk, book, extent. *(tenuity, diminutiveness, minuteness, smallness.)*

voluntary—*adj.* spontaneous, intentional, discretional, willing, deliberate, free, optional, unconstrained, chosen. *(coercive, forced, involuntary, compelled, compulsory, necessitated.)*

volunteer—*v.* proffer, originate, provide, offer, tend. *(suppress, withhold, withdraw, refuse.)*

voluptuous—*adj.* luxurious, licentious, highly pleasant, sensuous, hedonistic, sensual, self-indulgent. *(abstinent, sober, ascetic, monkish, unsensual, self-denying.)*

vulgar—*adj.* general, ordinary, vernacular, uncultivated, low, coarse, uncouth, underbred, popular, loose, public, plebian, unrefined, mean. *(scientific, restricted, accurate, select, cultivated, polite, stylish, elegant, aristocratic, strict, philosophical, technical, patrician, choice, refined, high-bred.)*

vulnerable—*adj.* unguarded, insecure, unprotected, weak, destructible, delicate, defenseless, easily wounded. *(protected, impervious, invincible, guarded.)*

W

wages—*n.* compensation, salary, payment, allowance, remuneration, stipend, hire. *(douceur, bonus, gift, premium, grace, gratuity.)*

wakeful—*adj.* vigilant, restless, alert, cautious, wary, awake. *(dozing, heedless, drowsy, somnolent, asleep.)*

wander—*v.* range, rove, roam, stray, err, straggle, navigate, travel, cruise, ramble, stroll, expatitate, deviate, depart, swerve, saunter, circumnavigate. *(stop, bivouac, lie, alight, moor, repose, remain, pause, settle, rest, perch, halt, anchor.)*

want—*n.* lack, insufficiency, shortage, neglect, absence, hunger, non-production, omission, deficiency, failure, shortness, scantiness. *(sufficiency, abundance, allowance, adequacy, affluence, supply, provision, production, supplement.)*

wanton—*adj.* roving, playful, loose, uncurbed, unrestrained, licentious, inconsiderate, heedless, gratuitous, malicious, wandering, sportive, frolicsome, unbridled, reckless, irregular, dissolute. *(unroving, unplayful, joyless, demure, discreet, self-controlled, formal, purposed, staid, cold-blooded, puritanical, determined, stationary, unsportive, unfrolicsome, thoughtful, sedate, well-regulated, austere, deliberate.)*

warlike—*n.* aggressive, militant, hostile, bellicose, belligerent, pugnacious, strategic. *(nonviolent, friendly, conciliatory, pacifistic, accommodating, peaceful.)*

warm—*adj.* thermal, irascible, ardent, fervid, glowing, zealous, excited, animated, tepid, genial, blood-warm. *(cold, starved, cool, passionless, chilly, frigid, unexcited, indifferent.)*

warmth—*n.* glow, zeal, excitement, earnestness, animation, vehemence, sincerity, irascibility, life, ardor, affability, emotion, fervor, heat, intensity, cordiality, eagerness, passion, geniality. *(frost, iciness, chill, calmness, indifference, insensitiveness, slowness, insincerity, good-temper, frigidity, congelation, coldness, coolness, torpidity, apathy, ungeniality, death, passionlessness.)*

waste—*v.* destroy, impair, pine, squander, throw away, lavish, attenuate, shrivel, wane, trifle, ruin, devastate, consume, decay, dissipate, diminish, desolate, dwindle, wither. *(repair, preserve, stint, protect, economize, hoard, augment, accumulate, flourish, multiply, develop, restore, conserve, perpetuate, husband, utilize, treasure, enrich, luxuriate.)*

watchful—*adj.* expectant, heedful, observant, circumspect, cautious, alert, vigilant, wakeful, careful, attentive, wary. *(invigilant, slumbrous, heedless, inobservant, uncircumspect, incautious, reckless, distracted, unwatchful, unwakeful, drowsy, careless, inattentive, unwary.)*

weak—*adj.* infirm, powerless, fragile, inadhesive, frail, tender, flabby, wishy-washy, watery, spiritless, injudicious, undecided, impressible, ductile, malleable, inconclusive, pointless, enervated, feeble, limp, debile, incompact, pliant, soft, vulnerable, flimsy, foolish, destructible, diluted, inefficient, unsound, unconfirmed, wavering, easy, unconvincing, vapid. *(vigorous, muscular, powerful, stout, sturdy, adhesive, fibrous, indestructible, intoxicating, spirited, wise, judicious, valid, determined, stubborn, inexorable, irresistible, telling, robust, strong, energetic, nervous, tough, lusty, compact, resistant, hard, potent, efficient, animated, sound, cogent, decided, unwavering, unyielding, conclusive, forcible.)*

weaken—*v.* enfeeble, dilute, paralyze, sap, emasculate, debilitate, enervate, impair, attenuate. *(invigorate, corroborate, develop, confirm, strengthen, empower.)*

wealth—*n.* riches, lucre, affluence, opulence, assets, influence, mammon, plenty, abundance. *(poverty, impecuniosity, destitution, indigence, scarcity.)*

wear—*v.* bear, sport, don, impair, channel, excavate,

rub, diminish, manifest, carry, groove, exhibit, consume, waste, hollow. *(abandon, renovate, increase, augment, expand, doff, repair, renew, swell.)*

weary—*adj.* tired, worn, faint, debilitated, toil-worn, fatigued, dispirited, exhausted, jaded, spent. *(vigorous, renovated, bouncy, hearty, fresh, recruited.)*

weather—*v.* withstand, surmount, survive, resist, bear, endure, suffer. *(collapse, fail, succumb, fall.)*

weave—*v.* braid, intermix, complicate, spin, intersect, loop, interlace, intertwine, plait. *(untwist, disentangle, simplify, dissect, segregate, unravel, disunite, extricate, enucleate.)*

weight—*n.* ponderosity, pressure, importance, influence, tonnage, consequence, impressiveness, gravity, heaviness, burden, power, efficacy, moment. *(levity, alleviation, insignificance, inefficacy, triviality, unimportance, worthlessness, lightness, portableness, weakness, unimpressiveness.)*

weird—*adj.* mysterious, mystic, strange, odd, uncanny, bizarre, queer. *(normal, common, orthodox, familiar, mundane, natural.)*

well—*adj.* hale, vigorous, sound, hearty, robust, healthy, strong, chipper. *(sick, ill, weak.)*

white—*adj.* pure, unblemished, stainless, clear, snowy, colorless, alabaster, unspotted, innocent. *(impure, ebony, black, inky.)*

whole—*adj.* entire, well, sound, perfect, undiminished, undivided, gross, total, complete, healthy, unimpaired, integral. *(imperfect, unsound, impaired, fractional, sectional, lacking, partial, incomplete, sick, diminished, divided.)*

wholesome—*adj.* salubrious, salutiferous, nutritious, healthful, invigorating, healing, salutary, beneficial. *(unhealthful, insalutary, unwholesome, detrimental, harmful, morbific, unhealthy, insalubrious, prejudicial, deleterious.)*

whore—*n.* prostitute, cyprian, trollop, night walker, wench, woman of ill-fame, bawd, hussy, fille de joie, harlot, courtesan, streetwalker, strumpet, Magdalen, punk, woman of the town, hustler. *(pure woman, lady, virgin, respectable woman.)*

wicked—*adj.* bad, sinful, iniquitous, unjust, irreligious, ungodly, sinful, atrocious, dark, unhallowed, evil, naughty, flagitious, corrupt, black, godless, immoral, criminal, unrighteous, profane, vicious, foul, nefarious, heinous, abandoned. *(virtuous, godly, religious, honest, honorable, good, sinless, immaculate, ethical, stainless, just, moral, upright, pure, incorrupt, spotless.)*

wide—*adj.* ample, spacious, remote, extended, broad, vast, immense, widespread. *(restricted, scant, small, narrow, limited.)*

wild—*adj.* undomesticated, uninhabited, savage, unrefined, ferocious, violent, loose, turbulent, inordinate, chimerical, incoherent, distracted, barbaric, haggard, untamed, uncultivated, uncivilized, rude, untrained, ferine, disorderly, ungoverned, disorderly, visionary, raving. *(domesticated, inhabited, populous, polite, reclaimed, tame, mild, regulated, rational, trim, coherent, sober, calm, tranquil, cultivated, frequented, civilized, refined, gentle, subdued, orderly, collected, sane, sensible.)*

willful—*adj.* deliberate, intentional, premeditated, wayward, stubborn, headstrong, contemplated, purposed, designed, preconcerted, refractory, self-willed. *(accidental, unpremeditated, obedient, manageable, considerate, amenable, thoughtful, undersigned, unintentional, docile, obdurate, deferential.)*

wisdom—*n.* erudition, enlightenment, information, judgment, prudence, intelligence, light, knowledge, learning, attainment, discernment, sagacity. *(illiterateness, indiscernment, folly, darkness, smattering, nonsense, ignorance, injudiciousness, imprudence, empiricism, inacquaintance, absurdity.)*

wit—*n.* intellect, reason, humor, imagination, levity, mind, sense, understanding, ingenuity. *(senselessness, dullness, stupidity, doltishness, vapidity, folly, mindlessness, irrationality, stolidity, inanity, platitude.)*

withdraw—*v.* go, retire, leave, retreat, depart, disappear, abdicate. *(arrive, appear, propose, reiterate, come, repeat.)*

withhold—*v.* keep, stay, restrain, detain, suppress, retain, inhibit, refuse, forbear. *(afford, provide, permit, incite, lavish, promote, grant, fur-*

nish, allow, encourage, concede.)

withstand—*v.* resist, thwart, endure, face, oppose, confront. *(surrender, falter, acquiesce, support, aid, back, yield, submit, encourage, abet.)*

witness—*n.* testimony, corroboration, corroborator, spectator, testifier, beholder, attestation, evidence, cognizance, eye-witness, auditor, voucher. *(incognizance, ignorance, ignoramus, alien, illiterate, stranger, invalidation, refutation.)*

woeful—*adj.* unfortunate, grievous, distressing, disastrous, tragic, mournful, doleful, anguished, miserable, pitiful, inadequate, worthless. *(fortunate, auspicious, beneficial, carefree, contented, generous, prosperous, enviable, glad.)*

wolfish—*adj.* savage, fierce, predatory, greedy, ravenous, merciless, pitiless. *(gentle, mild, harmless, generous, benevolent, compassionate.)*

wonder—*n.* miracle, surprise, awe, puzzlement, fascination, phenomenon, admiration, marvel, sign, surprise, prodigy. *(calm, apathy, anticipation, triviality, composure, expectation, indifference.)*

wonderful—*adj.* miraculous, astonishing, wondrous, fabulous, spectacular, awe-inspiring, unusual, startling, portentous, prodigious, strange, admirable, amazing. *(banal, normal, wonted, nondescript, every-day, regular, customary, expected, anticipated, current, natural, usual, expected.)*

wooly—*adj.* fuzzy, blurred, vague, hazy, foggy, clouded, murky, unfocused. *(clear, definite, well-defined, sharp.)*

word—*n.* message, report, news, promise, engagement, signal, warrant, declaration, term. *(idea, conception).*

wordy—*adj.* verbose, prolix, longwinded, talkative, garrulous, inflated, redundant, periphrastic, rambling. *(concise, succinct, brief, terse, trenchant, pithy.)*

work—*n.* travail, labor, toil, drudgery, product, result, issue, composition, operation, profession, business, chore, undertaking, project, feat, achievement. *(play, leisure, rest, non-performance, idleness, sloth, stall, collapse, non-production, fruitlessness.)*

worldly—*adj.* earthly, secular, profane, materialistic, mundane, temporal, carnal, shrewd, practical, urbane, experienced. *(unearthly, spiritual, metaphysical, heavenly, simple, naive, artless.)*

worn—*adj.* frayed, damaged, tattered, used, dingy, exhausted, threadbare. *(undamaged, fresh, unused, new.)*

worry—*v.* fret, brood, pester, harass, molest, annoy, tease, torment, importune, harry, plague, disquiet, vex. *(comfort, pacify, calm, soothe, gratify, please, quiet, amuse, reassure.)*

worsen—*v.* deteriorate, spoil, aggravate, decay, degenerate, contaminate. *(better, brighten, recover, improve, mend.)*

worship—*v.* revere, glorify, honor, respect, idolize, cherish, treasure, admire, venerate. *(dishonor, mock, blaspheme, scoff at, dislike, despise, hate.)*

worth—*n.* estimation, holdings, rate, value, merit, price, expense, importance, significance, estate, property. *(insignificance, worthlessness, inappreciableness, paltriness, triviality, demerit, uselessness.)*

worthless—*adj.* purposeless, unproductive, useless, valueless, meaningless, empty, trivial, reprobate, vile, trashy. *(important, worthy, essential, precious, virtuous, noble, advantageous, honorable, rare, costly, excellent, useful, lucrative.)*

wrap—*v.* envelop, enfold, cover, package, wind, conceal, roll up, bundle. *(unfurl, open, unwrap, unfold.)*

wrath—*n.* rage, anger, fury, indignation, resentment, choler, exasperation, irritation, vexation. *(pleasure, forbearance, delight, gratification, equanimity.)*

wreak—*v.* inflict, visit, exact, bring about, work, cause, exercise, effect. *(forbear, hold back, abstain from, desist from.)*

wreck—*v.* destroy, ruin, spoil, shatter, devastate, ravage, demolish, blast, smash. *(preserve, guard, secure, conserve, protect.)*

wrench—*v.* contort, jerk, twist, strain, blow, wring, sprain.

wretched—*adj.* dejected, depressed, mournful, forlorn, woeful, unfortunate, worthless, inferior, hopeless, pitiful. *(happy, glad, euphoric, affluent, noble, virtuous, comfortable, worthy, admirable.)*

wrinkle—*v.* crease, crumple, purse, furrow, fold, crinkle. *(flatten, smooth, straighten, iron, level.)*

wrong—*adj.* mistaken, faulty, untrue, inaccurate, inequitable, improper, inethical, unjust, unsuitable, erroneous, awkward, imperfect. *(perfect, correct, suitable, good, standard, ethical, fitting, right, fair, moral, beneficial, straight, appropriate.)*

wry—*adj.* distorted, askew, crooked, twisted, contorted, deformed, awry. *(straight, unbent, normal, supple, limber.)*

Y

yearn—*v.* crave, want, desire, wish, hunger for, long, covet, thirst for. *(revolt, shudder, recoil, loathe.)*

yet—*adv.* still, besides, hitherto, ultimately, at last, now, thus far, however, eventually, at last.

yield—*v.* supply, furnish, render, pay, submit, consent, acquiesce, grant, accede, assent, comply, bear, afford, succumb, give in, engender, resign, relinquish, produce. *(oppose, refute, resist, dissent, protest, retain, disallow, withhold, deny, claim, assert, vindicate, recalcitrate, strive, struggle.)*

yielding—*adj.* conceding, producing, submissive, unresisting, soft, surrendering, acquiescent, timid, crouching, spongy. *(nonproductive, waste, fallow, stiff, defiant, firm, unyielding, resisting, fierce, unbending.)*

yoke—*v.* connect, link, hitch, splice, mate, enslave, couple, subjugate, unite. *(release, dissever, divorce, liberate, enfranchise, manumit.)*

yonder—*adj.* yon, distant, faraway, thither, remote, faroff. *(near, close, nearby.)*

youth—*n.* minor, adolescence, juvenility, childhood, beginnings, start, youngster, kid, stripling.

youthful—*adj.* childlike, adolescent, juvenile, fresh, puerile, immature, maiden, early, unripe, virginal. *(elderly, aged, mature, antiquated, olden, time-worn, patriarchal, decrepit, ancient, decayed.)*

Z

zeal—*n.* zest, drive, enthusiasm, ardor, interest, ambition, earnestness, passion, heartiness, energy. *(detachment, indifference, apathy, coolness, carelessness, aimlessness, sluggishness, incordiality.)*

zenith—*n.* acme, crest, culmination, pinnacle, top, summit, maximum, climax, peak, height. *(bottom, nadir, depths, minimum, lowest point.)*

zest—*n.* enjoyment, relish, gusto, eagerness, delight, exhilaration, life, appetizer, flavor, sharpener, satisfaction. *(apathy, boredom, distaste, detriment, ennui.)*

zip—*n.* energy, vitality, animation, dash, zing, sparkle, punch, drive. *(sloth, lethargy, apathy, laziness, debility.)*

zoom—*v.* climb, soar, rise, ascend, escalate, mount, spiral, grow, increase. *(drop, descend, plummet, decrease, fall.)*

HOMONYMS

A

able, strong, skillful. **Abel,** a name.

accidence, rudiments. **accidents,** mishaps.

acclamation, applause. **acclimation,** used to climate.

acts, deeds. **ax or axe,** a tool.

ad, advertisement. **add,** to increase.

adds, increases. **adze or adz,** a tool.

adherence, constancy. **adherents,** followers.

ail, pain, trouble. **ale,** a liquor.

air, atmosphere. **ere,** before. **heir,** inheritor.

aisle, passage. **isle,** island. **I'll,** I will.

ait, an island. **ate,** devoured. **eight,** a number.

ale, liquor. **ail,** pain, trouble.

all, everyone. **awl,** a tool.

allegation, affirmation. **allegation,** uniting.

aloud, with noise. **allowed,** permitted.

altar, for worship. **alter,** to change.

amend, to make better. **amende,** retraction.

anker, a measure. **anchor,** of a vessel.

Ann, a name. **an,** one.

annalist, historian. **analyst,** analyzer.

annalize, to record. **analyze,** to investigate.

ant, insect. **aunt,** relative.

ante, before. **anti,** opposed to.

arc, part of a circle. **ark,** chest, boat.

arrant, bad. **errant,** wandering.

ascent, act of rising. **assent,** consent.

asperate, make rough. **aspirate,** give sound of "h".

assistance, help, aid. **assistants,** helpers.

ate, consumed or devoured. **ait,** an island. **eight,** a number.

Ate, a goddess. **eighty,** a number.

attendance, waiting on. **attendants,** those who attend, are in attendance.

aught, anything. **ought,** should.

augur, to predict. **auger,** a tool.

aune, a cloth measure. **own,** belonging to oneself.

aunt, relative. **ant,** insect.

auricle, external ear. **oracle,** prophet.

awl, a tool. **all,** everyone.

axe, a tool. **acts,** deeds.

axes, tools. **axis,** turning line.

aye, yes. **eye,** organ of sight. **I,** myself.

B

bacon, pork, **baken,** baked.

bad, wicked. **bade,** past tense of the verb TO BID.

bail, security. **bale,** a bundle.

bait, food to allure. **bate,** to lessen.

baize, cloth. **bays,** water, garland, horses.

bald, hairless. **bawled,** cried aloud.

ball, round body, dance. **bawl,** to cry aloud.

bare, naked. **bear,** animal, to carry.

bard, poet. **barred,** fastened with a bar.

bark, cry of dog, rind of tree. **barque,** vessel.

baron. nobleman. **barren,** unfruitful.

baroness, baron's wife. **barrenness,** sterility.

base, mean. **bass,** musical term.

bask, to lie in warmth. **Basque,** race of people in France or Spain.

bass, musical term. **base,** mean.

bay, water, color, tree. **bey,** governor.

beach, seashore. **beech,** a tree.

bear, an animal, to carry. **bare,** naked.

beat, to strike. **beet,** vegetable.

beau, boyfriend. **bow,** archery term.

bee, insect. **be,** to exist.

been, past participle of the verb TO BE. **bin,** container for grain.

beer, malt liquor. **bier,** carriage for the dead.

berry, fruit. **bury,** to inter.

berth, sleeping place. **birth,** act of being born.

better, superior. **bettor,** one who bets.

bey, governor. **bay,** sea, color, tree.

bier, carriage for the dead. **beer,** malt liquor.

bight, of a rope. **bite,** chew.

billed, furnished with a bill. **build,** to erect.

bin, container. **been,** of the verb TO BE.

binocle, telescope. **binnacle,** compass box.

birth, being born. **berth,** sleeping place.

blew, did blow. **blue,** a color.

bloat, to swell. **blote,** to dry by smoke.

boar, swine. **bore,** to make a hole.

board, timber. **bored,** pierced, tired.

bold, courageous. **bowled,** rolled balls.

boll, a pod, a ball. **bowl,** basin. **bole,** earth, trunk of tree.

border, outer edge. **boarder,** lodger.

bourne, a limit, stream. **borne,** carried. **born,** brought into life.

borough, a town. **burrow,** hole for rabbits, donkey.

bow, used in archery. **beau,** a boyfriend.

bow, to salute, part of ship. **bough,** branch of tree.

bowl, basin. **bole,** earth, trunk of tree. **boll,** a pod, a ball.

boy, male child. **buoy,** floating signal.

braid, to plait. **brayed,** did bray.

brake, device for retarding motion, a thicket. **break,** opening, to part.

bray, harsh sound. **brae,** hillside.

breach, a gap, a break. **breech,** part of a gun.

bread, food. **bred,** brought up.

brewed, fermented. **brood,** offspring.

brews, makes malt liquor. **bruise,** blemish.

bridal, of a wedding. **bridle,** a curb.

Briton, native of Britain. **Britain,** England, Scotland, Wales, Northern Ireland.

broach, to utter. **brooch,** a pin.

brows, foreheads. **browse,** to feed.

bruit, noise, report. **brute,** a beast.

build, to erect. **billed,** furnished with a bill.

buoy, floating signal. **boy,** male child.

burrow, hole for rabbit, donkey. **borough,** a town.

bury, to cover with earth. **berry,** a fruit.

but, except, yet. **butt,** a cask, to push with head.

by, at, near. **buy,** to purchase.

C

cache, hole for hiding goods. **cash,** money.

caddy, a box. **cadi,** a Turkish judge.

Cain, man's name. **cane,** walking stick.

calendar, almanac. **calender,** to polish.

caulk, to stop leaks. **cauk or cawk,** mineral.

call, to name. **caul,** a membrane.

can, could, tin vessel. **Cannes,** French city.

cannon, large gun. **canon,** a law, a rule.

canvas, cloth. **canvass,** to solicit, to examine.

capital, upper part, principal. **capitol,** statehouse.

carat, weight. **caret,** mark. **carrot,** vegetable.

carol, song of joy. **Carroll,** a name.

carrot, vegetable. **carat,** weight. **caret,** mark.

cash, money. **cache,** hole for hiding goods.

cask, wooden vessel. **casque,** a helmet.

cast, to throw, to mold. **caste,** rank.

castor, a beaver. **caster**, frame for bottles, roller.

caudal, tail. **caudle**, drink.

cause, that which produces. **caws**, cries of crows.

cede, to give up. **seed**, germ of plants.

ceiling, overhead of a room. **sealing**, fastening.

cell, small room. **sell**, to part for price.

cellar, a room under house. **seller**, one who sells.

censor, critic. **censer**, vessel.

cent, coin. **sent**, caused to go. **scent**, odor.

cerate, a salve. **serrate**, shaped like a saw.

cere, to cover with wax. **sear**, burn. **seer**, a prophet.

cession, yielding. **session**, a sitting.

cetaceous, whale species. **setaceous**, bristly.

chagrin, ill-humor. **shagreen**, fish skin.

chance, accident. **chants**, melodies.

champaign, open country. **champagne**, a wine.

chaste, pure. **chased**, pursued.

cheap, inexpensive. **cheep**, a bird's chirp.

chews, masticates. **choose**, to select.

choir, singers. **quire**, measure of paper.

choler, anger. **collar**, neckwear.

chord, musical sound. **cord**, string. **cored**, removed center.

chronical, a long duration. **chronicle**, history.

chuff, a clown. **chough**, a sea bird.

cilicious, made of hair. **silicious**, flinty.

cingle, a girth. **single**, alone, only one.

cion or **scion**, a sprout. **sion** or **zion**, mountain.

circle, round figure. **sercle**, a twig.

cit, a citizen. **sit**, to rest.

cite, to summon, to quote, to enumerate. **site**, location. **sight**, view.

clause, part of a sentence. **claws**, talons.

climb, to ascend. **clime**, climate.

coal, fuel. **cole**, cabbage.

coaled, supplied with coal. **cold**, frigid, not hot.

coarse, rough. **course**, route, **corse** or **corpse**, dead body.

coat, garment. **cote**, sheepfold.

coddle, to fondle. see **caudal.**

codling, apple. **coddling**, parboiling.

coffer, money chest. **cougher**, one who coughs.

coin, money. **quoin**, wedge.

colation, straining. **collation**, a repast.

collar, neckwear. see **choler.**

colonel, officer. **kernel,** seed in a nut.

color, tint. **culler,** a chooser.

complacence, satisfaction. **complaisance,** affability, compliance.

complacent, civil. **complaisant,** seeking to please.

compliment, flattery. **complement,** the full number.

confidant, one trusted with secrets. **confident,** having full belief.

consonance, concord. **consonants,** letters which are not vowels.

consequence, that which follows. **consequents,** deduction.

consession, a sitting together. **concession,** a yielding.

coolly, without heat, calmly. **coolie,** East Indian laborer.

coom, soot. **coomb,** a measure.

coquet, to deceive in love. **coquette,** vain girl.

coral, from the ocean. **corol,** a corolla.

cord, string. **chord,** musical sound. **cored,** taken from center.

core, inner part. **corps,** soldiers.

correspondence, interchange of letters. **correspondents,** those who correspond.

council, assembly. **counsel,** advice.

cousin, relative. **cozen,** to cheat.

coward, one without courage. **cowered,** frightened.

creak, harsh noise. **creek,** stream.

crewel, yarn. **cruel,** savage.

crews, seamen. **cruise,** voyage. **cruse,** a cruet.

cue, hint, rod, tail. **queue,** pigtail, waiting line.

culler, a selecter. **color,** a tint.

currant, fruit. **current,** flowing stream, present.

cygnet, a swan. **signet,** a seal.

cymbal, musical instrument. **symbol,** sign.

cypress, a tree. **Cyprus,** an island.

D

dam, wall for stream. **damn,** to doom or curse.

dammed, confined by banks. **damned,** doomed.

Dane, a native of Denmark. **deign,** condescend.

day, time. **dey,** a governor.

days, plural of day. **daze,** to dazzle.

dear, beloved, costly. **deer,** an animal.

deformity, defect. **difformity,** diversity of form.

deign, to condescend. **Dane,** native of Denmark.

demean, debase. **demesne,** land.

dents, marks. **dense,** close, compact.

dependents, subordinates. **dependence,** reliance.

depravation, corruption. **deprivation,** loss.

descent, drop downward. **dissent,** disagreement.

descendent, falling. **descendant,** offspring.

desert, to abandon. **dessert,** last course of a meal.

deviser, contriver. **divisor,** a term in arithmetic.

dew, moisture. **do,** to perform. **due,** owed.

die, to expire, a stamp. **dye,** to color.

dire, dreadful. **dyer,** one who dyes.

discous, flat. **discus,** quoit.

discreet, prudent. **discrete,** separate.

doe, femaie deer. **dough,** unbaked bread.

does, female deer. **doze,** to slumber.

done, performed. **dun,** a color.

dost, from verb TO BE. **dust,** powdered earth.

drachm, monetary unit of Greece. **dram,** small quantity.

draft, bill. **draught,** a drink, a potion.

dual, two. **duel,** combat.

due, owed, **dew,** moisture. **do,** to perform.

dun, color, ask for debt. **done,** finished.

dust, powdered earth. **dost,** from verb TO BE.

dye, to color. **die,** to expire, a stamp.

dyeing, staining. **dying,** expiring.

dyer, one who dyes. **dire,** dreadful.

E

earn, to gain by labor. **urn,** a vase.

eight, a number. **ate,** consumed or devoured.

eighty, a number. **Ate,** a goddess.

ere, before. **air,** atmosphere. **heir,** inheritor.

errant, wandering. **arrant,** bad.

ewe, female sheep. **yew,** tree. **you,** *pronoun.*

ewes, sheep. **yews,** trees. **use,** employ.

eye, organ of sight. **I,** myself. **aye,** yes.

F

fain, pleased. **fane,** temple. **feign,** pretend.

faint, languid. **feint,** pretense.

fair, beautiful, just. **fare,** price, food.

falter, to hesitate. **faulter,** one who commits a fault.

fane, temple. **fain,** pleased. **feign,** to pretend.

fare, price, food. **fair,** beautiful, just.

fate, destiny. **fete,** a festival.

faulter, one who commits a fault. **falter,** to hesitate.

fawn, young deer. **faun,** woodland deity.

feat, deed. **feet,** plural of foot.

feign, pretend. **fain,** pleased. **fane,** temple.

feint, pretense. **faint,** languid.

felloe, rim of wheel. **fellow,** companion.

feod, tenure. **feud,** quarrel.

ferrule, metallic band. **ferule,** wooden pallet.

feted, honored. **fated,** destined.

feud, quarrel. **feod,** tenure.

fillip, jerk of finger. **Philip,** man's name.

filter, to strain. **philter,** love charm.

find, to discover. **fined,** punished.

fir, tree. **fur,** animal hair.

fissure, a crack. **fisher,** fisherman.

fizz, hissing noise. **phiz,** the face.

flea, insect. **flee,** to run away.

flew, did fly. **flue,** chimney. **flu,** influenza.

flour, ground grain. **flower,** a blossom.

flue, chimney. **flu,** influenza. **flew,** did fly.

for, because of. **fore,** preceding. **four,** cardinal number.

fort, fortified place. **forte,** peculiar talent.

forth, forward. **fourth,** ordinal number.

foul, unclean. **fowl,** a bird.

four, cardinal number. **for,** because of. **fore,** preceding.

fourth, ordinal number. **forth,** forward.

franc, French coin. **Frank,** a name, candid.

frays, quarrels. **phrase,** parts of a sentence.

freeze, to congeal with cold. **frieze,** cloth. **frees,** sets at liberty.

fungus, spongy excresence. **fungous,** as fungus.

fur, hairy coat of animals. **fir,** a tree.

furs, skins of beasts. **furze,** a shrub.

G

gage, a pledge, a fruit. **gauge,** a measure.

gait, manner of walking. **gate,** a door.

gall, bile. **Gaul,** a Frenchman.

gamble, to wager. **gambol,** to skip.

gate, a door. **gait,** manner of walking.

gauge, a measure. **gage,** a pledge, a fruit.

Gaul, a Frenchman. **gall,** bile.

gild, to overflow with gold. **guild,** a corporation.

gilt, gold on surface. **guilt,** crime.

glare, splendor. **glair,** white of an egg.

gneiss, rock similar to granite. **nice,** fine.

gnu, animal. **new,** not old. **knew,** understood.

gourd, a plant. **gored,** pierced.

grate, iron frame. **great,** large.

grater, a rough instrument. **greater,** larger.

great, large. **grate,** iron frame.

greater, larger. **grater,** a rough instrument.

Greece, country in Europe. **grease,** fat.

grisly, frightful. **grizzly,** an animal, gray.

groan, deep sigh. **grown,** increased.

grocer, merchant. **grosser,** coarser.

grown, increased. **groan,** deep sigh.

guessed, conjectured. **guest,** visitor.

guild, a corporation. **gild,** to overflow with gold.

guilt, crime. **gilt,** gold on surface.

guise, appearance. **guys,** ropes, men.

H

hail, ice, to salute. **hale,** healthy.

hair, tresses. **hare,** a rabbit.

hale, healthy. **hail,** ice, to salute.

hall, large room, a passage. **haul,** to pull.

hare, a rabbit. **hair,** tresses.

hart, an animal. **heart,** seat of life.

haul, to pull. **hall,** a large room, a passage.

hay, dried grass. **hey,** an expression.

heal, to cure. **heel,** part of foot or shoe, the end of a loaf of bread, a scoundrel.

hear, to hearken. **here,** in this place.

heard, did hear. **herd,** a drove.

heart, seat of life. **hart,** an animal.

heel, part of foot or shoe, the end of a loaf of bread, a scoundrel. **heal,** to cure.

heir, inheritor. **air,** atmosphere. **ere,** before.

herd, a drove. **heard,** did hear.

here, in this place. **hear,** to hearken.

hew, to cut down. see **hue.**

hey, an expression. **hay,** dried grass.

hide, skin, to conceal. **hied,** hastened.

hie, to hasten. **high,** lofty, tall.

hied, hastened. **hide,** skin, to conceal.

higher, more lofty. **hire,** to employ.

him, that man. **hymn,** sacred song.

hire, to employ. **higher,** more lofty.

hoa, exclamation. **ho,** cry, stop. **hoe,** tool.

hoard, accumulate. **horde,** crowd.

hoarse, husky. **horse,** animal.

hoe, tool. **ho,** cry, stop. **hoa,** exclamation.

hoes, tools. **hose,** stockings, tubing.

hole, cavity. **whole,** all, entire.

holm, evergreen oak. **home,** dwelling.

holy, pure sacred. **wholly,** completely.

home, dwelling. **holm,** evergreen oak.

horde, crowd. **hoard,** accumulate.

horse, animal. **hoarse,** husky.

hose, stockings, tubing. **hoes,** tools.

hour, sixty minutes. **our,** belonging to us.

hue, color. **hew,** to cut down. **Hugh,** man's name.

hymn, sacred song. **him,** that man.

I

idol, graven image. **idle,** unemployed. **idyl,** poem.

I'll, I will. **isle,** island. **aisle,** passage.

in, within. **inn,** a tavern.

indict, to accuse. **indite,** write, compose.

indiscreet, imprudent. **indiscrete,** not separated.

indite, to write. **indict,** to accuse.

inn, a tavern. **in,** within.

innocence, purity. **innocents,** harmless things.

instants, moments. **instance,** example.

intense, extreme. **intents,** purposes.

intention, purpose. **intension,** determination.

intents, purposes. **intense,** extreme.

invade, to infringe. **inveighed,** censured.

irruption, invasion. **eruption,** upheaval.

isle, island. **I'll,** I will. **aisle,** passage.

J

jail, prison. **gaol,** British prison.

jam, preserves. **jamb,** side of door.

K

kernel, seed in nut. **colonel,** officer.

key, for a lock. **quay,** wharf.

knag, prong of deer's horns. **nag,** small horse, torment.

knap, elevation. **nap,** short sleep.

knave, rogue. **nave,** center, hub.

knead, work dough. **need,** want. **kneed,** having knees.

kneel, to rest on knee. **neal,** to temper by heat.

knew, understood. **gnu,** animal. **new,** not old.

knight, title of honor. **night,** darkness.

knit, unite, weave. **nit,** insect's egg.

knot, tie. **not,** word of refusal.

know, understand. **no,** not yes.

knows, understands. **nose,** organ of smell.

L

lack, to want. **lac,** gum.

lacks, wants, needs. **lax,** loose, slack.

lade, to load. **laid,** placed, produced eggs.

lane, a road. **lain,** rested.

Latin, language. **latten,** brass.

lax, loose, slack. **lacks,** wants, needs.

lea, meadow. **lee,** shelter, place.

leach, to filtrate. **leech,** a worm.

lead, metal. **led,** guided.

leaf, part of a plant. **lief,** willingly.

leak, ooze. **leek,** onion-like vegetable.

lean, not fat, to rest, to slant. **lien,** mortgage.

leased, rented. **least,** smallest.

led, guided. **lead,** metal.

lee, shelter, place. **lea,** meadow.

leech, a worm. **leach,** to filtrate.

leek, onion-like vegetable. **leak,** ooze.

lesson, task. **lessen,** to diminish.

levee, bank, visit. **levy,** to collect.

liar, falsifier. **lyre,** musical instrument. **lier,** one who lies down.

lie, falsehood. **lye,** strong alkaline solution.

lief, willingly. **leaf,** part of a plant.

lien, legal claim. **lean,** not fat, to rest, to slant.

lightning, flash in the sky. **lightening,** unloading.

limb, branch. **limn,** to draw.

links, connecting rings. **lynx,** an animal.

lo, look, see. **low,** not high, mean.

loan, to lend. **lone,** solitary.

lock, hair, fastening. **loch** or **lough,** lake.

lone, solitary. **loan,** to lend.

low, not high, mean. **lo,** look, see.

lusern, a lynx. **lucerne,** clover.

lye, strong alkaline solution. **lie,** falsehood.

lynx, animal. **links,** connecting rings.

lyre, musical instrument. **liar,** falsifier. **lier,** one who lies down.

M

made, created. **maid,** unmarried woman, female servant.

mail, armor, postal service. **male,** masculine.

main, principal. **mane,** hair. **Maine,** a state.

maize, corn. **maze,** winding course.

male, masculine. **mail,** armor, postal service.

mall, walk. **maul,** to beat.

manner, method. **manor,** landed estate.

mantel, chimney piece. **mantle,** a cloak.

mark, visible line. **marque,** a pledge.

marshall, officer. **martial,** warlike.

marten, an animal. **martin,** a bird.

martial, warlike. **marshall,** officer.

maul, to beat. **mall,** walk.

mead, drink. **meed,** reward. **Mede,** native of Media.

mean, low. **mien,** aspect.

meat, food. **meet,** to encounter, a match. **mete,** apportion.

Mede, native of Media. **mead,** drink. **meed,** reward.

meddle, interfere. **medal,** a reward.

meddler, one who meddles. **medlar,** a tree.

meed, reward. **mead,** drink. **Mede,** native of Media.

meet, to encounter, a match. **meat,** food. **mete,** apportion.

mettle, spirit, courage. **metal,** ore.

mew or **mue,** to melt. **mew,** fowl enclosure.

mewl, to cry. **mule,** an animal.

mews, cat cries. **muse,** deep thought.

mien, look aspect. **mean,** low.

might, power. **mite,** insect.

mighty, powerful. **mity,** having mites.

mince, to cut. **mints,** coining places, candies.

miner, worker in mines. **minor,** one underage.

mints, coining places, candies. **mince,** to cut.

missal, prayer book. **missel,** bird. **missile,** weapon.

mite, insect, small. **might,** power.

mity, having mites. **mighty,** powerful.

moan, lament. **mown,** cut down.

moat, ditch. **mote,** small particle.

mode, manner. **mowed,** cut down.

morning, before noon. **mourning,** grief.

mote, small particle. **moat,** ditch.

mowed, cut down. **mode,** manner.

mucous, slimy. **mucus,** secretion of mucous membranes.

mue, to molt. **mew,** fowl enclosure.

mule, an animal. **mewl,** to cry.

muscat, grape. **musket,** gun.

muse, deep thought. **mews,** cat cries.

mustard, plant. **mustered,** assembled.

N

nag, small horse. **knag,** prong of deer's horns.

nap, short sleep. **knap,** elevation.

naval, nautical. **navel,** center of abdomen.

nave, center, hub. **knave,** rogue.

navel, center of abdomen. **naval,** nautical.

nay, no. **neigh,** whinny of a horse.

neal, to temper. **kneel,** to rest on knee.

need, necessity, want. **knead,** work dough. *kneed,* having knees.

neigh, whinny of a horse. **nay,** no.

new, not old. **gnu,** animal. **knew,** understood.

nice, fine. **kneiss,** rock similar to granite.

night, darkness. **knight,** title of honor.

nit, insect's egg. **knit,** to unite, to form.

no, not so. **know,** to understand.

none, no one. **nun,** female devotee.

nose, organ of smell. **knows,** understands.

not, word of refusal. **knot,** a tie.

nun, female devotee. **none,** no one.

O

oar, rowing blade. **o'er,** over. **ore,** mineral.

ode, poem. **owed,** under obligation.

o'er, over. **oar,** paddle. **ore,** mineral.

oh, expression of surprise or pain. **owe,** be indebted.

one, single unit. **won,** gained.

onerary, fit for burdens. **honorary,** conferring honor.

oracle, seer. **auricle,** external ear, chamber of heart.

ordinance, a law. **ordnance,** military supplies.

ore, mineral. **o'er,** over. **oar,** paddle.

ought, should. **aught,** anything.

our, belonging to us. **hour,** sixty minutes.

owe, to be indebted. **oh,** expression of surprise or pain.

owed, under obligation. **ode,** poem.

P

paced, strode. **paste,** flour and water mixed.

packed, bound in a bundle. **pact,** contract.

pail, bucket. **pale,** whitish.

pain, agony. **pane,** a square of glass.

pair, a couple, two. **pare,** to peel. **pear,** a fruit.

palace, princely home. **Pallas,** heathen deity.

palate, roof of the mouth. **pallette,** artist's board. **pallet,** a bed.

pale, whitish. **pail,** bucket.

pall, covering for the dead. **Paul,** man's name.

pare, to peel. **pair,** a couple, two. **pear,** a fruit.

passable, tolerable. **passible,** with feeling.

paste, flour and water mixed. **paced,** strode.

patience, calmness. **patients,** sick persons.

paw, foot of a beast. **pa,** papa.

paws, beasts' feet. **pause,** stop.

peace, quiet. **piece,** a part.

peak, the top. **pique,** grudge. **peek,** to peep.

peal, ring. **peel,** to pare.

pealing, tolling. **peeling,** shredding.

pear, a fruit. **pair,** a couple, two. **pare,** to peel.

pearl, a precious substance. **purl,** a knitting stitch.

pedal, lever worked by foot. **peddle,** to sell.

peek, to peep. **peak,** the top. **pique,** grudge.

peer, nobleman. **pier,** column, wharf.

pencil, writing instrument. **pensile,** suspended.

pendant, an ornament. **pendent,** hanging.

philter, love charm. **filter,** to strain.

phiz, the face. **phizz,** hissing noise.

phrase, expression. **frays,** quarrels.

piece, a part. **peace,** quiet.

pier, a column, wharf. **peer,** nobleman.

pique, grudge. **peak,** the top. **peek,** to peep.

pistil, part of a flower. **pistol,** firearm.

place, position. **plaice,** a fish.

plain, clear, simple, meadow. **plane,** aircraft, tool.

pleas, arguments. **please,** to delight.

plum, a fruit. **plumb,** perpendicular, leaden weight.

pole, stick. **poll,** vote.

pool, water. **poule** or **pool,** stakes played for.

pore, opening. **pour,** cause to flow.

poring, looking intently. **pouring,** raining, flowing.

port, harbor, wine. **porte,** Turkish court.

praise, commendation. **prays,** entreats, petitions. **preys,** feeds by violence, plunders.

pray, to supplicate. **prey,** plunder.

presence, being present. **presents,** gifts.

pride, self-esteem. **pried,** moved by a lever, snooped.

prier, inquirer. **prior,** previous.

pries, looks into. **prize,** reward.

prints, impressions. **prince,** king's son.

principal, chief. **principle,** doctrine.

prior, previous. **prier,** inquirer.

prize, reward. **pries,** looks into.

profit, gain. **prophet,** a foreteller.

purl, a knitting stitch. **pearl,** precious substance.

Q

quarts, measures, **quartz,** rock crystal.

quay, wharf. **key,** lock fastener.

queen, king's wife. **quean,** worthless woman.

queue, pigtail, waiting line. **cue,** hint, rod.

quire, package of paper. **choir,** church singers.

quoin, wedge. **coin,** money.

R

rabbet, a joint. **rabbit,** small animal.

radical, of first principles. **radicle,** a root.

rain, shower. **reign,** rule. **rein,** bridle.

raise, to lift. **rays,** sunbeams. **raze,** to demolish.

raised, lifted. **razed,** demolished.

raiser, one who raises. **razor,** shaving blade.

rancor, spite. **ranker,** stronger, more immoderate.

rap, knock. **wrap,** enclose.

rapped, knocked. **wrapped,** enclosed.

rapping, striking. **wrapping,** a cover.

rays, sunbeams. **raise,** to lift. **raze,** to demolish.

raze, to demolish. **raise,** to lift. **rays,** sunbeams.

razed, demolished. **raised,** lifted.

razor, shaving blade. **raiser,** one who raises.

read, to peruse. **reed,** a plant.

real, true. **reel,** winding machine, to stagger.

receipt, acknowledgment. **reseat,** to sit again.

reck, to heed. **wreck,** destruction.

red, color. **read,** perused.

reek, to emit vapor. **wreak,** to inflict.

reel, winding machine, to stagger. **real,** true.

reign, rule. **rein,** bridle. **rain,** shower.

reseat, to seat again. **receipt,** acknowledgment.

residence, place of abode. **residents,** citizens.

rest, quiet. **wrest,** to twist.

retch, to vomit. **wretch,** miserable person.

rheum, thin, watery matter. **room,** space.

Rhodes, name of an island. **roads,** highways.

rhumb, point of a compass. **rum,** liquor.

rhyme, poetry. **rime,** hoar frost.

rigger, rope fixer. **rigor,** severity.

right, correct. **rite,** ceremony. **write,** to form letters.

rime, hoar frost. **rhyme,** poetry.

ring, circle, sound of bells. **wring,** to twist.

road, highway. **rode,** did ride. **rowed,** did row.

roads, highways. **Rhodes,** name of an island.

roan, color. **rown,** impelled by oars. **Rhone,** river.

roe, deer, fish eggs. **row,** to impel with oars, a line.

roes, eggs, deer. **rows,** uses oars. **rose,** a flower.

Rome, city in Italy. **roam,** to wander.

rood, a measure. **rude,** rough.

rote, memory of words. **wrote,** did write.

rough, not smooth. **ruff,** plaited collar.

rouse, stir up, provoke. **rows,** disturbances, tiers.

rout, rabble, disperse. **route,** road.

row, to impel with oars, a line. **roe,** a deer, fish eggs.

rowed, did row. **road,** highway. **rode,** did ride.

rows, uses oars. **roes,** deer, fish eggs. **rose,** a flower.

rude, rough. **rood,** measure.

ruff, collar. **rough,** not smooth.

rum, liquor. **rhumb,** point of a compass.

rung, sounded, a step on a ladder. **wrung,** twisted.

rye, grain. **wry,** crooked.

S

sail, canvas of a boat. **sale,** act of selling.

sailer, vessel. **sailor,** seaman.

sale, act of selling. **sail,** canvas of a boat.

sane, sound in mind. **seine,** fish net.

saver, one who saves. **savor,** taste.

scene, a view. **seen,** viewed.

scent, odor. **sent,** caused to go. **cent,** coin.

scion or **cion.** sprout. **sion** or **zion,** a mountain.

scull, oar, boat. **skull,** bony framework of the head.

sea, ocean. **see,** to perceive.

seal, stamp, an animal. **seel,** to close the eyes.

sealing, fastening. **ceiling,** overhead of a room.

seam, a juncture. **seem,** to appear.

seamed, joined together. **seemed,** appeared.

sear, to burn. **cere,** wax.

seas, water. **sees,** looks. **seize,** take hold of.

seed, germ of a plant. **cede,** to give up.

seen, viewed. **scene,** a view.

seine, a net. **sane,** sound in mind.

sell, to part for price. **cell,** small room.

seller, one who sells. **cellar,** basement.

sense, feeling. **scents,** odors. **cents,** coins.

sent, caused to go. **scent,** odor. **cent,** coin.

serf, a slave. **surf,** breaking waves.

serge, a cloth. **surge,** a billow.

serrate, notched, like a saw. **cerate,** salve.

session, a sitting. **cession,** a yielding.

setaceous, bristly. **cetaceous,** whale species.

sew, to stitch. **sow,** to scatter seed. **so,** in this manner.

sewer, one who uses a needle. **sower,** one who scatters seed.

sewer, a drain. **suer,** one who sues.

shear, to clip. **sheer,** to deviate, pure, see-through.

shoe, covering for foot. **shoo,** begone.

shone, did shine. **shown,** exhibited.

shoo, begone. **shoe,** covering for foot.

shoot, to kill. **chute,** a fall.

shown, exhibited. **shone,** did shine.

side, edge, margin. **sighed,** did sigh.

sigher, one who sighs. **sire,** father.

sighs, deep breathings. **size,** bulk.

sight, view. **site,** position. **cite,** to summon.

signet, a seal. **cygnet,** a swan.

silicious, flinty. **cilicious,** made of hair.

silly, foolish. **Scilly,** name of islands.

single, alone. **cingle,** a girth.

sit, to rest. **cit,** a citizen.

skull, bony framework of the head. **scull,** oar, boat.

slay, to kill. **sley,** weaver's reed. **sleigh,** vehicle.

sleeve, cover for arm. **sleave,** untwisted silk.

slight, neglect, small. **sleight,** artful trick.

sloe, fruit, animal. **slow,** not swift.

soar, to rise high. **sore,** painful.

soared, ascended. **sword,** a weapon.

sold, did sell. **soled,** furnished with soles. **souled,** having a soul or feeling.

sole, part of foot, only. **soul,** spirit of man.

some, a part. **sum,** the whole

son, a male child. **sun,** luminous orb.

sow, to scatter seed. **sew,** to stitch.

sower, one who scatters seed. **sewer,** one who uses a needle.

staid, sober, **stayed,** supported, remained.

stair, step. **stare,** to gaze.

stake, a post, a wager. **steak,** meat.

stare, to gaze. **stair,** step.

stationary, motionless. **stationery,** paper, etc.

steel, metal. **steal,** to thieve.

sticks, pieces of wood. **Styx,** a fabulous river.

stile, stairway. **style,** manner.

straight, not crooked. **strait,** narrow pass.

style, manner. **stile,** stairway.

Styx, a fabulous river, **sticks,** pieces of wood.

subtle, cunning. **suttle,** to carry on business of a sutler.

subtler, more cunning. **sutler,** trader.

succor, aid. **sucker,** a shoot of a plant, slang for a victim.

suer, one who sues. **sewer,** a drain.

suite, train of followers. **sweet,** having a pleasant taste, dear.

sum, the whole. **some,** a part.

sun, luminous orb. **son,** a male child.

surcle, a twig. **circle,** a round figure.

surf, dashing waves. **serf,** a slave.

surge, a billow. **serge,** cloth.

sutler, trader. **subtler,** more cunning.

suttle, to carry on business of a sutler. **subtle,** cunning.

swap, to barter. **swop,** a blow.

symbol, emblem. **cymbal,** musical instrument.

T

tacked, nailed. **tact,** skill.

tacks, small nails. **tax,** a tariff.

tale, story. **tail,** the hinder part.

taper, a wax candle, lessen. **tapir,** an animal.

tare, a weed, allowance. **tear,** to pull to pieces.

taught, instructed. **taut,** tight.

teal, a water fowl, grayish-blue. **teil,** a tree.

team, two or more horses, squad. **teem,** to be full.

tear, moisture from eyes. **tier,** a rank, a row.

tear, to pull to pieces. **tare,** weed, allowance.

teas, different kinds of tea. **tease,** to torment.

tense, rigid, form of a verb. **tents,** canvas houses.

the, adjective. **thee,** thyself.

their, belonging to them. **there,** in that place. **they're,** they are.

threw, did throw. **through,** from end to end.

throne, seat of a king. **thrown,** hurled.

throw, to hurl. **throe,** extreme pain.

thrown, hurled. **throne,** seat of a king.

thyme, a plant. **time,** duration.

tide, stream, current. **tied,** fastened.

tier, a rank, a row. **tear,** moisture from eyes.

timber, wood. **timbre,** crest, quality.

time, duration. **thyme,** a plant.

tire, part of a wheel, weary. **Tyre,** city. **tier,** one who ties.

toad, reptile. **toed,** having toes. **towed,** drawn.

toe, part of foot. **tow,** to drag.

told, related. **tolled,** rang.

tole, to allure. **toll,** a tax.

ton, a weight. **tun,** a large cask.

too, also. **to,** toward. **two,** couple.

tracked, followed. **tract,** region.

tray, shallow vessel. **trey,** three of cards.

tun, a large cask. **ton,** a weight.

two, a couple. **to,** toward. **too,** also.

U

urn, a vase. **earn,** to gain by labor.

use, to employ. **yews,** trees. **ewes,** sheep.

V

vain, proud. **vane,** weathercock. **vein,** blood vessel.

vale, valley. **veil,** to cover, netting.

vane, weathercock. **vein,** blood vessel. **vain,** proud.

Venus, planet. **venous,** relating to the veins.

vial, a bottle. **viol,** violin. **vile,** wicked.

vice, sin. **vise,** a press.

W

wade, to ford. **weighed,** balanced.

wail, to moan. **wale,** a mark. **whale,** a sea animal.

waist, part of the body. **waste,** destruction.

wait, to stay for. **weight,** heaviness.

waive, to relinquish. **wave,** a billow.

wall, a fence. **wawl,** wail, bowl.

wane, to decrease. **wain,** a wagon.

want, desire. **wont,** custom, habit.

ware, merchandise. see **wear.**

wart, hard excrescence. **wort,** beer.

way, road, manner. **whey,** curdled milk. **weigh,** to balance.

weak, not strong. **week,** seven days.

weal, happiness. **wheal,** a pustule. **wheel,** circular body.

wear, to impair by use. **ware,** merchandise.

weasel, an animal. **weazel,** thin, weasen.

ween, to think. **wean,** to alienate.

weigh, to balance. **way,** road. **whey,** of milk.

weighed, balanced. **wade,** to ford.

weight, heaviness. **wait,** to stay for.

wen, a tumor. **when,** at what time.

wether, a ram. **weather,** state of air.

what, that which. **wot,** to know.

wheel, circular body. **wheal,** a pustule.

whey, thin part of milk. **way,** road, manner. **weigh,** to balance.

Whig, name of a party. **wig,** false hair.

whist, a game of cards. **wist,** thought, knew.

whole, all, entire. **hole,** a cavity.

wholly, completely. **holy,** sacred, pure.

wig, false hair. **Whig,** name of a party.

wight, a person. **wite,** blame.

wist, thought, knew. **whist,** a game of cards.

won, gained. **one,** single, unit.

wont, custom, habit. **want,** desire.

wood, substance of trees. **would,** was willing.

wort, beer, herb. **wart,** hard excrescence.

wot, to know. **what,** that which.

wrap, to enclose. **rap,** knock.

wrapped, covered. **rapped,** knocked.

wrapping, a cover. **rapping,** knocking.

wreak, to inflict. **reek,** to emit vapor.

wrest, to twist. **rest,** quiet.

wretch, miserable person. **retch,** to vomit.

wring, to twist. **ring,** a circle, a sound.

write, to form letters. **wright,** workman. **right,** correct.

wrote, did write. **rote,** a memory of words.

wrung, twisted. **rung,** sounded.

wry, crooked. **rye,** a grain.

Y

yew, a tree. **you,** person spoken to. **ewe,** a sheep.

yews, trees. **use,** employ. **ewes,** sheep.

yolk, yellow of egg. **yoke,** collar for oxen.

your, belonging to you. **you're,** you are.